Customer-Driven Services Management

Customer-Driven Services Management

Second Edition

S. Balachandran

Response Books
A division of Sage Publications
New Delhi/Thousand Oaks/London

First published in 1999.
This second edition published in 2004 by

Response Books
A division of Sage Publications India Pvt Ltd
B-42, Panchsheel Enclave
New Delhi 110 017

Sage Publications Inc
2455 Teller Road
Thousand Oaks, California 91320

Sage Publications Ltd
1 Oliver's Yard, 55 City Road
London EC1Y 1SP

Published by Tejeshwar Singh for Response Books, typeset in 10.5 pts Minion Condensed by Innovative Processors, New Delhi, and printed at Chaman Enterprises, New Delhi.

Library of Congress Cataloging-in-Publication Data

Balachandran, S., 1932-
    Customer-driven services management/S. Balachandran.—2nd ed.
        p. cm.
    Includes bibliographical references and index.
    1. Customer services—India—Management. I. Title.
HF5415.5.B354   658.8'12'0954—dc22   2004   2004004750

ISBN: 0-7619-3255-0 (US-PB)   81-7829-389-7 (India-PB)

Production Team: Leela Gupta, R.A.M. Brown and Santosh Rawat

CONTENTS

CONTENTS

Dr. C. RANGARAJAN

GOVERNOR
ANDHRA PRADESH

RAJ BHAVAN
HYDERABAD-500 041

July 2, 1999

FOREWORD

The service industry is emerging as the most dominant sector in every economy in the world today. This is true of India as well. The contribution of the services sector to the GDP now in India stands around 45 per cent. Much of the management literature evolved during the period when manufacturing was the most dominant sector in an economy. It is in this context, management principles and prescriptions relating to strategy and structure came to be discussed. All firms and organisations have as their objective the delivery of something that is of value to their customers. In the past, this was mostly in the form of products. But the times are changing. The emerging business environment is defined by new technology, intense global competition and constantly changing market place. In this new business climate, the consumer is more often a purchaser of service than a product. Services can be both intermediate and final. Banking, insurance and transportation, to name a few, are basically intermediate. But in attending a theatre or getting a hair cut, the service that is provided is final. It has often been said that in a well functioning economic system the consumer is the sovereign. Speed and quality are the ultimate tests of consumer satisfaction. In the newly emerging service dominated economies, the management principles require a relook. This is precisely the focus of this book by Shri S. Balachandran. The title of the book brings out the essence of what needs to be done. The services must be customer driven. After explaining the different characteristics of service as a desirable end of consumers, the book deals with a few selected service industries such as general insurance, life insurance, public services, hospital and tourism. Shri Balachandran's book fills a gap in management studies.

CR ~ -

(C. Rangarajan)

PREFACE TO THE SECOND EDITION

Services continue to dominate economies the world over. Business process outsourcing (BPO) has become among the fastest growing sectors in India. Outsourcing helps organisations to cut costs. At the same time, it adds to social costs in terms of lost jobs. It also affects the terms of trade. Countries are presently engaged in reconciling these contradictory pulls within and between nations. The World Trade Organisation's (WTO) agendas are full with items relating to these unresolved contradictions.

Technology is driving these changes. Technologies throw up new possibilities every day. New products and new applications are constantly emerging. Keeping a book on services up-to-date, is therefore, a difficult task. The revisions that have been made are mainly in Chapter 9 on Managing Information. I have also added 'Logistics' among the select service industries, because the dimensions of this business are growing rapidly.

S. Balachandran

PREFACE TO THE FIRST EDITION

The services sector has always been a vital component of all economies. It has become more so these days. From the agricultural and the industrial economy, the emphasis has now shifted to the service economy. In India, the service industry had been given due recognition, as crucial to its economy. The first acts of nationalisation, as part of planned economic development, had been of services like banking, insurance, railways and airlines.

Till the early 1980s, literature on management dealt mainly with manufacturing and operations and did not pay much attention to services. By the 1980s, it was realised that the management of services needed a different approach from that of the management of manufacturing and trading. Articles and books began to appear, focussing on the service industry. In May 1993, I published a book entitled *Excellence in Services*.

Since then, the scenario in the services industry has undergone a sea change in India, keeping pace with the developments elsewhere in the world. Cellular phones, paging services, satellite communication, software, the Internet, credit cards and education are some of the areas in which growth has been very high and in which international presence and participation is becoming increasingly strong. Video libraries, found at every nook and corner in the 1980s and early 1990s, have practically vanished, giving way to satellite television and the cable operators. Incidental to this growth in the business of entertainment and information processing, is the expansion in software production (serials, chat shows, news, etc.), marketing of these, venues for shooting, studios and supporting services like editing, special effects, computer graphics and computer imaging. Words like the Internet, cyberspace, e-mail, web sites, surfing, artificial intelligence, virtual reality, connectivity and bandwidth, are indicative of the extent of one's awareness of the Global Information Infrastructure (GII), which is the symbol of both the present and the future. This book takes note of new developments in the business of services, in order to keep abreast with the latest developments. It is possible however, that in the intervening period between the time the book is written and it is published and read, further significant changes may have occurred.

Some of the words that have become common jargon over these six years are liberalisation, deregulation, globalisation, etc. The meanings and implications of these words are not easily understood by those who are not exposed to the complexities of economic strategies. Yet, what all these words mean is that competition is going to be intense. It also means that the market for Indian business is the international market. Services operating within India, like hotels, tourism, transportation, banking, insurance, software and communications, will have as customers, not Indians alone, but people and organisations from all over the world. The orientation necessarily, will have to be global.

It is obvious, that for a sustained competitive advantage in any business, the focus will have to be as much on service as on technology. This is probably what Mr Parvinder Singh, Chairman of Ranbaxy meant, when, while accepting *Business India*'s Businessman of the Year award, on 14 December, 1998. He said, 'The era of knowledge-based competition is upon us'. Service support makes even better price realisation possible. This is an area in which Indian industry has much to do.

Many of the ideas in this book will be relevant also to the service components of manufacturing industries, like marketing, customer care, retail management, purchasing, vendor development, office administration, warranties, franchising and relationships management. The impact of these practices will not remain confined to the Indian market. They will apply to intra-office transactions worldwide.

Concepts and principles of management found to be effective in the western industrialised world may succeed in Indian factories. One cannot be sure of this happening in the service sector. The reason is that matters relating to the provision of services are heavily people-oriented and, therefore, the local ethos has a role to play in its effectiveness. There are substantial differences between people in India and people elsewhere, in their behaviours as customers or as employees or as suppliers. Foreign entrants into the Indian business scene have learnt this at some cost of time and money.

This book also deals with reengineering. Many seem to think that reengineering is just another fad for what is basically Total Quality Management (TQM). The strongest argument that supports this view is that the Japanese do not appear to have gone in for reengineering. Despite some confusion on its scope and potential, reengineering has caught the imagination of entrepreneurs and professional managers. While examining the possibilities of a new concept that has done a lot of good elsewhere, it would be wrong to neglect such an important sector such as services which, all over the world, continues to grow at a faster rate than the rest of the economy, contributing to the GDP, to employment and to costs, more than the other sectors. Even in heavy industry, the application of reengineering has been in inventory movements and storage, in delivery schedules and procedures, in processing payables and information, in response to customer complaints, and so on. These are all services. Reengineering tries to enhance the quality of these services

Reengineering essentially deals with processes. The quality of a service is determined by its process. Service is rendered by people from the service organisation to people outside the service organisation. Service is also rendered by people within the organisation to other people within the organisation, who are internal customers. It is the interaction between these two sets of people that creates service and satisfaction from service. Information handling is a service within the organisation, that can enhance the quality of management as a whole and of performance at any level. The accuracy of information and the speed of processing it, can do a lot to enhance the quality of that service and the satisfaction therefrom. Many problems in business arise because the information available at any point of time is dated. The processes cause these problems. Attention being given to the processes will eliminate some of these problems.

This book focusses on quality, which is determined by the customer. The management of Indian service businesses will deal with Indian employees, but their customers may not be Indians alone. The quality standards to be aimed at will be global. The thrust of management has to be driven by the customer in the driver's seat. The title of the book reflects this focus.

Quality is the outcome of processes. People manage these processes. The focus on people is a necessary corollary. The book also deals with Marketing, as it is a critical factor. Marketing services is different from marketing other products.

I have tried to include illustrations and examples from service industries. However, Indian business is secretive and reluctant to reveal information. So, I have had to take recourse to cases published in journals or books.

The service industry is a mix of great variety. The nature and behaviour of the customer of a hotel is very different from that of a hospital or of an insurance company. In the latter, the associated emotions are of anxiety, sadness, depression and fear. The ways of catering to needs of these people cannot be the same as in the case of a hotel or tourist destination. In the case of couriers, banking and transportation, the attitude is more rational; considerations more economic than sentimental. Concepts and principles relevant to services have to be adapted for the uniqueness of each service operation or business. A separate chapter deals with some service businesses in detail, to highlight the distinctive differences in the characteristics of customers and strategies.

In the foreword to my earlier book, Dr M.B. Athreya, the well-known Indian management guru, had noted, 'As the economy opens up, it is increasingly being recognised that growth has to come not only from products, but also from services like tourism, banks, leisure, etc.' In the Harvard Business Review of September–October 1997, Peter Drucker, looking at the future, noted that in the developed world 'the critical work force will be contractors, experts, consultants, part-timers, joint venture partners and so on', and that 'new concepts, methods and practices, will be in the management of society's knowledge resources, education and health care, both of which are over-administered and under-managed.' The editorial of *Business India* (30 November to 13 December 1998) states, 'Brand Equity is an agglomeration of tangibles and intangibles. In these days of transition to a knowledge economy, it is the latter that has begun to matter more.' In his keynote address to the World Congress on Total Quality on 8 January 1999, the Rt. Hon Lord Swraj Paul remarked, 'It is clear that the 21st century will be an international century. People will move longer distances in shorter times. More importantly, managements will move goods, money, information and ideas farther than ever before over the world'. Managing information is one of the biggest services. In fact, the present and the future are often referred to as the information or the knowledge age.

The emphasis on the service business in today's world is very clear. I have written this book in the hope that it will make a humble contribution to the understanding of this business and lead to both better administration and better management. The book deals with concepts within which innovative practices can develop. It also deals with practices that give meaning to concepts. It should be of use both to academics familiar with the concepts and to practitioners aware of the practices.

In preparing this book, I have benefited from the supportive suggestions made by Mr Ranjan Kaul of Response Books. There are many others to whom I owe a lot for the information and the ideas that have gone into this book. It is difficult to identify and name them all. My children, Sangeetaa and Rajesh, and daughter-in-law, Bhavna, have been understanding enough to allow me to invest the time and effort in writing. They have had to tolerate a lot in terms of messy surroundings.

S. Balachandran

1 SERVICES TODAY

If one were to compare the market place of any town, small or big, with what it was, say, 20 years back, one would notice

- a large number of boutiques, travel agents, tour operators, one-minute photo services, xerox and telephone booths (providing STD and international calls facilities), computer classes, cybercafes, courier services, fast food joints—businesses almost non-existent 20 years ago,
- video games parlours which provide simulated experiences of skiing and Formula one racing, as if one is actually participating in a competition on the Alps or on the racing track,
- shops offering designer dresses, hoardings on auto-finance and cellular phones, name boards having words like cyberspace and the Internet,
- many shops with elaborate displays, more space for customer movement, more expensive decor, more lighting, more ornaments like plants, curios and water fountains—physical factors which are considered to be as important as the goods stocked, to provide customer satisfaction. Some shops also have arrangements for children to be looked after, while their elders shop without distraction,
- that purchasing has become much more convenient with many restaurants, shops, chemists, etc., accepting credit cards and providing home delivery services. Shopping can now be done sitting in one's drawing room, because of teleshopping through the telephone or the television. Tickets on airlines or railways can be booked through the Internet and are delivered at home. Books can be bought and magazines subscribed to, through cards and the Internet. Transactions in the capital market can also be made online, and now even education is available online. One can study at one's leisure and the examination will be conducted when one is ready to take the test.

These are indicators of how the business of services has been growing, occupying more and more of the market place. *They are varied. Most of them are new.*

Substantial space in the business press is devoted as a regular feature, to developments relating to communication via cellular phones and the Internet. Already, a large numbers of students, professionals and businessmen own or have access to a space, called a home page or website. Not only business organisations, but even students have e-mail addresses. No newspaper or journal is considered worthwhile unless it is on the Internet. Residents in the USA can read the *Hindu* of Chennai, the *Times of India* of Mumbai and the *Statesman* of Calcutta, before the residents of these cities receive them at their doorsteps. Indians can read the *Time, Newsweek* or any magazine published anywhere, without subscribing to them. Even spiritual needs can be met through the Internet. The Siddhivinayaka temple of Mumbai and the Dnyaaneshwari, are on the Internet, occupying cyberspace. Both customers and vendors and even marriage partners are found 'by surfing the Net' and they enter through the 'electronic door'. E-commerce is expected to overtake all other forms of retail selling. Government departments are competing in setting up websites. In this set up, there are web servers and website designers providing space, access and technical knowhow. Plenty of transactions, whether commercial, personal, governmental or otherwise, are taking place through these information highways, manning which is becoming one of the biggest services.

❏ *What is 'Service'* ❏

Several definitions of 'service' exist. All of them emphasise the following:

A service is intangible, yet provides satisfaction to the customer. Good service makes the consumer 'feel good'. To understand 'service' therefore, it is necessary to understand what makes people feel good. As we examine it in detail later, the scope and form and variations of service will be found to be infinite.

It is performed by people, not manufactured by machines. It does not come out of a process in a factory, but is experienced during the interaction of one person with another.

The service may or may not be tied to tangible goods. Maintenance and repairs are services tied to goods. Consultancy is not. Transportation and hotel services, providing intangibles like convenience and comfort, are tied to tangibles. Tourism is not.

If the service is tied to tangible goods, *the ownership of the goods does not pass from seller to buyer.* The buyer only acquires the right to certain benefits from what the seller offers. One may have the right to use the hotel room or a rail berth for a period of time, but the ownership of the room or the berth does not pass on to the user, even during that period of time. The ownership remains with the hotel or the railways. Libraries and leasing companies only lend. The ownership of what is lent does not transfer.

A doctor offers service. There is no tangible good that he produces or offers. He uses knowledge, which is intangible. He prescribes treatment which may cure. The treatment may or may not involve medicines, but he does not deal in medicines, like a chemist. The knowledge he uses remains with him. The patient only gets the benefit of that knowledge. The satisfaction is not only in the form of relief from sickness, but also in the manner of the doctor's attention, the behaviour of the attending nurse, the gentleness of the injection, the apparent thoroughness of the examination and so on—all intangibles.

❑ *Classification* ❑

Economic activities are broadly classified into five groups as follows:

1. The *Primary* sector refers to what comes directly as an output from land and nature. Agriculture, forestry, farming, mining, etc., belong to this sector.
2. The *Secondary* sector deals with the conversion of outputs from the primary sector. This includes manufacturing, engineering, construction, power generation and food processing.
3. The *Tertiary* sector deals with ancillary and support services like restaurants, hotels, laundry, maintenance, repairs and entertainment.
4. The *Quaternary* sector deals with facilitating the activities, as well as an exchange of products with the other sectors. These include transportation, communication, commerce, insurance, finance, administration and packaging.
5. The *Quinary* sector includes activities that change and improve people, like health care, education and beauty.

All economic activity is directed towards the production of goods and services. The primary and secondary sectors are involved essentially in the production of tangible goods. The other three sectors are essentially service sectors.

Even within manufacturing establishments, activities like human resources management, administration, logistics, marketing, information processing, accounting, repairs and sales are service activities. However, the costs of these activities are accounted for in the secondary sector, because the business is mainly of that kind.

❑ *Categories* ❑

The service sector can be divided into four categories:

- Production services, like repairs, maintenance and transportation of goods, growing almost at the same rate as industry.
- Business services, like banking, insurance, advertising, accountancy, finance, market research, credit cards, software, business centres, call centers and information processing, growing at rates faster than industry.
- Consumer services like health care, travel, leisure, beauty, entertainment, information, investments, education, consultancy and brokerage.
- Public administration and defence. Although this is a function of the government, administration is an important activity within all organisations, manufacturing or otherwise.

The boundaries of the variety of service businesses tend to get blurred. Insurance, banking, mutual funds, investment businesses overlap in many ways. Pensions, in the sense of regular periodical payments from a future date, can be arranged through the Unit Trust, Life Insurance Corporation of India (LIC), Mutual Funds or even through banks. Fixed deposits have effectively become current accounts, earning interest and can be placed with not only banks, but also public limited companies. Some non-banking companies abroad even provide cheque facilities. Travel agencies are into insurance business and also banking operations, particularly foreign exchange dealings. Thomas Cook had identified that in the 1990s, globally and particularly in Asia, the thrust will be in financial services, funds management, and security. They anticipated that issuing tickets may become routine and as easy as using a vending machine.

The SCICI was created as a subsidiary by the ICICI in 1986, as an agency dedicated to financing the needs of the shipping industry. Over the years, the SCICI diversified into financing other industries like automobiles, oil, steel, engineering, electronics and chemicals. It had developed expertise in shipping, aquaculture, transport and also entered into the sphere of merchant banking. In 1997, SCICI merged with the ICICI. The concept of Universal Banking recognises that separate classifications like retail banking, developmental banking and commercial banking, are not very relevant in 2003. The ICICI and the Industrial Development Bank of India (IDBI) have found that development banking functions have become insignificant. ICICI has become the bank. IDBI is contemplating such a change. These institutions have lost their unique roles, mainly because new regulatory policies have made it possible for capital being sourced globally.

Digitalisation of voice, images, data and text, has blurred the boundaries between telecommunication, computers, media and consumer electronics, generating competition between cable networks, cellular telephones, wireless radio and TV broadcasting, and satellite companies. They are all part of the GII, providing and facilitating entertainment, information, communication and commerce.

❑ *Range and Variety* ❑

The business of service ranges from

- multicrore hotel chains to wayside *dhabas* in the hospitality segment,
- airlines and shipping companies with a huge infrastructure of support systems, to owners of fleets of lorries, cars and buses, and to single-car-owner/taxi-driver in the transportation segment,
- a multifacility business centre with satellite linkages to receive data and transmit output to countries across the globe, to a single machine xerox facility, in the secretarial segment,
- a multidisciplined fully equipped general hospital, to speciality hospitals for specific diseases (for diabetes, eyes and heart), to diagnostic centres, to family physicians, in the healthcare segment,
- advisers on restructuring, on strategies for growth, on mergers and acquisitions, on arranging finance locally or globally, on interior furnishing and decor, on installing office systems, on tax management, on market information, on business opportunities, on technology, operating with a single person and an Internet connection or with plenty of professionals, located at several offices around the world, in the consultancy segment.

There are services which are

- supplier dominated, like education, healthcare, food and repairs, where the skills of the supplier are the source of service,
- production-intensive or scale-intensive services like travel, insurance, networks and phones,
- specialised technology services, like science-based laboratories providing designs or special effects for films.

With organisations becoming more complex, many services are contracted out. Services available include sweeping and cleaning office premises, providing flowers, maintaining plumbing systems or electric systems and airconditioners, running canteens, providing chauffeur-driven cars and so on. The Group 4 Securitas of the UK provides services in the areas of security, gas meter reading, escorting prisoners to court and so on. The adoption of Indian children (by childless couples, single women, or by others out of enlightened social consciousness), has given rise to a new advisory service—to find the children, to verify the bona fides of the intending adopters and to complete legal formalities. Well-known auctioneers like Sotheby's and Asprey's have set up offices in India to provide valuation for Indian art objects and to auction paintings and sculptures. One of the growing businesses in India, with a growth rate of about a 100 per cent, is information processing, which is essentially secretarial work. What is recorded by doctors on their dictaphones in the US, is received in India via satellite, transcribed and sent back via satellite, to be on the doctor's desk when he opens his clinic the next morning.

Education, as a service, is changing very rapidly. It is no longer an interaction between a teacher and students within the confines of a classroom, using textbooks and blackboards. Large numbers of students are being enrolled in India for courses of universities in England, the US, Australia, and elsewhere with facilities for local tuition and examination, both learning material and question papers being the same as in the headquarters of the university and in similar centres elsewhere, worldwide. Audio and video cassettes are available that substitute for text books, notes and lectures, to cover the curriculum for an entire course of a recognised educational institution. TV channels are developing their own programmes to provide such inputs in their daily broadcasts. In the quest for access to the most advanced levels of knowledge, the customary barriers of distances, costs and admission processes are breaking down. In the wake of such distance education becoming possible, there is a rise in the number of universities set up within the last couple of years to cater to young Indians aspiring for foreign degrees.

Event management is a new and big business. There are expected to be approximately 2,500 to 3,000 events per year, including conferences and launches. Both private and government organisations are involved in it. The business which was estimated to be Rs 30 billion in 2000, is expected to be worth Rs 300 billion by 2005. Live entertainment alone is expected to be worth Rs 50 million. When a major event takes place, the cost of conducting it is met through entry fees, sponsorships, broadcasting rights, advertising rights. People even pay to be associated with that event. The economics of producing a film is different in 2003 compared to say, in 1983. Associated businesses include, advertisement of products within the film, sponsorship for launching and for promotion of film and songs, and rights to songs. Many advertising agencies like O&M, MaaBozell, Maadhyam and Clea PR have set up separate divisions to take care of events. Events constitute a special niche business of some companies like CPV Cause Celebre, Wizcraft, Plus Events, DNA Networks, Procam, Showbiz, Fountain head and A! Media Power Productions. The business prospects are attractive. Therefore, the number of companies entering the business is likely to grow from 30 to about 150 in two years. However, it is also a fairly risky business. ABCL is an instance, of difficulty in survival, despite strong brand equity.

Managing events is not easy. It needs lot of expertise. Mistakes can be as embarrassing as the 'eminent' key speaker being introduced on the basis of the wrong data sheet!

Seminars and conferences, hosted by government firms or rather non-corporate agencies, are usually entertaining, if not comical. Professionalism, being a far fetched term with them, they leave a funny giggle in the stomach of journos who are expected to attend them and take down serious notes. Take the bridge engineers seminar hosted in the city the other day. The piazza of the auditorium was crammed with coloured valises meant to be given as gifts to guests. However, the attendants handling the valises were not sure who exactly the gifts were meant to be given to and ended up making a mockery of the whole thing. They made some of the guests wait indefinitely, while the seminar had already begun. One of the guests miffed and huffed at being kept waiting, finally decided to get inside without the largesse.

Emcees invariably end up bungling up the simple procedures of seminar manouevring. At yet another conference, the host called all the distinguished guests, all in a row (like children getting into a school bus) back up the stage, long after they had finished their speeches, only for the pallid roses.

Source: *Sunday Midday*, 15 November 1998.

❏ *Value Addition* ❏

One goes to a restaurant to eat food. However, eating may not be the only purpose of the visit. The food may be incidental to the main purpose of celebrating an event or negotiating a business deal or a social get-together. The sense of satisfaction at the end of the visit would depend not so much on the quality of the food—which is, no doubt, important—but on other factors, like promptness and courtesy shown by the staff, the general ambience of the place, the music, the noise level, the privacy available (if privacy was important) and the respect and recognition shown. These constitute service (intangibles that matter) and determine whether the customer will return, if there is a similar occasion. Food of similar quality can be had at many places. However it is service that distinguishes one restaurant from another. In fact, the quality of service influences one's perception of the quality of the food, both positively and negatively. *Service adds value.*

Airlines offer to carry people from one city to another. The aircraft and the space around the seats are tangible. Probably all major airlines offer the same tangible facilities. But passengers have preferences for some airlines. These may be due to convenience of timings, punctuality, safety precautions, check-in and baggage delivery arrangements, care during flights and transit and so on. These factors provide satisfaction as much as, if not more than, the extent of legspace or the cuisine. These are essentially service elements and intangible. They add value.

The Jawaharlal Nehru Port at Nhava Sheva off Mumbai is one of the most modern in terms of lengths of berths, draft, cranes and other handling equipments. It is built with enough capability to handle large-size shipments. However, ships are generally reluctant to call at this port because the turnaround time is among the worst in the world. Turnaround depends on the way the available equipments and facilities are used. These constitute service. Efforts have been made in 2003, to improve these services, so that more ships would dock at this port.

Even those who produce and sell goods have found that competitiveness is enhanced, or reduced, by the nature of service that accompanies the sale of goods. The excellence of the product will not hold the market and customers' loyalty if deliveries are not made on schedule, billings are wrong, documents are improper, packaging is defective, queries are not answered, shipments are to the wrong addresses, or credits are not given as agreed upon. Technical differences between products are becoming less significant. For example, there may be little to choose between one make of TV and another, in terms of technical data and characteristics, which in any case, most users do not understand. Computer dealers sell the hardware largely on the strength of what they offer in the areas of

- help in planning and installing support facilities,
- training of the staff of the client organisation,
- help in programme development to suit the client's needs,
- speed of response in the event of breakdown or problems cropping up.

Market information, advertising and promotion are as important as the quality of goods, to ensure market penetration and dominance. The periodical studies of the Audit Bureau of Circulation are critical to the revenues of any newspaper or magazine. Similar ratings from recognised agencies, are important for companies seeking capital from Indian or foreign markets. The popularity of a departmental store depends very much on the quality of display and billing and delivery procedures. These are services.

Managers throughout the world are unanimous that in the future years, superior service will be the key differentiation in the battle for the minds, hearts, and credit cards of the customer. It will remain the focus of all strategy. Developers and builders promote the new colonies, not merely on the strength of design or the quality of the houses, but security, health clubs, Internet and piped-gas connections, etc. Some even offer day and night international standard golf courses, aqua club including fishing and a range of water sports, amusement parks, adventure clubs including sky sports like hang-gliding or rock climbing and trekking, multipoint video conferencing with link up via satellite, hi-tech communication, subsidised transport services including helicopters, health care including doctors and diagnostic centres, electronic surveillance systems, infra-red fencing systems, uninterrupted power supply, LPG supply and a lot of other facilities. Examples are Sahara in Goregaon (Mumbai) and Santosa near Noida, New Delhi.

The Matsushita Electric Co. of Japan had set up service stations throughout India, even in the days when import of electronic goods were severely restricted, in order to maintain the competitive position of the 'National' range of audio and video equipment, which were coming in from the Middle East countries. A manufacturer of fertilisers conducts farmer contact programmes, field demonstrations and crop seminars, using video films, on efficient urea management. A cement manufacturer believes that it has to focus on marketing and logistics for competitive advantage. The superior strength of its product is not enough to get leadership in the market. It runs workshops for masons and contractors on various aspects of concrete mixing and applications.

Service has more economic impact than is commonly imagined. Many are losing out because the service provided is mediocre. In fact, even good service, after some time, would be seen as mediocre. The challenge therefore, is to be continuously upgrading the level of service and thus add value. Given below is an extract showing how car manufacturers in India were gearing up for competitive advantage by adding value through services.

> But where price does not remain the ultimate factor in purchase decisions, value-for-money is manifested in a number of other factors. After-sales service, for instance. For General Motors, this translates to a complete ownership experience .... To this end, the company has set up Opel Club, an exclusive club for Astra owners. The club membership entitles the car owners to exclusive benefits and privileges, through special offers from other brands such as Airtel, Lufthansa, Nokia, the Welcomgroup, Reebok, Sita Travels and HCL-Frontline. Special events from members are also to be organised by the Club. Two of these have already happened, one each at Delhi and Mumbai.
>
> G.M. has also launched a Customer Assistance Programme for its customers. In the event of a breakdown at a location far away from Opel dealer service facilities or authorised service outlets, all the car owner needs to do is to call the customer assistance number printed on his Opel Club card.
>
> Honda, on its part, plans to offer the famous 'Honda after sales customer care'—a complete value package to take care of service, spare parts and customer care from one location.
>
> '... The latest strategy for market share includes wooing auto finance companies with attractive incentive packages, ...like 30 day credit period, cash incentives of Rs 7000 to Rs 8000, one-year free service, free fuel up to 600 litres, 'old car for new', holiday packages, cellular phones, et al.'
>
> Source: *The Economic Times*, 25 December 1996.

The increasing importance of services in the economy and in the value addition to business is reflected in the number of specialised diploma courses that have been developed by universities and other institutions that cover the management of services. Insurance and banking have always been important service businesses. Banking was a subject in commerce courses, but specialised qualifications could be obtained only through the Indian Institute of Bankers or the Insurance Institute of India, similar to the qualifications provided by professional associations like the Institute of Chartered Accountants of India, the Institute of Cost and Works Accountants, or the Institute of Company Secretaries. A number of institutions have recently begun offering diplomas and degrees in insurance. It is now considered an essential subject in most of the finance disciplines. There are also courses available in the management of materials, inventories, logistics, advertising, events, sales, retailing, purchasing, hospitals, hotels, travel and tourism and so on, conducted by variety of academic institutions.

❏ *Growth* ❏

Services is the fastest growing segment of the economy, worldwide. In the US, 75 per cent to 80 per cent of new jobs are in the service sector. The contribution of the service sector to the GNP has increased compared to the rest of the sectors. The richest man of the late 1990s, Bill Gates, is from the service industry. The World Trade Organisation (WTO) reports that the world's largest industry is tourism with over 613 million people travelling in 1997 and an expected 1 billion by the year 2010.

In India, the same trends are seen. In the Yellow pages of the Mumbai Telephone Directory, the number of entries for the service industry exceed the entries for manufacturing, by nearly 2:1. In the 'Appointments' columns, the advertisements for jobs for services exceed those for manufacturing by almost the same ratio. The jobs in the service sector were just about the same as in manufacturing in 1980. It was 160 per cent by 1990. Out of the 27.79 crores of persons employed in the organised sector in 2002, 1.43 were in agriculture, 6.44 in manufacturing and 17.97 in the services industry, including finance and insurance (1.65), social services (11.56), construction (1.14), retail (0.5) and transport (3.12). The number will be more, if it is noted that only 5 per cent of the retail trade is in the organised sector. It is estimated that for every 10 lakhs of rupees invested, the number of jobs created in manufacturing is 13, in agriculture 45 and in services 89. Jobs in the service sector, particularly at higher levels, command the highest salaries and have the heaviest demand.

The contribution of the service sector to the economy had risen from about 30 per cent in 1970–1971 to over 50 per cent in 1988–1989. The growth rate of the service sector has been about 37 per cent compounded, between 1984–85 and 1988–89, and was expected to continue to grow at a minimum of 25 per cent. Some services like credit cards and couriers, had been growing at 35 per cent to 40 per cent, while the software industry and cellular phones had been growing at much higher rates (exceeding 50 per cent). In 1998, when a general recession hit the Indian industry, software and IT companies were surging upwards in the Indian stock markets. Even in 2003, the IT related services grew at much more than 50 per cent. Call centres are growing at more than 80 per cent. A survey conducted by the CII indicated that in the six months from April to September 2003, the cellular phones business had grown by 180 per cent, housing finance by 35 per cent, project consultancy by 45 per cent and software exports by 40 per cent. The number of new restaurants opening each year in Delhi is 170 compared to an average of 35 a few years back. Experts find it difficult to estimate future trends with any accuracy.

A study made in 1997 by Merrill Lynch, termed Global Satellite, estimates that the satellite operation industry will emerge as the main means of delivering advanced digital telephony, high speed Internet access and multichannel digital television. It is expected that the industry will triple in the next five years from $4.5 billion to $14.7 billion, or even to $31 billion, if 'direct to home' television is included. The number of computers connected to the Internet was expected to go up from 50 million to 200 million by 2000 AD. This may turn out to be an underestimate as new uses are being found for the Internet. Electronic commerce was expected to cross $ 300 billion by 2000 AD, according to the WTO. The sales of *Encyclopedia Brittanica* dropped more than 50 per cent between 1990 and 1996 in the face of the alternative offered by CD-ROMs. The costs of producing a CD-ROM was $1.50 compared to $200 to $300 in the case of the *Brittanica*, including binding. CD-ROMs were available at $50 while the *Brittanica* cost $1500 to $2000. The *Brittanica* almost wound up. The attempt to recoup their position was by pursuing the electronic route.

❏ *Globalisation* ❏

The world is moving towards becoming a single market. The European Community, the ASEAN, Pacific Rim, the SAPTA, the NAFTA, are all movements in this direction. The WTO, which has replaced the General Agreement on Tariffs and Trade (GATT), is also pushing for removal of tariffs and trade barriers, permitting increasingly freer movement of money, labour and goods across national boundaries. International bodies like the World Bank (WB) and the International Monetary Fund (IMF), also put pressure on aid-receiving countries to move in this direction. Communist countries provide the strongest evidence of how closed communities do not survive. A hard-core communist country like Cuba has also begun to open up. India has recognised the compulsions of global interdependence, although some groups contend that the security of nationhood is at stake, if restrictive controls are removed. *The increase in competitiveness, that comes from globalisation, will require increasing emphasis on the quality of services as much as of goods.*

The movement of service across national boundaries is relatively free. Big finance is arranged by international consortia pooling their resources from operations all over the world. A crisis in Korea (1997) or Brazil (1999) had its repercussions in the financial markets throughout the world. More than 60 per cent of the credit cards business in India comes from foreigners travelling in India. Access to broadcasts is difficult to regulate. Governments find it difficult to regulate the 'air invasion' (TV or radio) from across the boundaries, via satellite or otherwise. When trade is international, all services that enable trade, like insurance, banking, transportation, communication, practically the whole of the Quaternary sector, has to be international. In December 1991, 26 nationalised banks and 11 branches of foreign banks in India were linked to the SWIFT—Society for Worldwide Interbank Financial Telecommunications— global network, joining 3,000 financial institutions in 74 countries to help do business with each other, using standardised messages. This network carried over 1.5 million messages per day, including customer bank transfers, documentation credits and traveller's cheques. Airlines like Swiss Air and Cathay Pacific have moved entire departments to India, to handle and control their worldwide activities in accounting for revenue or for reservations. A ticket booked in Brazil is accounted for in Chennai (India). Some of these departments might become separate companies to perform similar services for other airlines as well. The Tata Energy and Resources Institute (TERI) had set up an institute in Washington to advise the WB on the environmental concerns of underdeveloped countries.

Information and knowledge know no boundaries. They travel between the minds of people through fax, telephones, Internet, cyberspace and satellite TV, through papers and discussions at conferences and seminars and through journals. Universities across countries exchange course materials, libraries and professors. Access through satellite is also easy. Medical reports are referred to specialists via electronic media and opinions are obtained in no time at all. Money moves across the globe almost instantaneously, depending on market conditions, exchange rate fluctuations etc., which are monitored continuously and communicated globally through channels like the Reuters, BBC, CNN and ABN. Many financial and industrial institutions employ personnel only to monitor these fluctuations and transfer funds between markets and currencies in order to derive maximum advantage, for booking profits, as well as to hedge against imbalances in portfolios. The loan of $100 million obtained by the IPCL in August 2003, was arranged by a consortium of banks, led by the State Bank of India (SBI) and included the ANZ Investment Bank (Australia & New Zealand), the Emirates Bank (UAE), Bumiputra Commerce Bank (Malaysia), National Bank of Kuwait, Syndicate Bank (India), Bank Muscat International (Muscat), SBI International (Mauritius), Indian Overseas Bank (India), and MizuhoFinancial Group (Japan). The funds of each of these companies must have been mobilised from different parts of the world.

An indicator of the momentum towards globalisation is that several law firms, established many years ago, have begun to open offices abroad. Cadawalader Wickersham & Taft, Wallstreet's oldest firm, opened its office in London in September 1996. Freshfields, Allen & Overy, Linklaters & Paines, Clifford Chance, all UK firms, recently hired offices in the USA. Dorsey has added German, Belgian and Irish lawyers in its Brussels office.

The business of service is what makes the market truly global. Since it is global, the expectations of customers are high. The standards by which they are evaluated are international. The customer, whenever possible, exercises his option in favour of the best, from wherever available. One may not have much choice about infrastructural services like roads, telephone, warehousing or retailing, but there is choice about music, TV, information, entertainment, medical care, banking and insurance services. Tourists have choices regarding places to visit. Those connected with these services can ignore this factor only at a grave risk to their businesses, even if the business is offered only within India. However, for those who transact internationally, the challenge is greater. They will have to continuously strive to match and excel the best possible international standards.

❏ *World Trade in Services* ❏

One of the major issues in the negotiations in the WTO relate to services. The services sector, including insurance, forms part of the negotiations. Services are traded through: (*a*) cross border supplies, when the service is provided across the border (for example, consultancy advice is sent to the client); (*b*) consumption mode when the consumer moves across the border to access the service (tourists); (*c*) commercial presence when facilities are set up in the importing country (banks, insurance and service centres); and (*d*) when people go across the borders to provide the service (software specialists). There is a controversy with regard to the movement of people.

Countries, including developed countries, hesitate to open up their services sector. India, for example, does not favour the entry of foreign companies to be in the audit or news gathering business. Developed countries, including the USA and many in Europe, are not in favour of BPO operations being shifted to India or to the Philippines, or of Indian software engineers going there, because these cause loss of jobs locally. Services constitute two-thirds of the domestic product of the European Union and account for 110 million or two-thirds of the total employment.

❏ A Different Model ❏

Theories of management appropriate for managing industrial establishments, have been found to be inadequate in dealing with the issues of service management. The model for managing services had to be different from the model for managing industries. The main reason is that in the industrial model, the focus was on production, locations, logistics, sales promotion, advertising, revenue and costs. The objective was to keep operating costs low and maximise profits, which could be done through technology, machines and systems. The emphasis was not so much on people. In the service model, technology and machines yield place to people, who deliver services. Strategies and systems, in the industrial model, were assumed to be capable of rendering satisfactions to the customer. The third component in the process was people. In the services management model, both strategies and systems have to be aligned to the needs of the role of the people in delivering satisfactions. Middle managers and supervisors assume great importance.

❏ Summary ❏

Service is intangible, performed by people, providing satisfaction to customers. Services vary considerably in variety and size. Boundaries between different kinds of services have become blurred. This is the fastest growing sector in the economy. It provides the competitive edge in the market place. It does not recognise geographical boundaries. It is truly global in its reach and impact. The model for service management is different from the model for industrial management.

2 THE DISTINGUISHING CHARACTERISTICS

Every economic unit produces either goods or services (or both), for the benefit of the community outside it. The nature of services is distinctly different from the nature of goods. Therefore, the methods and principles relevant to the management of services have to be different in several aspects. People perform services, while goods are manufactured. Apart from this, services are distinguished from goods mainly by five factors, such as intangibility, inseparability, heterogeniety, perishability and ownership.

❑ *Intangibility* ❑

Goods are tangible in the sense that they have physical dimensions and attributes and can be seen, felt or tasted. Services have none of these and are therefore, intangible. For example, in the case of an educational institution, one can see and evaluate the building in which it is located, the facilities within, the library, its academic affiliations and the qualifications of the faculty. However, none of these tangibles determine the nature and the quality of the education imparted by that institution. These are only adjuncts for its main purpose, which is education. The 'product' (of education) is to be evaluated in terms of the development of the knowledge, intellect and character of the alumni. This development may be perceived, but cannot be measured. The marks obtained in a test are not a correct measure of the development. The critical factor that constitutes education is intangible. Municipal schools in villages sometimes have very dedicated teachers, and provide better education than some of the expensive public schools which, because of excessive pocket money, may have misguided students from wealthy backgrounds who value arrogance instead of humility. Doctors providing medical treatment in government hospitals are often as qualified as doctors in private hospitals. The shabbiness of government hospitals is not indicative of the sincerity or adequacy of the medical attention provided. The latter is intangible.

One cannot see, feel, smell, touch or measure a service performed. *It can only be experienced from the effects produced on the person receiving the service.* Most of the hotels are constructed and furnished with a lot of care. The design and interior decoration do not make a guest feel good about his stay there. These do not necessarily ensure that the lights work when put on, or that hot water is available when needed, or that lizards do not jump out of the cupboard. When one wakes up thirsty at midnight and finds the water jug empty, the experience is not mitigated by the fact that the jug is made of pure crystal.

When a doctor examines a patient and makes a decision about diagnosis and treatment, what we see him doing are things like tapping the chest, listening to the sounds, looking at the throat and reading the instruments or reports. He is not paid for doing these observable activities. He is paid for the knowledge, the experience and the training that he brings to bear during these observable activities, his deductions and diagnosis and the remedy that he prescribes. This application of knowledge and arriving at a diagnosis is intangible. If the patient is cured, the effect of the service rendered by him is experienced as good. Otherwise, it is experienced as bad and second opinion is sought. It does not matter what the doctor's qualifications are. The patient's satisfaction with the medical service does not depend upon the prestige of degrees added to the doctor's name or the hospital in which he works.

The service that a cinema offers is in terms of providing pleasure, through the screening of films. The pleasure is an intangible experience. The courtesy shown by a waiter in a restaurant, or by an airhostess on a flight, the comfort of airconditioning in a hotel, the speed of response of a nurse and the promptness of a maintenance man, are all intangible. There is no way of measuring these, except in terms of the customer's evaluation. If he says the service is bad, there is no way of proving it otherwise, except perhaps, through many other customers with different evaluations, of the same transaction.

One might ask whether the service provided by a car rental service is not tangible. The answer will become clear if one compares the purchase of a car to the hiring of a car. In the first case, the purchase is made after comparisons are made among different makes and models, the comparison being on factors like roominess, safety features, performance, fuel consumption, maintenance costs and colour. In the second case, the rental firm is selected on the basis of an assumption or reputation that the car supplied will not break down, that the chauffeur will be competent and polite, and so on. The tangible part is not what the buyer is buying in the second case. After deciding to dine out, the restaurant is chosen on the basis of whether the experience, not merely the food, is likely to be satisfying or not, consistent with the main purpose, viz., celebration, entertaining guests or just having a good time. The relevant factors are intangible.

The characteristic of intangibility lies on a continuum, with pure goods at one end and pure service at the other, with most products lying between the two extremes. When an almirah is being bought, the considerations are essentially its strength, space, size, security, etc., all tangible, measurable factors. When a refrigerator is being bought, the considerations are essentially functional, i.e. its ability to cool and to preserve food. The considerations will also be the arrangements for repair, in case anything goes wrong, which are intangible factors of service. When a motorcar is being bought, there are more intangibles as regular services and repairs will be more frequent. When a lawyer is being selected for a case, the consideration is his competence, a factor which is purely intangible and cannot be measured.

Services can also be distinguished between 'pure intangibles' (education, consultancy, information, museum, security services, placement agencies), services which add value to tangible products (repair, laundry, decor, advertising, insurance), and services that make available tangible products (retailing, credit cards, financing, warehousing, mail order, transport).

It is difficult to provide a sample of the service that is on offer. One's experience of a service is a totality, the effect of all the elements present at the time. It is not possible to duplicate the totality, as a sample. The totality would require the entire infrastructure to be in place. A courier cannot demonstrate his service, until all his systems and linkages for collection and delivery at all connected places are operational. A retail shop cannot open with only 10 shelves as a sample of what it might be when it has all its scheduled 200 shelves full. The experience of a tour operator, when he is checking out a hotel, is not the sample of what his clients will experience, when 50 of them arrive together in the hotel a few days later. Researchability is poor when sampling is difficult. Test marketing before introducing a new service, is also difficult. Intangibles cannot be specified or described accurately. Without that, there can be no patent or copyright, and it then becomes difficult to prevent the competition from copying and matching one's service. Competitors are able to imitate and adapt one's innovative concepts. These are some of the implications of the characteristic of intangibility

❑ *Inseparability* ❑

A physical product like soap or oil, is produced in a factory, bought in a retail shop and consumed in a customer's premises, at his convenience. The experience of a refrigerator or new fruit drink, is not when it is bought at the shop, but when it is used at home. There is a gap in time and space between production, purchase and consumption. In a restaurant, one of the factors that constitutes service, providing customer satisfaction, is the courtesy of the waiter. In this case it is the behaviour of the waiter with the customer that is of relevance not his behaviour elsewhere. Courtesy is what the customer perceives at a particular time, not before or after. It is shown by the waiter and perceived by the customer simultaneously. There is no gap either in time or space between the production and the consumption of the service. They are not, and cannot be, separated. The service product, being an intangible, exists only during the interaction.

When one goes to an event like a musical show or a beauty contest, the satisfaction depends on how clearly one is able to witness the various details of the event and how well one is able to hear what is going on, plus the comforts (atmospheric and physical) provided during the show. All these are the outcomes, not only of the arrangements made by the organisers, but also of the behaviour of the rest of the audience, the position of one's seat, the movements of the performers on stage and off stage, and so on. None of these would be the same if the show were to be repeated on another day or even after another hour. The experience was as it occurred (produced) and as it was experienced (consumed). Both happened together and could not have been separated. If the same events were recorded and watched later on one's video player, the experience would not be the same.

When a car is being repaired by a mechanic, the mechanic's skills are applied directly to the job. The effectiveness of the repair job can be tested only on the performance of the repaired car. The satisfaction with the service and an evaluation of its quality takes place only when the performance, after repair, is experienced. An advertisement does not exist till it is seen and read. The advertisement is as good or as bad as the impact it has on the reader. That impact depends also on who the reader is and his frame of mind at that time. If the advertisement is not seen, either because its size is small, or it is dwarfed by a bigger splash, or it is in a corner of a page not normally read by many, or any other reason, for all practical purposes, there is no advertisement.

Education takes place in the interaction of the teacher and the student. Both teaching (production) and learning (consumption) take place together. If there is no learning, there is no teaching. The product exists only when the consumption takes place. In a class of many students, a teaching session of one hour may cause different levels of learning among the students. What the teacher did in that one hour would be the same for all students, but each student would have received it differently. The product (of teaching) was different to each student, depending on the nature of his consumption (learning).

The production and consumption take place mostly at the producer's premises and with his equipment. Examples are laundry, car rental, beauty parlour, museums, and parks. There are exceptions when the barber or the courier or the doctor visits the customer's premises to provide the service. Even then, the equipment remains the possession of the producer. Where the user has to use his equipment, the service is pure and can be provided at the consumer's premises like TV or radio broadcasting, telephone and the Internet. Even banking has started providing service at the consumer's premises.

The implications of the concept of Inseparability are several. First, *one cannot manufacture service somewhere and transport it to be delivered to the consumer at another appropriate place and hour.* A service organisation's manufacturing facility is effectively operated in the presence of the consumer and together with him. When a fast food service like McDonalds opens an outlet in Mumbai, the food is being franchised and its quality maintained. The service elements consisting of speed of delivery, courtesy, freshness, cleanliness, etc., cannot be created or controlled at any place other than in the Mumbai premises. These cannot be manufactured elsewhere to be 'delivered' in Mumbai.

Second, *sales are direct.* There will be no intermediary. Services cannot be stored and warehoused, like manufactured goods, which are produced in a factory and delivered later to the consumer through a retail outlet. The service provided at the McDonalds outlet in Mumbai is that of the franchisee. The franchisee may be trained to McDonalds' standards, but the service provided in New York cannot be made available in Mumbai.

An important outcome of this characteristic is that *the service product cannot be experienced before the purchase. In fact, the customer has to make the purchase, before it is even produced.* When one engages a consultant, the purchase is made. The product, by way of the consultant's advice, is made only thereafter. The client organisation cannot later on claim that the consultant's work was not satisfactory and refuse to pay. The doctor's fees has to be paid whatever the final outcome of the treatment is. Similarly, school fees have to be paid, even if the student fails. One cannot walk out of a restaurant without paying, on the ground that the food or the floorshow was not satisfactory.

❑ *Heterogeneity* ❑

Due to the factor of inseparability, it is not possible to produce a service in advance, according to specified standards. Both production and consumption of a service being done by human beings, the service (as experienced), may not be of a consistent quality. What is 'excellent' to one, may not be so to another. What is 'excellent' for one at a particular time, may not be so to the same person at another time. In a cinema, while one person may be sitting on the edge of his chair thoroughly engrossed, another may be snoring away, thoroughly bored. In a class, the quality of teaching is as varied as the students who attend the class. The same teacher will not explain a topic in the same way everyday. Even if the words and the examples are the same, the tone, enthusiasm, and the emphasis may differ. *Standardisation is difficult.* In the case of goods, the quality can be checked at the gate before the product leaves the premises and reaches the customer. Not so, in the case of services.

An optician sells glasses to correct vision. However, what is bought by the customer is not merely better vision, but also fashion and appearance. That is why he chooses between different kinds and colours of glasses as well as between different kinds and types of spectacle frames. The consumer may need help in making these choices. An optician who is technically good at determining the proper refractive index of corrective glasses, has to enhance his 'service' with a large range of frames and tints of glasses, which the consumer can try out. A choice cannot be made from a catalogue or even from looking at the display shelf. The choice depends on the 'fit' of the frame to the face of the customer, as seen by the customer himself. The service must also include speed of delivery, depending on the urgency of the consumer. *Each customer requires a different kind of service.*

A good service organisation may provide elaborate training to its staff on the ways in which they should try to serve their customers. The hotel receptionist, the telephone operator, the hospital nurse, the tourist guide, the room service attendant, the shop salesman, the theatre usher, the cabin steward and the bank clerk, can be given practical instruction on strict routines of work-related behaviour, so that what they do at work, would reflect the service standards of the organisation they represent. Yet, the warmth of the smile cannot be guaranteed. What the tourist wants to know and what the guide is explaining, may be completely different. Different guides in an agency may effectively render different kinds of service depending on each tourist's interests and requirements.

In a beauty parlour, the beauticians may be very skilled, but what each customer needs will be different. Not all opt for the latest fashions. Each shape and face is different and there cannot be a standard routine for each customer. The result of the beautician's efforts will be seen only after the job is completed. What the beautician may consider perfect, could be most disgusting to the owner of the face.

A garage may have a routine of repair and maintenance. Yet, it is the mechanic who has to listen to the sounds of the machine and decide how many turns of the screw are required for fine tuning. Whether the decision is perfect or not cannot be guaranteed, however experienced and competent the mechanic may be. Even if there is an electronic machine to help him in say, wheel balancing or engine tuning, it is the mechanic who has to adjust the machine. If he is not in a proper frame of mind, his concentration and performance will be affected. The service of the garage varies according to the mechanic doing the job and his frame of mind at that time.

In conducted tours, in restaurants, in theatres and in aircraft, the experience of the service is influenced by others present. The behaviour of other people may give one either pleasure or irritation. It also influences one on the evaluation of the service received. The irritating experience may be attributed to the poor service provided. The efforts of the tour agency or the restaurant manager may be affected or even overlooked due to the behaviour of other people present.

One of the major problems faced by every 'service' organisation, is the effectiveness of prescribed routines in ensuring the consistent quality of service. Elimination of the human element in the process, even partially, may improve the consistency. Electronic instruments, automated teller systems (ATMs), stores that display prices and allow self service, are attempts to standardise procedures and achieve consistency in the quality of service. Even if these attempts succeed, customers may respond differently. The response to the same stimulus can be very different. This response is the 'consumption' which determines the product and cannot be standardised.

❏ *Perishability* ❏

The demand for fire crackers is very high during the Diwali season. Manufacturers of crackers make them well in advance, stock them at various places, and sell the whole stock during the season. If the crackers are not consumed, they can remain in stock and be sold later when consumers are available as they do not perish during storage and retain their full value. Vegetables, though perishable over time, can also be stocked for later consumption, through processes like refrigeration and canning. However, *the supply of services cannot be so stored.* If an advertisement is not seen or read, it dies. The money spent on it is wasted. If the available seats in a cinema are not used during a show, the vacant seats cannot be added on to the next show. If the supply is not used, it perishes. The loss of revenue cannot be recovered. Similarly, the seats in an aircraft, the rooms in a hotel, the space in a ship, the facilities in a diagnostic centre, the time at the beauty parlour, all perish, if not used when available. What is unsold, cannot be carried forward to the next day. The income which is lost, cannot also be made on a subsequent day and this loss of income is permanent and irrecoverable.

The ability to carry stocks, gives the manufacturer of goods some level of stability in operations, despite fluctuations in demand. If the supply is short at any time, he can arrange deferred deliveries. The consumer can buy and store the product till he is ready to consume it. The stability in operations helps to improve the recovery of costs. Such stability is not possible for the producer of services, because of the characteristic of perishability. If an airline has only 20 per cent occupancy, the costs of operation do not come down to 20 per cent. If the courier does not get business which he is equipped to handle, his costs of establishment will remain the same. If the funds in a bank are not used on a particular day, that much interest is a permanent loss to the bank. If the telephone is not used, that much income is lost to the telephone company. None of these can become additional business the next day.

A museum's capacity to handle visitors, is limited by the strength of the staff and the space available for visitors to move and view the exhibits. If the number of visitors is less than this capacity on any day, it cannot handle that much more the next day. If there is 'too much of a crowd', the visitors will be dissatisfied. Those who are not admitted on any day because of limited capacity, may not come back the next day.

Perishability is less if the service facility is mobile. A mechanic, who works for more than one contractor, is less perishable than one who stays only in the same workshop. A restaurant which supplies home-delivery of food is less perishable than one which serves only within its own premises. The supplies in a circulating library are less perishable than in a reading room. An advertisement by way of a loose insertion in a newspaper, is less perishable than one which is printed within its columns. Advertisements and newspapers on the Internet being less mobile, are more perishable. However, in relation to those who browse, they are not perishable at all. This is a different segment and the dynamics are different.

Supply of service has to be understood as the capacity to produce, not as a quantity of output. In a service business, capacity is sold, while a manufacturer sells inventory. Capacity can be utilised only when customers are present (The concept of inseparability). The implication from the concept of perishability is that there is a need to ensure that the service offered is used on a continuous basis. The demand has to be consistent with supply, not merely on an average over a period of time, but all the time. *Anything short of maximum at any time, is an irrecoverable loss.* Also, if demand is more than supply, the business is lost. Hotels and airlines have firm arrangements with other hotels (nearby) and airlines (on the same routes) to take up the excess bookings, so that customer loyalties are not lost. Very often, the demand comes without prior notice, like the arrival of 260 passengers because of delayed or diverted flights, or of casualties after a major disaster or the pressure on the telephone system when idols of Lord Ganesh reportedly drank milk. At any level of capacity, the service will become woefully inadequate.

❏ *Ownership* ❏

This concept has been explained at some length in the earlier chapter.

❏ *Other Features* ❏

Services are performed by people, but service businesses are not low tech. One of the fast-growing areas of the service segment relates to computers. Computers are high tech. Maintenance and repair services are high tech in the aircraft industry or nuclear power plants. There are a lot of high tech applications in the business of cinema, theatre, music concerts, advertisements, medicine and surgery. Some of the action scenes of modern films like the *Titanic* (with 14 Oscar nominations) or *Jurassic Park*, are not shot in the studios but are created in the computer room.

Service businesses have high labour impact, but not necessarily high labour content in total output. The quality, determined in terms of customer satisfaction, is influenced by the people. However, the labour cost as a proportion of the total cost of producing the service would, in several cases, be low.

❏ *Barriers to Entry* ❏

Barriers to entry are those obstacles that prevent potential entrants from disturbing the existing market structure. The more the barriers, the safer the existing players are from competition.

Five kinds of barriers are postulated, particularly in the context of manufacturing.

- *Cost* : Newcomers may have higher average costs compared to existing firms.
- *Initial Capital Requirements*: This will vary according to the type of business.
- *Scale*: New entrants may have to produce large outputs relative to the total size of the market, to remain competitive. Multinationals have the capability to do so.
- *Product Differentiation*: Specialised products may be needed by various segments of the market.
- *Legal*: These constitute patents, franchises, licences, etc.

Due to the vast range in the service industry, it is difficult to generalise. Broadly speaking, the barriers to entry in services are low. In other words, the chances of new competition are high. The capital investments are high only in some services like hospitality and transport. Even in the services requiring capital, the investment does not have to be big, unlike manufacturing industries, where a minimum size of turnover would be necessary for the feasibility of operations. A small-scale operation can also be viable. Since services are people oriented, the regulatory procedures are also not very rigid or cumbersome. Product differentiation is difficult because of the non-availability of patents. There are not too many hassles in starting a consultancy or a clinic or a beauty salon.

In India, several years ago, in the field of insurance, there were legal barriers to start an insurance company, but there were no barriers to becoming an insurance consultant, advising on what insurance to buy and helping to recover claims. The consultant used his knowledge to help the client. Knowledge is an important input in most of the advisory services, like export procedures, tax management, education, medicine, law, finance, organisation development and quality management, which have practically no barriers for entry. The capital required is low. One can choose the scale of operations, whether it is limited clientele who are directly looked after, or large segments with infrastructure of office and assistants to support. One can even go international through the Internet.

❏ *Summary* ❏

To summarise, the distinction between goods and services are as below:

Goods	Services
Are manufactured	Are performed
Are tangible	Are intangible
Patents possible	Patents not possible
Barriers to entry, could be high	Are generally low
Produced and then consumed	Produced with customer participation
Can be sampled before purchase	Cannot be sampled before purchase
Can be stocked and sold later	Cannot be stocked and sold later
Moved to places convenient to the customer	Customer moves according to supplier's convenience
Purchaser acquires full rights to use them	Purchaser has limited rights to use them
Ownership can be transferred	Ownership is not transferred

3 DEVELOPING THE SERVICE PRODUCT

❏ *The Product Personality* ❏

By definition, a service is not produced. It is performed. Therefore, to refer to service as a product may not seem quite appropriate. Yet, such a reference makes it possible to apply to the service business concepts relating to the processes of developing, managing and marketing of goods.

A product is basically something that a producer offers to a consumer to provide satisfaction of the consumer's needs. To the manufacturer or producer, the product is an aggregate of technical/physical features and characteristics. To the consumer, it is an aggregate of utilities, values, expectations and perceptions, a complex cluster of value satisfactions. One buys satisfaction and state of mind rather than just goods and services; well-being rather than simply a package holiday or a designer outfit; security rather than just an insurance policy or a warranty; even beautiful feet rather than simply shoes; confidence rather than cosmetics.

A product is not merely a physical commodity. People endow it with attributes, beyond the functional characteristics of the product. A soap is valued not merely for its ability to clean and protect the skin, but also for its shape, colour, fragrance and the status that its use symbolises. The packaging, labelling, price, and the image created through promotional efforts, all add up to make the product occupy a specific position in the mind of the consumer. Functional utility is only one element of the complex product personality.

❏ *Core and Peripherals* ❏

The product has a core constituent. These are the technical characteristics to perform the basic functions for which the product is made. The peripherals have no great functional utility, but they add value. The core constituent of a television set will be its engineering, circuitry, etc., that provide steady and clear images and sound. The peripherals would be the design of the cabinet, positions of the controls, remote control facilities, the guarantees, etc. The peripherals are also referred to as the associated features that augment the product.

Different pharmaceutical companies market the basic generic medicine (core). The associated features that distinguish one from the other, would be in the strength of the drug, its form (i.e., liquid, capsule, pill or powder), additives (for taste or as a base), packaging (bottle, strips, cartons), labelling and so on. The brand name makes a difference (in the value) in the minds of the consumers. The name Colgate or Glaxo or Lupin may create notions of quality differently from that of a new manufacturer. The associated features may also raise the price of the core (generic) product, several times.

In an event, a live performance by A.R. Rehman or a presentation by film artistes may be the core attraction. The associated features that would enhance the value of that event would be

- the location and venue,
- the celebrities who may attend,
- the arrangements for car parking,
- the broadcasting arrangements (of value to sponsors and advertisers),
- the chance of ticket holders winning lucky prizes,
- the values of such lucky prizes, if any.

It is possible to compare two events on these kind of features and say that one is more attractive than the other.

❑ *Product Differentiation* ❑

Products may be differentiated through claims made by the manufacturer. Cooking oils refer to effects on cholesterol levels to differentiate themselves. Toothpastes are differentiated on the basis of clove oil, flouride and so on. These differentiations create distinctive value. When differentiation is effective, nothing else is equal. Competition on price is avoided because competition is only among equals and not among unequals.

Products also may be customised to meet the specific requirements of the consumer. This is done particularly for high value industrial products, which may be fabricated or modified to meet specific needs. This is not done for mass produced items. In the service sector, the opportunity, as well as the need, for customisation is very high. There is practically no mass production in the service business. Every service transaction is a specific response to a specific need of a specific customer.

How does one hospital for instance, differentiate itself from another? People prefer one hospital to another because of reasons such as proximity and the level of charges. Apart from these, one tends to prefer a hospital with a reputation of providing good medical facilities, in terms of equipment and specialist doctors. This is differentiation in the product or value of the services on offer. However, a particular patient may not need all of the available services. The hospital has to provide that service which is specifically required by the patient at a particular time.

❏ Packaging and Labelling ❏

Packaging and labelling are very important in goods. Packaging provides protection, attractiveness and identity. Brands are easily identified by just looking at the packaging. The packaging of goods is as important as the design and colours in the case of a car. It has to look good. Book covers constitute packaging and have a lot of influence in attracting the attention of the prospective reader. Labelling helps in identification and also provides information about distinctive features, technical data, usage instructions, precautions, etc. In the service business, the place from which the service is rendered, the appearance of the people providing the service, the equipment and the forms used, the displays and the decor etc., constitute the packaging. They influence initial reactions and are as important as packaging of goods.

❏ The Service Product ❏

A service product is what the service provider offers. It is a kind of promise, which will be experienced only after purchase. It is not a physical entity. Physical tangible entities may be associated with some service products. However, a service product is made up of a number of intangible elements. It is not enough to pay attention to the tangibles. A well built hotel is not necessarily an enjoyable place to stay. The intangible elements are far more important.

A choice has to be made as to what elements have to be incorporated in the core service offer, which will become the product. For example, the offer in a courier service would be

- delivery of articles at designated destinations (city limits only, major cities only, anywhere within India, anywhere in the world) within specified time limits,
- arrangements for collection of articles (limited hours, 24 hours, collection at specified points of collection or from the customer's premises),

- nature and size of articles that would be accepted (letters only, anything, no gold and diamonds),
- payment requirements (strict cash, credit till end of month).

Every combination of elements makes a different product. The options are many. No great effort is needed to modify the features of a product at any time. In a theatre, the elements will include, apart from the shows (language, quality, timings), climate control, accoustics, cleanliness, quality of seating, courtesy of ushers, elevator service, reservation facilities, car park facilities, conveniences in lobby, decor, nature of patronage, information on forthcoming programmes, and a lot more details on reception, waiting, comfort, ambience, etc. Satisfaction increases when one is recognised as a patron by the officials in the theatre; when one can have the seats of one's choice, whenever required; when the others in the theatre are of an acceptable kind and so on. Some people avoid certain theatres, because of the 'crowds' there.

A product in tourism is the place of destination as well as what one may experience while proceeding to and staying in that destination. Excellent destinations like Kumarakom and Thekkady in Kerala or Belur, Halebid and Agumbe (hill stations) in Karnataka, become less attractive because of the bad conditions of the approach roads. Sentosa Island off Singapore, is packaged as a place where there are no shops, no skyscrapers, no offices—a place of peace and tranquillity, to relax and be with nature, so different from Singapore. Travelling by cable car to this island is part of the package. Places in Rajasthan, like Jaisalmer, are being offered as tourism products, to experience the life styles of Maharajas, living in real palaces, with kingly appurtenances, travelling in the 'Palace on Wheels', the luxuriously fitted up railway train, going hunting (with cameras, of course) on elephant back and so on. The 'Palace on Wheels' has by itself become a tourism product and is being made available in many circuits in India.

The tourism product may be developed with an emphasis on art, architecture, culture, religion, history, sports, temples, leisure, life styles, etc. The Himalayas is a product not only for adventure tourism and sports, but for nature lovers and for those looking for peace and quiet. Varanasi is a product based on religion, the Ganges, Buddha and capturing the essence of Indian heritage. Temples and architecture form the basis of the tourism circuit in South India. The accommodation provided is as much part of the package in the African safari tours, as the bushes and the wild life. Many pay more to live in the tents in open country 'with nature' instead of in five-star comfort. Unusual or beneficial experiences like a dinner aboard the huge boats called *valloms* on its backwaters and Ayurvedic treatment, have become part of the tourism product in Kerala.

The product in a museum is not merely the collection of artefacts, but include the manner of display, convenience of visiting hours, space for visitors to move about, guidance on how to reach specific displays, opportunity for detailed study and explanations provided about exhibits. The experience in a museum can be enhanced several times by more detailed explanations through panels or electronically regulated images and sounds. A museum has the potential to make people not only aware of, but also get increasingly interested in the subjects exhibited.

In the case of a retailer, the range of what he has in stock is probably less important than reliability for genuineness, purity, etc.; displays, convenience to inspect and choose, behaviour at times of scarcity, delivery, billing and payment procedures. In the case of a dealer in computers, the hardware and software are important, but they alone would not give him a distinctive competitive advantage. These are not difficult to replicate. His distinctiveness would be in the areas of help to adapt, availability in the event of problems (technical support), reliable information, etc. All these are augmented elements of the core product. Cellular phone services are augmented when messages are flashed on it like pagers, and through billing procedures, facilities for free toll and roaming (country wide or worldwide), etc.

People use credit cards not merely because to avoid carrying cash, but because they get statements of expenses ready for submission to the tax authorities. A car rental agency can offer a choice of different makes of cars, which provide not merely transportation, but also status satisfaction. Business travellers avoid hotels which do not provide facilities in the room, to link their laptops to their home offices. Marriage halls provide not only a range of decorations and menus to choose from, but also accommodation for guests and priests to perform the rituals as per one's faith. The parents (or couples) only need to arrange the money.

❑ 'Servuction' ❑

This new word is not found in dictionaries. It has been coined to refer to the production of services, as the word 'production' is normally used in the context of goods. The following elements have been identified as relevant in 'servuction' (see C.H. Lovelock et al. 1981).

- The invisible factors are the organisational policies and systems, which influence the nature and quality of the service made available.
- The visible factors are (a) environment in its widest sense, including both the internal and the external; (b) the contact persons and service

providers in support to the contact persons; (c) the customer who is the direct recepient of the service in question; and (d) the co-customers whose behaviours affect the experience.

❑ *Developing a Product* ❑

A product has to be designed keeping in view the expectations and needs of the consumer. The experience of satisfaction has to be achieved during use, as well as during purchase. The production process must be defect-free, according to the specifications of the design. Also, there should not be any deterioration or damage during storage or transportation before the finished product reaches the customer.

While designing and offering a product, the following factors are to be taken into account:

- The market segment being catered to (See Chapter 5 for segmentation).
- What is the core product? This depends on the segment chosen.
- What should be the mix of the elements in the product?
- Nature of differentiation with other products.
- Extent of augmentation.
- Extent of customisation.
- Packaging and labelling.

The steps in developing a service product are

- Determine what the customer values as benefit (Benefit concept).
- Determine which of these benefits could be offered (Service concept).
- Decide on the precise service offer, which includes form and levels of the benefits to be offered (Service offer).
- Decide on arrangements for delivery of the service (Delivery system).

Benefit Concept

The product has to provide benefits to the customer. One needs to be clear on who the customer is and what his needs are. Segmentation helps in this process. The expectations (needs) of the customer include a number of functional and psychological dimensions. The needs of a traveller on business are different from those of one travelling on holiday with the family. In the latter case, the needs of the family are important. The children and/or wife are also customers. Thomas Cook began in 1841 as a travel agency. It has now become a one-stop travel shop, providing itineraries, bookings for travel and for stay, currency in various denominations, help in passport and visa formalities, arranging for conferences and sightseeing, and also receiving and delivering mail to travellers on long holiday tours, covering several destinations.

In the UK and the USA, the cooperation between business houses and educational institutions is becoming closer, each trying to meet the requirements of the other. Industry is in a position to help the educational system update courses by feeding back latest knowledge from their research work and other market experiences. Both industry and the education system benefit. This is the synergy that has developed between Stanford University and the Silicon Valley. Siemens and Dow Jones are also doing the same.

In India also there is a similar trend. There are plans for high-class academic institutions being established, with the cooperation of industry. This has happened in relation to tourism, hotels, retail management, capital markets and advertising. The Indian Oil Corporation as well as the Larsen & Toubro have tied up with management institutes to provide courses specially designed to meet the requirements of their businesses. There is already a close link between industry and management schools, whereby

- practising managers teach in the schools and,
- the student is allowed to gain practical experience at work even during his academic days.

A principal of a school wanting to help students who could not complete the course, began short duration courses for various jobs in hotels and hospitals, like bell boys, housekeeping and front office jobs, with the help of hotels and hospitals in the neighbourhood. Almost all of the students were taken up immediately and some of them could even get jobs in the Gulf countries. The school became a very valuable intermediary, meeting the needs of employers as well as those seeking employment. The demand was from both sides. Education thus becomes more relevant to, and less distant from, the realities in the shopfloor or the market place and therefore more satisfying to the customers (potential employers as well as students). The product was of better quality.

Fidelity Institutional Retirement Services Co. (FIRSCO) manages corporate retirement plans for 5700 clients with 3.8 million individuals, handles thousands of calls everyday about options and transactions. Believing that satisfied employees will create satisfied customers and thereby contribute to continued profit growth, FIRSCO started the Service Delivery University (SDU) to give every employee 80 hours of developmental activity. The SDU has grown and provided, in addition to a foundation course as a core curriculum (technical, regulatory, industry information), five colleges that offer high level courses on different subjects (Customer Service, Operations Management, Marketing and Sales, Risk Management and Leadership), requiring cognitive thinking.

The Indian Institutes of Technology (IITs) are in a position to help industry to develop products in the infotech and telecom businesses. This activity is not education. However, the IITs' strength, which is research and knowledge, is being made available to industry for commercial application. The need of industry is being met. Several scientific educational institutions were involved in the development of the SLV and guided missile programmes of India, contributing with research and testing reports. In course of time IIT research may be influenced by the needs of the industry, creating a mutually beneficial relationship.

Service Concept

Once the benefit concept (what the customer values as benefit) is clear, the service provider has to decide the benefits which he would like to offer. He may choose to provide only a part of it or the whole of it. Thomas Cook started with part and then gradually expanded towards the whole. The decision of the provider depends on the available resources.

The benefit from a restaurant may vary in the kinds of food offered, (Indian, Continental, Chinese, Thai or Mexican), the large spread (salads, seafoods, cold meat) price, courtesy, waiting, comfort of seating, privacy, exclusiveness, and so on. One restaurateur may in his service concept include (a) authentic Goanese food, Chinese food, or Punjabi Koliwada; and (b) quick service, with little attention paid to seating or ambience or courtesy in service. Another may conceive of service in terms of quick, clean, simple wholesome lunches for business executives, without much of a choice in menu, but offering convenient seatings and atmosphere, to enable serious business discussions as well. Variations in service may be in terms of (a) seating facility, (b) waiter service or self service; (c) delivery of food to the customer's work place; (d) daily/monthly payment of meals; and (e) payment before/after service. These choices are to be made keeping in mind

- the market segment proposed to be served,
- the resources one has and can muster.

A new airline focussed on personalised service, being familiar with their regular customers and their habits. Cabin crew and pilots were briefed on their passengers. The patronage became regular and the personalised service easier. However, when the airline fleet was modernised from Constellations to Boeing 747s with much bigger capacities and the routes increased in number, personalised service became impossible. The service offer had to change. In the case of Singapore Airlines, the benefits provided included

- reclining seats (for the first time, gaining competitive advantage),
- choice of food for economy class (normally only First Class had the choice),
- menus changed every week (four times more often than industry practice),
- more cabin crew than average,
- ultramodern fleet (in 1998, this airline was among the first to use Boeing 777s),
- purchases home delivered anywhere in the world,
- inflight office fax,
- priority passenger gets magazines related to his hobbies/profession.

Product development may also be done by not providing benefits. Deccan Airways, which offers to fly passengers at about half the rates of other established airlines, proposes to cut down on in-flight services, baggage bookings, checking in procedures, etc. Some foreign airlines do not even sell tickets in advance. One can walk into the airport and get into the earliest available aircraft, like shuttle bus services between cities leaving every half hour. This is possible, if there is a market segment which seeks benefits of this nature. One would imagine that such passengers may be businessmen travelling light, not only between small cities, but also between metro cities.

A prestigious hotel uses mechanical equipment (to reduce staff) as well as tinned food and ready mixes, while another of the same class chooses to offer additional personalised attention and only fresh raw materials. These are different benefits on offer, both perfectly marketable and potentially satisfying.

Delivery System

Once the choices with regard to offer are made, the proposed service must be delivered consistently, a 100 per cent, all the time. The delivery system, which makes this possible, is probably the most important part of product development. The reference here is not to delivering a packet or a letter but to the arrangements made through people, equipments and systems, so that the proposed services are performed as intended. If the delivery system is not perfect, the promised service will not happen. A promised service (promise raises expectations) not fulfilled, is much worse than not offering the service in the first place.

Service is delivered

- by people,

- using equipment and other physical facilities,
- through systems.

All these have to be in place. Otherwise there will be no service in reality.

A courier service may ensure consistent performance of its offer, by having tie-ups with other national or international couriers, or seek to manage with its own staff and equipment, if it is big enough in size and spread, like Blue Dart or Elbee in India. If it offers a 'track and trace' facility, it has to establish a system that continually records the movement of the package, however small, even when it goes across the hands of other agents. It cannot otherwise trace a missing item.

The Star Alliance between United Airlines, Lufthansa, Scandinavian Airlines System, Air Canada, Thai International, Air Nippon and ten other airlines, offers an integrated worldwide transport network, trouble-free seamless, global travel in 500 cities in 106 countries. Passengers on any of the member airlines can accumulate frequent flying credits, enjoy star airport lounge facilities, have one stop checking for up to four sectors, easy transfers for connecting flights, and similar specified benefits. Similar alliances exist between other airlines as well, like One World (American, British Airways, Cathay Pacific, Iberian, Qantas and others), or Sky Team (Air France, Alitalia, Delta, KLM, Korean, Mexican, and others). It should not happen that an official of one of the associated airlines is not aware of the arrangements and the nature of authentications required.

These arrangements, whereby the service is offered or sold by one, but effectively rendered by another is similar to the arrangements in manufacturing, whereby products are made in different places, even in different continents and sold under different brand names. Nike shoes are made in Taiwan. Shoes are made in Agra for Bata and other reputed brands.

Some travel agents do not limit their services to the issue of confirmed tickets, but extend it to check-in and other boarding formalities. Rail passengers would be met at the railway stations and seen to their berths. One firm posted their employees at Sahar airport in Mumbai to receive outgoing international passengers booked through them and to help them in completing departure formalities. This service was available only to First Class and Business Class passengers. They chose to enhance the product for higher class passengers. In this case, posting their employees at the airport was not enough. There had to be a foolproof method that made it possible to identify the passengers. The person posted had to be familiar with the routines at the airport and also have the ability to overcome any problem that may develop. If a passenger was aware of and expected this service and for some reason could not find this person or found that the person was not familiar with the procedures, he would be dissatisfied.

A consumer utility company had arrangements with a number of banks to collect payment from customers. In 1996, the company scrapped these arrangements and, with the permission of the Reserve Bank of India, announced the Electronic Clearance facility whereby a consumer could just give the bill to his banker duly endorsed and the bank would remit the amount to the company. The system looked very convenient to consumers, was faster, and avoided a number of steps compared to the earlier process. However, when the bills reached the consumers, there was utter confusion. They did not understand the new format of the bill. Unaware of the change, many went to the collecting banks as before, who refused to accept. They were told of the new procedures. Many of them had not seen the press release issued some time back. There was not enough space to sign on the bill, particularly in the case of corporates, where two signatures and rubber stamps had to be affixed leaving the MICR line clear. The staff in many banks were not familiar with the procedures agreed to by their Head Offices, but not communicated clearly to all the branches. Some Head Offices did not want to accept this system and therefore sent no instructions to the branches. Consumers with these banks had additional problems now, as they had to go the company's offices, located at distances. More than two months later, the system had still not been properly implemented. The service concept was excellent but the delivery system had failed.

❑ *Product Range—Breadth and Depth* ❑

Developing a service product calls for attention on

- core,
- peripherals,
- delivery system.

The provider of a service, like any other businessman, has to ask the question, 'What business am I in?' From the answer to this question, he will decide on the core, peripherals and the range of products to offer. The service concept then emerges. From the concept to the service offer, the gap is filled by decisions on the combination of elements, both tangibles and intangibles, to be included. Different combinations create different products. Singapore's Changi airport is ranked among the world's best. The experience is enhanced by the offer of a complimentary 2-hour tour for transit passengers, arranged by the Civil Aviation Authority and the Tourist Promotion Board.

Product ranges are looked at in terms of breadth and depth. Different kinds of products add breadth. Different varieties of the same product add depth. An icecream parlour providing different varieties of icecream has depth. If it also provides milkshakes, it has added breadth. An insurance company which offers policies covering death or survival, with variations in the ways in which money may be paid, has depth. However, if it also offers insurance policies, linked to stock market indices and if the policy coverage is in terms of physical objects like houses or gold, then breadth is created. A food store may add breadth by offering cookery classes or advice on calorie-based menus.

Product depth is created by retaining the core and adding peripherals. Breadth is created through new core products. A beach resort may add depth by increasing the number of water sports or beach-based activities. When it also seeks to attract local patrons through coaching arrangements, the range becomes broader. It may offer to become the outlet for local talent in folk art and handicrafts, through display and marketing facilities. Then the range becomes still broader. A motor car dealer adds depth when he arranges finance facilities for purchase, and breadth when he arranges facilities for paying taxes, teaching driving, a breakdown service, etc.

A hotel identified a potential market if they could offer benefits for companies to conduct in-house training programmes. Offering this service, the hotel provided

- a large air-conditioned hall with excellent accoustics, a white board, projection equipment, etc.,
- space for smaller groups working simultaneously,
- clean but modest living accommodation for participants,
- wholesome food.

They thought that the rooms would be empty throughout the day, as everybody would be attending the conference or training session. Therefore, there would be no need for room service, except for morning tea. Lunch, breakfast and dinner would always be at fixed intervals, for the whole group, as part of the conference arrangements. These would be buffets and not a-la-carte.

They could cut down on dining room staff. Cheap arrangements were made for laundry, because most of the participants were not senior executives and would otherwise, hang their washing from the windows. Another hotel, identifying itself as a leisure resort, had room service that would guarantee service within 10 minutes, faster than in the restaurant, plenty of indoor and outdoor and water-based games, and arrangements for outings.

Laundry services may include in their offers minor repairs like darning, stitching on of buttons, stitching up holes in trouser pockets, redoing stitches that are getting undone, and so on. Repair services may add depth to the product range through (a) offering free regular services, in the nature of preventive maintenance; (b) guaranteeing repair jobs done and the parts replaced; (c) providing substitute equipment when the original is taken away for repairs; (d) promising attention within specified time limits. A trainer in computers offered to his students, who were mostly working people, that they could come in whenever they were free after work. The attention was individual and hours flexible. He also agreed to help them with any problem that they encountered at work with computers. The consultation was free, therefore, he had added both depth and breadth.

The retail business illustrates the possibilities in product development in services. Some experts in retail management claim that big chains like Walmart or Marks & Spencer, located outside the city limits, with plenty of parking space and a big range of displays, are not suited to India as the Indian customer is not willing to travel more than 3 to 4 km to do his shopping. The neighbourhood shop is still the popular one, being familiar and assumed to be trustworthy. The Indian customer's behaviour is characterised by the lack of familiarity with brands and new products; suspicion about price, quality and reliability; and dependence on the salesman. Current experience does not seem to validate such claims. Big malls with thousands of square feet of space, are becoming the norm in cities. Business houses are entering into the retail trade with big investments in property and creating brands across several cities, like Shoppers Stop, West Side, Life Styles, Giants, Subhiksha, Margin Free, Food World and Big Bazaar. Some of them occupy nearly 100,000 square feet in space and stock more than a 100,000 different items. The product range in such retail outlets will include not merely shopping, but entertainment and games, particularly for accompanying children who are not interested in shopping.

It is not safe to generalise about the behaviour of Indian customers. The differences between the customers in Mumbai and in Bangalore are as divergent as between two continents. What would apply to a retail food store, would not apply to a retail apparel shop, where the frequency of purchase is less and the selection process more elaborate. However, the growth of Kids Kemp (Bangalore), Shoppers Stop (Mumbai and Bangalore), Chirag Din (Mumbai), the Food World chain (Bangalore, Chennai and Hyderabad), Nanz (Delhi and Punjab), suggest that there is a trend in favour of big size, multiple outlet, retail chains with own brands. The DLF Galleria in Gurgaon (Haryana), as a mega complex, over an area of 3.77 acres, with open-to-sky green walks through galleries, 230 shops and 300 offices, a grand atrium at the ground floor and four roof top restaurants, may be the beginning of the grand plazas for shopping. A similar concept in Mumbai, the Century Bazaar, though on a much smaller scale, did not survive the novelty for too long in the early 1960s. The world's first megaplex called Kinepolis, had 25 screens, 7500 seats, located off the ring road circling Brussels, 15 minutes from downtown. It expanded the market by 40 per cent.

Service is usually provided at the premises of the service provider. The customer has to go to the doctor's clinic, or the beautician's salon, or the consultant's office. If the provider can go to where the customer is, there is added value to the service. Upgradation, through depth, is achieved by taking the service to the customer, outside the premises of the service provider—an activity which may often be considered a problem. Examples are hotels that meet the guests at the airport, mobile vans carrying library or post office or banking or medical facilities into the interiors, mobile cinemas, telemarketing and home delivery, collection centres for payment of telephone bills, laundries offering to clean carpets at home. Units of the Unit Trust of India and bookings for new cars were made available at petrol stations and select departmental stores. Customs formalities, which used to be done at the port of entry, are now done at places called inland ports, much closer to the ultimate destination or to the place of origin, avoiding the need for unpacking and repacking for the sake of customs scrutiny, en route. *These services, being nearer to the client, are much more satisfying.*

The new 'core' product to add breadth, sometimes, may have no direct connection to the main business. For example, a bank offered the following services to its account holders:

- payment of bills (electric, telephone) and taxes,
- buying of tickets (air, rail or bus).

These are not banking services, but have the effect of attracting and retaining customers. Petrol stations are adding retail stores within the same premises, so that essential shopping can be done, while the vehicle is being attended to. These stores will become popular if there is enough parking space for cars, because the time for filling petrol and for shopping are not the same. The latter involves choices and bargaining.

❑ *Flexible Options* ❑

Wherever possible, the 'core' offer could be the bare minimum service, uniformly valued by customers in a given segment at the lowest price with wrap on supplements or options which may be chosen by individuals who need them, at a concessional price. In tourism, travel may be the core, with options to change from the standard itinerary, extending or curtailing stays at specific centres, special visits (to monuments, people, places, acquaintances, religious centres) and language guides. In education, there could be core subjects with several options for additional credits (subjects to be studied) and students can choose the pace of their studies. This kind of syllabus is called the 'cafeteria'. Standard coaching may be through interactive CDROMs, with personal interaction (with guides or professors) being the options. This is customisation, popularly known as 'tailor-made'. Such options already exist in many services like beauty parlours, tailors, restaurants, hospitals, consultants, transportation, banking and insurance. However, advances in electronics and infotech, make many more such options possible, even in mass produced items like cars.

❑ *Guarantees* ❑

Service is intangible. *The customer does not know what he is getting, until after the service is bought, performed and experienced.* He has some expectations about the service that he is buying, and faith that he will get what he expects. Yet, there is uncertainty about whether the service will match the expectations. Some uncertainty exists at the time of purchase of goods also. One way to overcome the uncertainty and reassure the customer is to provide guarantees. Mail order services offer full money-back refunds, if the product is returned within specified periods.

Unlike tangible goods however, the scope for giving guarantees is limited, in the services business. A rewashing can be done, if the original wash is not satisfactory. However, nothing can be done if the fabric is damaged by the laundry or if the haircut or beauty treatment is not satisfactory. If a trouser stitched by a tailor to order, is not to the user's liking, can one really fault the tailor? The nature of the cloth, or the design selected, as well as the shape of the user's body may have something to do with the 'fit'. Even if the tailor agrees to forego the tailoring charges, the cost of the cloth is still a waste. The colour on a repainted car, rarely resembles the colour chosen from the sample card. The paint manufacturer escapes liability because there is an appropriate caution printed on the sample card. The garage cannot be blamed, as they have used the specified paint. One way to avoid such variations may be to apply samples of paints on the car body before making choices. This practice is common while choosing colours for painting buildings. Another method may be to choose the colour, not from the sample card, but from a painted car. Then the garage can be held responsible for the final product matching the expectations. These methods enable sampling which may lead to better satisfactions, but then the choice is limited to small ranges.

Consultants will find it impossible to refund fees, if their advice is not found acceptable. There has been an instance of a doctor refunding the fees when the patient complained that his arthritis had not been cured, but this is rare. Transporters, airlines, lorry services and postal services may refund charges at least partially, if they do not keep to agreed schedules. They may also make refunds if they damage the contents. In both cases, the refund may not help the client much and also may have a deterrent effect on the service provider. The client may even have a case for compensation and consequential damages. Consider for example, the case of a person who was to report for work in California, USA, on Sunday and was scheduled to fly out of Kolkata on Saturday. He was not able to do so because of the flash strike by the Air Traffic Controllers on Friday when all flights out of Kolkata were cancelled. The consequences cannot be evaluated and no compensation can be adequate.

Guarantees are meant to ensure performance. Refunds are not adequate for non-performance or for defective service. For example, 20 cartons of training material sent from Mumbai to Delhi 20 days earlier, were not delivered till the evening prior to the start of an international training programme. Copies had to be made from the material in these cartons to be used in the programme. If these cartons had not been delivered, the programme would not have started. People had come from several countries to attend the programme. There would have been no way to compensate for the disaster that the programme would have become and the disgrace which the organisers would have had to face. Cash compensation is inadequate when a doctor amputates, by mistake, the healthy leg or when the police neglect its protective function and there is riot, disablement or death. When one misses an early morning flight because the telephone does not wake him up as programmed, the consequences are several. It could mean the loss of a contract or a career. Failure of a courier to deliver a document in time may mean missing deadlines for admission, tournament entries, conference participation, immigration rights, etc., with irreversible consequences on one's future.

Performance is important. The whole 'product' has to be designed for non-failure. It is necessary to accept that a 100 per cent performance or zero per cent failure is possible. Cliches like 'to err is human' or 'mistakes will occur' mitigate this effort. Aeroplane manufacturers for example, have to provide a 100 per cent safety in their designs, to the point of asserting confidently that an accident that occurred (TWA 800 in July 1996) could not be due to mechanical or engine failure.

Safety systems in industry cannot be less than a 100 per cent reliable, as the consequences of an industrial accident are almost incalculable. The effects of the gas leak in the Union Carbide plant in Bhopal in 1984 had not abated even in 2003, 19 years later. The response of the relevant personnel to an alarm has to be immediate and correct. They should know what to do, where equipment is located, and how to operate it. An investigation to a major fire in a petro-chemical plant revealed that the delay in attending to the fire was because certain keys could not be found. These failures were avoidable, but in this case, could not be avoided because the systems were not functional. In many cases, regular drills will point out the areas of weakness and ensure performance when required.

The John Hancock Centre in Chicago, 97 storeys high, called the City in the Sky, has a swimming pool on the 44th floor. The thousands that utilise the various facilities in the centre, have no doubts about its stability. The architects, engineers and contractors, have taken care of that. It is a 100 per cent more reliable. One may compare this with the number of houses and bridges that collapse in India, sometimes even before usage. Every 'accident' must be seen as a failure in promise, a service improperly performed and also avoidable.

❑ *Delivery System* ❑

In services, the delivery system is an integral part of the product. It is the delivery system that translates the service concept into reality. It has been mentioned earlier in this chapter that for the customer to receive the service as proposed to be offered, there have to be

- equipment,
- people,
- systems.

All these have to be in place, properly tuned, trained and adjusted and ready to perform. These arrangements by themselves do not constitute service, but constitute preparedness and readiness to do that service, when the offer is accepted by a customer.

The courier service promises that documents will be delivered on time. The office and staff, the procedures for collection, the documentation, the arrangements for transport from one station to another, have all to be in place to enable the service of 'delivery on time' being rendered. A courier offerred concessional rates, almost equalling postal rates, to organisations which had to mail thousands of letters to all their clients, if the entire business was given to them. They got the business, but they did not have the capability of handling such large volumes. The delivery system was not in place. Deliveries were delayed and they subsequently lost the business.

New projects of interest to the public are often announced in the press with a list of telephone numbers from where more information can be available. There should be people manning those telephones from the moment the announcement appears, and they should have <u>all</u> the information requested. Several hotels advertise the offers they have for New Year's Eve. When enquiries are made for details or bookings, one hears a visibly annoyed voice and the telephone going dead immediately, or one has to listen to recorded music till the electronic system automatically switches off the line. The hotel should have anticipated the rush of enquiries and provided for a dedicated attendant to handle them. If a service is to be offered, arrangements must be made to ensure that it is possible to render that service.

Technology and equipment does facilitate the performance of service, but does not ensure it. For example, the recorded answering service (of airlines or railways) will not be satisfactory if

- the recorded message is not updated regularly,
- the message had been recorded by a person who does not articulate clearly,
- the recording machine is not functioning satisfactorily,
- there is an unduly long wait before being connected to the machine.

Several organisations have installed electronic systems to replace the telephone operator. Not properly monitored, they can be sources of intense dissatisfaction. In one case, the voice requests you to dial 9, if you do not know the extension number and want the operator's assistance. When 9 is pressed, after a short pause, you are informed that the operator is busy and you have to dial again and the line goes dead. In another case, when the required extension number is dialled, after a short spell of music, the system reverts back to the start of the sequence, with the words 'Welcome to ... '. The reason apparently is that the required number is not free.

The story will indicate a system, not properly monitored can add to one's frustrations.

Technology and equipment cannot function better than the systems and people that support them. The telephone department has a system that identifies subscribers who have arrears, repeats the warnings a few times and then disconnects the telephone, if the bill remains unpaid. However, it is no service if the repetition of warnings comes within fifteen minutes of each other, or if the payments made are not fed into the computer system promptly. It is important that the routine of warning and disconnection is disrupted as soon as the bill is paid. If the system does not enable this, the service becomes a disservice. The reminder becomes a threat causing anxiety.

'Systems' refers to the arrangements for the flow of information and material, to the points where the service is being delivered. When a car is being given for repairs or service, the jobs to be done on the basis of the owner's complaints have to be informed to the various persons who have to do those jobs, later in the day or night, or may be during the week or fortnight. The system to ensure this will become more impersonal and elaborate as the size of the garage becomes larger. If the service is being provided by a franchisee or authorised agent, the manufacturer has to supply

- details of the nature of services/repairs to be done,
- the characteristics of the equipment to be used,
- the warranties to be honoured,
- likely causes of usual complaints,
- necessary parts to be replaced,
- technical competence,
- the parameters to be maintained while checking results.

The manufacturer should also get feedback from the agents about

- the nature of complaints,
- frequency of complaints,
- difficulties experienced during service/repairs.

This enables the manufacturer to revise and update its manuals and instructions. Airlines have to keep their booking agents informed of the changes in flight schedules. If the carrier fails to do so, the agent will fail in his service to the passenger, who reporting at the airport according to the time written in the ticket, may find that the aircraft has left half an hour earlier as per the revised schedule.

Systems should, as far as possible, be self-regulating, simple and quick to respond. For example, if the inputs include numbers, then it is useful to introduce a control digit also in the input system. An airline received an instruction for a ticket by Flight No. 163. The ticket was issued for Flight No. 663, which also flew on the same sector. The error went undetected because manual verification required by the system was not done, there having been a change of personnel. Foreign exchange transactions are subject to a number of regulations which change frequently. Import/export rules are quite complex and change frequently. A customer who contacts a foreign exchange dealer or someone enforcing the import/export regulations, relies on the other person, who may only be a clerk, to know, interpret and apply the rules correctly. The clerk's employer cannot know that the clerk is advising the client correctly. An error can be harmful to the customer or to the government. Manuals and files with instructions are not adequate. They are cumbersome to handle and not easy to retrieve. A computer with a checklist can be made part of the processing system.

The experience narrated in the box below is not an exception. Many services, particularly essential ones, are organised without taking into account the convenience of the customers.

Paying At TMCH

TMCH is a speciality hospital. Patients from all over India come here to consult. Treatment, being mainly exposure to rays or injections, is possible without admission as an in-patient. The corridors of TMCH are always full with patients and their accompanying relatives, mostly standing and in varying degrees of suffering, waiting for tests, for treatment, or to consult the doctors.

Murali had taken his mother to TMCH to consult Dr Rao, who advised her to return the next day for some tests. She was asked to get four tests done. One of these involved a minor surgery, when a piece of flesh was to be cut for laboratory study.

For each of the first three tests, she had to go to the specific testing room, where the nurse prepared a receipt, which had to be taken to the cashier (in the cash department) and brought back with the cashier's signature, before the test could be done. There were queues to get the receipt, to pay cash and do the test. Murali's mother waited at one place while Murali stood in the queues each time.

The test rooms and the cashier were on the same ground floor, but the laboratory was in the seventh floor of an adjacent building. The receipt had to be brought down to the cashier and taken back to the laboratory. There were queues for the lifts.

Murali spent about three hours waiting in the queues. The tests hardly took 45 minutes of a patient's time. All the while, his mother was alone in the crowded corridors. When he mentioned this experience to Dr Rao and wondered what patients, without healthy relatives, would have done, Dr Rao smiled and said 'They manage.'

Systems in a repair shop will include ways to

- receive and record complaints from customers,
- assign persons to inspect and determine the nature of repairs to be carried out,
- collect equipment from customer's premises, if necessary, and deliver it back,
- make estimates and adhere to costs and time schedules,
- inform customer about (*a*) times when personnel will visit him; (*b*) estimates; and (*c*) variations therein.

The events described in the box emphasise the scope for making services more customer-friendly.

A manufacturer of consumer durables had made arrangements to

- note down customer's complaint and say that the mechanic would visit him the next day
- convey the complaint to the appropriate workshop personnel who were expected to visit the premises of the customer within 24 hours

The 'next day' is a very long period during which the customer has to remain on the premises and be available if and when the mechanic calls. If the mechanic does not come, he feels cheated and angry. He will make an enquiry as to why the mechanic did not turn up and perhaps become agitated. The person who wrote down the complaint earlier will, most likely, bear the brunt of the customer's temper for which he can do nothing, not even explain why the mechanic did not turn up. He would then either apologise and promise to find out what went wrong or give details of the repair shop to be contacted directly. The repair shop personnel may then say, with an air of apology, something like

'There was too much work' or 'The message did not reach us' or 'We had the wrong address'. None of these excuses will satisfy the customer, who spent a full day expecting, but not receiving, a service which had been promised. He will see the organisation as inefficient, indifferent or even unreliable.

While deciding on the service offer, the questions to be asked would be:

- How quickly can the mechanic be sent?
- How accurately can the time of visit of the mechanic be estimated?
- How can the person receiving the complaint, become aware of this time?
- In case the expected visit does not materialise, can the customer be informed about the change?
- Is it better to send the mechanic to the customer's premises or to get all the equipment to the workshop?
- How to ensure that the details of the customer's complaint are correctly noted, so that the mechanic equips himself adequately?
- Will the mechanic who visits, have the skills and the tools to do the work at the premises, or else to estimate the cost of repairs?

A provider of office equipment promised that the mechanic will reach the client's premises within 90 minutes of a complaint. He organised separate cells at nodal points in the city, with a few mechanics and a mobile van with essential spares. All complaints were to be received at a central location, from where the complaints would be routed to the different cells, according to the location of the client's premises. The central location had, in its computer system, full details of the client and the equipment he had. Every cell would be in contact with all the mechanics in the field every half hour. (This story relates to the early 1990s when cell phones and pagers had not yet become popular.) The mechanics had instructions to report back regularly, their movements and the progress of their assignments. On the basis of this information, the cell would direct a mechanic to the client concerned. If the 90 minutes deadline could not be met, the client would be informed about the delay. Every mechanic had with him enough material to attend to the common complaints, but if there was something unusual, he could call for the mobile van, which had more spares. If the repair could not be done even then, the mobile van would provide a substitute equipment to the client and take away the original to the workshop for attention. This level of service needed a clear communication system in place and the personnel had to conform to the procedure laid down of reporting.

In insurance, the delivery system is more complicated. At the time of buying the policy of insurance, the coverage has to be clear, complete and specific. Otherwise, when the event insured against happens, it will be noticed that the warranted exclusions, declarations etc., have nullified the intended arrangement. This is what people complain about as 'The small print takes away what the big* print giveth'. Systems have to be developed to ensure that both the insured and the insurer have the same understanding about what is on and what is not. The second stage of the delivery system is at the time of making the claim. For example, the Overseas Medical Insurance scheme, (which assures free medical attention for Indians travelling abroad), becomes non-functional if

- the appropriate endorsements or evidences are not carried by the traveller,
- the appropriate endorsements or evidences are not properly authenticated,
- the updated list of authorised doctors and hospitals at the overseas centre are not available,
- the persons to be contacted in case of need, are not known or are not available at given addresses,
- the necessary authorisations are not forthcoming.

These deficiencies cannot be anticipated or asked for by the insuring person. The system of the insurance company should automatically deliver all the details and instructions, so that the benefits of the coverage become available as promised.

Since the service product is made and delivered by people, there are risks of consistent standards not being maintained (concept of heterogeneity). The delivery system should seek to ensure that, no matter who delivers it, the service is

- at promised levels,
- beyond expectations,
- rendered without being asked,
- consistent without failure,
- at increasingly higher levels.

A customer's experience with a bank and courier company is given in the following box.

The Credit Card

Mr B had a credit card issued by ABC Bank. Purchases through the card were debited to his savings account with that bank. After some years, Mr B was advised that, for reasons of adhering to international practice, card holders' accounts would not be debited, but they would be required to settle accounts, as advised in their monthly statements. Mr B found that even if he sent a cheque promptly on receipt of the statement of outstandings, the next month's statement would contain a demand for service charges, which was attributed to failure to settle within the stipulated dates.

Mr B's card was valid up to the end of February. On 27 February, Mr B wanted to make a purchase on the card. The shop refused to accept the card as 'it was only valid for another 24 hours'.

On 4 March, Mr B went to his bank to collect the new card as was the practice in the previous years. After a search, he was told that the card was not there. On enquiring when the card would be expected, the person on the next table volunteered the information that this year, credit cards were being sent directly to the holders. Mr B then contacted the credit card department and was told that the cards had already been sent on 26 February. He was given two telephone numbers of the courier service where 'Mr Rao would be able to help'. Mr B rang up the first number. The response was that the courier did not operate at that location any more. Mr Rao was available at the second number He said that he was trying his best, but could not promise any specific date because the volume was large. Mr B insisted that he wanted it immediately as he was going out of town on tour. Mr Rao agreed to deliver it within two days. It did not arrive for the next four days, when Mr B left on tour.

'Consistently' refers to the continued maintenance of a promised level or quality of service. The provider may choose the level at which the service should be and offer accordingly, but must deliver at that level, regularly, without fail. It is not enough to be performing, on an average level. Even a 90 per cent strike rate has a 10 per cent failure, which can be very damaging. Imagine the airlines or the railways allowing themselves 10 per cent accidents. A garage may be very good at tuning up engines, but may not bother to wipe the car body clean, before returning it to the owner. What it chooses not to do, need not be done, but there should be no relaxation in the perfection of the tuning job. If the person who is the specialist in tuning or the equipment required is not available, it is better to announce that the quality of the job may suffer.

Earlier in this chapter, reference has been made to architects, engineers and contractors, ensuring 100 per cent non-failure. While the target has to be no failure, they may still occur. An unexpected circumstance can happen. When failure occurs, it is advisable to

- apologise for the failure,
- explain the reason for the failure to the customer.

This is preferable to denying the failure. A flight can get delayed for a number of reasons, but the announcements usually attribute the delays to 'technical reasons'. These announcements are seen to be false and invite ridicule. The reasons may range from the non-arrival of aircraft to non-arrival of pilot. It is better to state the real reason as nobody likes to be told lies. People like to know what is happening, however, unpleasant. Patients do not like to be misinformed about the true state of the disease. When the doctor says, 'Everything will be OK', there is no reassurance. There is on the contrary, heightened anxiety, because the behaviour of the doctor and the nurses may suggest that there is some seriousness; enough to be hidden. Stating the reasons conveys reassurance that the failure was not due to lack of effort or concern.

❏ *Benefits* ❏

The elements to be included in the product have to be such as will provide satisfaction to the customer. What the customer needs or values is known only to him. The provider of the service has to become aware of these. At a time when Broadway theatre was losing money because of the salaries and union rules, a Boston-based theatre group of 65 persons, made $ 4 million by targetting high schools, showing them literary adaptations. Students in distant towns, who did not normally get to see theatre, were enthusiastic. The quality of education also improved. A pizza joint began to sell its pizza at more than $3 a piece, compared to the 89c in the supermarket, when it made its pizzas in the shape of logos for corporate gifts, and mascots for sports events, or in the form of Disney characters.

The needs and expectation of customers are not always the same. In a sports event for example, there would be sports enthusiasts looking forward to quality performance and top level competition. There would be socialites, looking forward to the experience of the venue and the contacts. Race courses and cricket grounds attract a lot of socialites. Participants would be concerned with organisational matters like convenience of schedules, proper communication about arrangements, transport from and to venue, adequate practice facilities, ground conditions, etc.

❏ *Understanding Expectations* ❏

Market research is the traditional method of finding out customer needs. A variety of techniques, like surveys, questionnaires, interviews, observations etc., have been developed to do market research in relation to goods. There are limitations in using these, in the case of services. For example, surveys are carried out to find out reader habits and preferences. Readers are asked what they would like to have in the newspaper or magazine. Suggestions for improvement are also asked for. If a preference is shown for news analysis, is the preference for the kind written by Arun Shourie, or of Girilal Jain or of M.V. Kamath or Inder Malhotra, all of whom are renowned columnists and respected political commentators, but who are very different in style and in perspectives. Crosswords are asked for, but is the preference for the kind of crosswords in *The Statesman*, or *The Indian Express* or *The Hindu*? When a film becomes a hit and another producer tries the same formula, it does not always work.

Market research, in relation to services, is like trying to get objective data about preferences while choosing a wife or husband. The 'right' person is such a vague combination of perceptions that articulation, however detailed, may not convey adequately. TPR ratings, in the case of TV programmes, at best, might indicate the popularity of TV channels or programmes. They may help advertisers choose slots or media. They do not help producers improve popularity.

Test marketing is another technique where the sample of the product proposed to be made, is given to a few customers and their responses elicited. In the matter of services, samples cannot normally be made. Some newspapers prepare dummy editions before regular publication to guage public reaction. Film makers release trailers. Travel agents are given free flights by airlines or taken to travel destinations to be promoted. These are really in the nature of promotional efforts, because the product has already been designed and the comments of these users are unlikely to cause substantial changes.

Advertisement dummies can be shown to selected experts, before finalising campaigns. A visual TV advertisement, raved about by experts for its innovation and impact before its release, made no impact on the viewing public. Viewers did not understand the message. The impact of an advertisement depends on the position it has in the page, the matter in the rest of the space, or the position in the series before a TV programme and those preceding and following. These are not constants. They cannot be sampled or predetermined.

Breakthrough products rarely come out of asking customers what they want. People cannot envision what does not exist. Successful companies probe problems and transfer their understanding to the innovative process. When Akia Morita asked his engineers to develop a cassette player which could fit into his hip pocket, he was not acting on research data. A report in August 2003 states that the tourism department was planning a luxury train to be called the Deccan Odyssey, on the lines of the Blue Train in South Africa, Royal Scotsman in the UK or the Oriental Express in the Far East, with facilities of conference room, suites, health and fitness centres, etc., with a tariff of US$ 2000 or so for a week long tour. Will this be popular? One cannot have samples of this train for the public to react. The whole train and infrastructure at all the stations of call, with the trained staff, will have to be in position, before one can find out whether there are buyers. You cannot depend on its popularity elsewhere.

One market research technique uses the data gathered by those in contact with the customer like sales personnel, front office staff, billing clerks, room boys, ushers, messengers, telephone operators. At all these contact points, some messages are available as to what the customer (a) expected; (b) got or; (c) missed. These messages are not usually in the form of clear statements, but are often implied in enquiries or comments. When a customer enquires about how to contact another room, or to go to a venue within the same hotel, it means that he had experienced some difficulty in that respect. The instructions were either not clear or not easily noticeable and perhaps needed to be positioned more prominently.

If a customer enquires about the arrangements for cleaning the room, he is not making a routine enquiry. He is actually expressing dissatisfaction with what he had experienced. A customer once asked the lobby manager what they did to keep cockroaches and spiders out of the rooms and got a detailed account of the hotel's practices. The lobby manager did not realise that the enquiry was not a consultation, but a complaint. The customer had killed a big black spider in his room that morning.

It is customary to test customer satisfaction through surveys, which list down a number of elements of the service and ask the user to rate these elements on a scale ranging from excellent to poor, identified by words or by numbers. The responses do not really help the management to know what is happening or what needs to be done. What exactly is the level that the management would like to call 'excellent'? If the majority of responses are 'good', what can the management do to improve it to 'excellent'?

Customers express themselves subtly and indirectly, even if asked directly, 'How did you like the service?' or 'Hope you enjoyed being with us' are meaningless questions that will elicit casual answers like 'Okay'. Formal feedbacks and questionnaires thus fail to communicate much. A teacher cannot expect a student to tell him that the class was not interesting. However, the teacher can gauge it from the way the students sit in the class, from the earnestness with which he is accosted, from the 'light' in the student's eyes, from the comments made between friends, from the nature of discussions during a break, from the spontaneity of the response to a joke. When a student tells a faculty member, in an in-house programme, 'The lecture was very good, Sir. You are very knowledgeable. Your level is much higher than ours', the real meaning is, 'We did not understand you'.

While satisfying customer's needs is the primary drive for product development, the job, as stated by the British architect, Sir Denys Lasdun is 'to give the client on time and on cost, not what he wants, but what he never dreamed he wanted and, when he got it, recognised it as something he wanted all the time'.

Doing without being asked. When one asks for a service, it means that

- it was expected,
- it was not received,
- there was suspicion that it may not be received.

Asking therefore, is preceded by dissatisfaction. When the service is then provided, it does not matter at what level it was provided. The perception of the customer will still be that he would not have got what he received, had he not insisted on getting it; and that there was an attempt to cheat him out of what was legitimately due to him. There is no satisfaction. Any service that comes automatically is more satisfying. When buying provisions, if a pretty carry-home bag is given only after asking for it, there is no satisfaction. If it is given without the customer asking for it, it may produce a smile. If one does not get it, but sees that some others are being given, the dissatisfaction is quite intense, because therein lies a message that one customer is less important than another. A greeting card or a calendar or an invitation (for a sale) from a shop, received at home is very satisfying because there is in that action, a recognition of being a patron. If while buying a washing machine, a packet of washing powder is given, without being expected, there is satisfaction. A hotel had arranged separate buffets for the two conferences it was hosting. Some members noticed that the spread on the other table was bigger. No amount of explanation could remove the sense of having been discriminated against.

Keep Upgrading. If a service is experienced as better than the expectations, then the service has to be maintained at that level. It cannot slip back from that level. The service must aim at a still higher level to make the experience continually exciting. Excitement or delight occurs when something pleasant and enjoyable happens without having been asked for and not even expected. Frequent customers compare service experiences from competing providers and keep raising their expectations. The standards therefore, have to be continually moving up.

In areas like information technology and electronics, where technologies are changing rapidly, there is much scope as well as need for upgrading benefits. New applications are found almost every day. Product development has to be flexible, almost continuous, sensing, testing and integrating up to the last minute.

❏ *Complaints* ❏

People in contact with customers can pick up a lot of data on customer needs, expectations and experiences, if they are sensitive enough to listen to the comments and complaints that are not explicitly expressed. A customer who does express a complaint explicitly, is indeed doing a great service to the service provider. It is found that generally very few customers complain. They just switch brands. An airline once subjected all their 300 passengers in its Jumbo jet to a series of problems including flight cancellations and loss of luggage. Only six complaints were received at their headquarters.

Every complaint provides an opportunity to augment the product, by adding a new element to the service, or improving the delivery. Customers should be encouraged, to record their experiences of the services provided. The comments, to be useful, should be precise and detailed. If someone says, 'I was waiting for a car. The driver had reported to the Reception, but I got no information. When I checked with Reception, I was told that no driver had come. I lost more than two hours', there is enough data to pinpoint failure and make correction.

A complaint does not necessarily mean that there is a fault or neglect on the part of an individual. It may only be revealing an omission in designing the product or the system. People concerned with providing the service tend to interpret a complaint as an accusation against themselves and therefore try to

- explain away the failure,
- decry the customer's demand as unreasonable,
- look for the person who could be faulted and punished,
- hush up the complaint at lower levels.

There is an attempt to find scapegoats. Employee errors do not account for more than 20 per cent to 30 per cent of customer complaints. A multistorey building repeatedly complained that the doors of the lifts were not closing properly and that the maintenance men were not rectifying the error on a permanent basis. On investigation, it was found that the problem was being caused because dust from the civil works being done by the residents of the building, was settling down on the floor of the lift and the grooves of the door channel. The maintenance people had to work more with the brooms than with other tools, to set matters right; yet, they would recur. Delays in banks are not always because of employees being indifferent but often due to unclear instructions and ambiguous authority. A cheque had been dishonoured because another cheque credited to the account had been kept in suspense without being credited, because the account number on the paying slip was unreadable due to an ink smudge on it. The account holder had not been informed before dishonouring the cheque. The system caused the lapse. Several unpleasant scenes at the airport can be avoidable if the supporting systems are improved. Many of the unruly scenes are caused by misbehaving passengers, while the butt of the accusation is borne by the staff, described as 'indifferent' and 'impolite'. Most of the complaints of indifference in service emanate from the procedures being unsuitable for speedy response to unanticipated situations as can be seen in the example below.

> Mr Mark McCormack, Chairman, International Management Group, narrates the story of the gift of flowers ordered by a friend of his to be delivered to him every month, being repeatedly sent to his office instead of to his house. Every month he would write to the agency to change the address, he would get an apology, an assurance of revised instructions having been noted and a fresh set of flowers at his house. This went on for twelve months.

A complaint is an indication of inadequacy, which may be due to

- design of the delivery system,

- the customer himself neglecting instructions,
- faulty perceptions.

There could be scope in improving conformity by customers to instructions through

- removal of ambiguity,
- prominent display,
- adding illustrations for better understanding.

Medicine packs have instructions which are unreadable. Even the word POISON, is not always noticeable. Instructions in parks or museums are cluttered with a lot of redundant words. They are also placed at places which may easily be missed. It would appear that these are meant more to meet legal requirements than to inform or help the user of the facilities. Buses, for example, have instructions for passengers, which otherwise abut advertisement messages and perhaps, have faded letters. Instructions on highways are hidden under all kinds of posters. Insurance claims procedures are not known to claimants, sometimes not even to the clerks in the insurance offices. Rules to be observed in hospitals, for municipal services, for admissions and even in offices, are as told by some people from time to time. Government employees do not have copies of the fundamental and supplementary rules, that govern their conduct and terms of employment. Cooperative Housing Societies do not give their members copies of the bye laws or the relevant Act and Rules. Apart from lawyers, very few citizens know the Civil and Criminal Procedure Codes that regulate public behaviour. Tourists do not know the laws of the country that they are visiting. Beach resort hotels in Mombasa, Kenya, which attract tourists from all over the world, have clear instructions displayed at almost every corner, about the dress to be worn in the town and in the various areas of the hotel, written in many European languages and also illustrated with sketches.

When complaints are made, most of the time and effort (estimated to be 95 per cent) is spent to make amends for that complaint and apologise. Only 5 per cent is spent in analysing it and improving the product and its delivery. It is often assumed that the designs are alright and there has only been negligence or non-adherence to the prescribed routines. An attempt is then made to find out the 'guilty' person to be punished, so that others may learn the lesson and be more careful. It is safer to assume that there is need for strengthening of the product and the systems supporting it. *The problem is to be fixed, not the person.* The opportunity provided by the complaint to identify the elements and to augment the product will be lost, if the person remains in focus. Every complaint should cause some movement towards avoidance of such a complaint in future. Those who complain are more loyal to the company than those who do not.

❏ *Regulatory Authorities* ❏

In the liberalised regime in India, there will be a number of authorities, to ensure a level playing field among the various players as well as to protect the interests of the customers of the players. These authorities are themselves rendering services to their customers who are the players in the various fields like insurance, telecom, or petroleum. They are constituted to direct and regulate all operations, to act as a watchdog in the era of transition from a regulated regime to a deregulated regime and an effective market regulator thereafter. How will it lay down its policies? These policies are the products. They have to identify who their customer is, the business organisation or the customer of the business organisation. They also have to define the products they offer, which should be beneficial to the customers. The products have to be so designed as to satisfy the expectations of the customers. Fixing rates, for example, in the case of telecom, cannot be arbitrary and uneconomical. The pressure to gain competitive advantage should not lead to reckless actions like price wars, which often damage the service provider and also the market, more than anyone else. In December 1998, the three oil distribution majors in the public sector had objected to the 3000 km pipeline being laid by the Reliance from Jamnagar to Hyderabad, on the ground that it is 'reckless entry' and that the monopoly is not against the principle of the oil pipeline having to be a national carrier.

❏ *Summary* ❏

A service product is the offer made to the customer, promising benefits. It is constituted of elements, some of which are the core and the others peripherals. Infinite options are available in creating depth and breadth in the product range. The delivery system is an integral part of a service product. It should deliver consistently as promised, without being asked for by the customer. Performance beyond expectations and continuous upgrading are facilitated through attention to customer complaints. Customisation improves attractiveness. Guarantees have limited value.

4 KNOWING THE CUSTOMER

❏ *Who is a Customer* ❏

A customer is one who buys. A consumer uses what is bought and can be different from the customer. The decision to buy is made by the customer, while the consumer's needs may influence the buying decision. For our discussion however, the two words will be used interchangeably.

The customer of an educational institution is the student. He is the one who benefits directly from the service of education. The parent is also a customer as he has a role in the choice of the educational institution, which is a decision to buy the service offered. Society that benefits from the student's education, is also a customer. In some institutions, the students are drawn from limited segments, defined in economic, geographic, linguistic or even religious terms. Trained personnel from vocational and technical schools are 'bought' by employers, during campus recruitment. Business houses are customers of management schools, being interested in (*a*) buying the trained managers that the management schools produce; and (*b*) using the knowledgeable faculty both (as trainers) to train their employees through short duration courses and (as consultants) to enhance effectiveness of management Some management schools have multinationals as their customers. Some others cater to the needs of smaller organisations operating at district and state levels. The management school has to keep in mind the expectations and needs of all the potential customers.

The customers of a credit rating agency are the corporates whose credits are rated, as well as those who rely on those ratings, like security analysts and financial institutions who invest. The customers for credit cards are both the holder who uses it to buy as well as those who honour the cards in business. Both have to be satisfied, if the credit card business is to do well. What constitutes the 'convenience option', is different for the two. Their concerns will be different from that of the one who issues the card. If the trader experiences problems with respect to the card, the buyer's convenience is not possible.

Many support and advisory functions within organisations are service functions. Examples are legal, administrative, personnel, HRD, accounts, audit, training, purchase and stores. All of them exist because someone else can perform their jobs better. That someone else constitutes the customer for the service function. The service function is effective only if the customer is satisfied. If the customers of the audit department are not satisfied, the reports generated by the audit department would remain the subject of endless correspondence, with no effect on systems and procedures. In one sense, even management is a service function, whose customers include all the subordinates of the manager.

❏ *Buying Process* ❏

A customer buys because he wants to satisfy a need. Therefore, before buying, he has to

- become aware of a need to be satisfied,
- want that need to be satisfied (he has the option of living with the unfulfilled need),
- search for alternatives that can give him what he wants,
- gather data on what each of the alternatives have and do not have (advantages, disadvantages, cost-benefit),
- compare the data so collected,
- evaluate the best among the alternatives.

The process of making a buying decision would thus, appear to be rational, based on data, logic and reasoning. In reality however, much of the processes are not rational. They are often perceptual and influenced by individual preferences, values, paradigms and other personality characteristics.

❏ *Needs are not Uniform* ❏

A hungry person needs food, but one person's need may be frugal, for simple fruit, while another's may be related to rich and/or exotic food. Another person's need may be for a quick meal to get back to work, while yet another may need to combine mealtime with social or business contacts. One may need to be 'recognised' by the choice of the eating place and therefore, not be seen in a cheap joint, while another may not have such a need. *Each person has his peculiar set of needs.* Not only is one person's needs different from another's, but the same person's needs will change from time to time. The needs in the presence of the family members is different from the needs in the midst of friends. A businessman going to a meeting is different from the same person returning after the meeting. It would be wrong to assume that the need of a person in the middle of a desert is water. It could be direction.

❑ Needs are not Known ❑

Several things that people need are not known to them, particularly if such needs are not of immediate concern. Pleasures of the present take precedence over needs of the future. Any doctor will confirm that people neglect their health and practically invite disease. Financial consultants are aware as to how elderly persons find themselves inadequately prepared for the impending days of retirement. The conflict between environmentalists and developmental agencies are manifestations of the same phenomenon, at a national level. *Short-term interests override long-term concerns.*

❑ Needs and Wants ❑

Very often, one would not have been aware of some needs, because the possibility of satisfying such a need was not known. For example, car drivers never felt the need for intermittent and varying speeds of windscreen wipers until they were provided. The cable TV is meeting the need of, among other things

- good TV programmes 24 hours a day,
- instant contact with events worldwide,
- keeping up with the Joneses.

The intense demand experienced in 1991 for Star TV and CNN via dish antennas and cable networks, did not exist in 1990. These needs could not have arisen all of a sudden in 1991. The first need for 24 hours entertainment was perhaps, being met partially, through videocasettes. Due to this, people wanted VCRs and VCPs, cassette libraries and cable TV connections. The second need was being met through radio, until the possibility of speedier and more intimate (live, visual) contact became known. The third need was expressed in wanting colour TV sets, as soon as they became available in 1982.

Thus, needs may be met in different ways and each way generates a different kind of want. A person may want to buy a car because of the need for (*a*) transport; (*b*) status; or (*c*) collecting allowances from the employer. The need for transport may be met by arranging a taxi, or sharing with others having cars. The need for status may be met through staying in a posh locality, buying a bungalow, carrying a cellular phone, wearing expensive clothes, etc. One goes out in search of a purchase when a want has arisen. A need which is not felt, does not generate a want and therefore, there will be no purchase.

❑ *Search for Alternatives* ❑

When the desire for a colour TV arises, for example, to meet the need of keeping up with the Joneses, a person has many options to choose from. If there are no options, no decisions have to be made. To know these options is the next step in the buying process. Ideally, one can shop around, ask questions, study literature, etc. With the help of 'shopping agents', one can scour on the Internet to find on-line merchants that sell what you want and report the prices.

However, there are limitations. Not all items can be easily specified. We can specify a book by its title, author, year of publication and binding and order according to availability and price. However, if one is searching not for a specific book, but a book on a specific subject, there is a problem. Not many booksellers can help, not even some who claim to have 100,000 titles on stock and promise delivery within four days. Librarians are familiar with this problem. It is not enough to mention 133 MHZ Pentium laptop with 16 megabytes of memory and 1 gigabyte hard disk, when wanting a computer. Weight, size, battery type, screen pointing device, modem, CD ROM drive speed, video RAM are also important. When such detailed specifications are made, there would perhaps be only one product that meets these.

All outlets do not deal in all products. They may deal only in some brands. Even in respect of the brands they handle, they may not have all the models in stock. One cannot walk into all shops to find out price differentials, credit possibilities, service arrangements, etc., which may be relevant in making the decision to purchase. The buying decision is not only about what to buy, but also about from whom to buy. What happens often in practice, is that the buying decision is based on some information, collected through friends and a few known dealers, but is mostly incomplete.

Some studies reveal that consumers do not engage in extensive search for alternatives: it was found that 47 per cent of those purchasing new durables, visited only one store and made the purchase there. Those buying houses, for example, depend on advertisements or friends or agents. Those choosing hotels or couriers or films or motor garages, do not go round making elaborate enquiries. The search for alternatives is neither thorough nor complete. *It is limited to a point where one says, 'I think I have got enough information'.*

Five reasons are postulated for the low level of search. The first could be, ignorance about the availability of information. The second could be the lack of awareness about what information may be relevant. To search, one must know what to search for. How does one, for example, get information about a consultant? What information is to be asked for? From where can it be found? The third could be the incapacity to handle the information, particularly if the information is technical. The fourth of course, is inertia or indifference. The fifth could be a sense of urgency to decide. There is not enough time to search.

❏ Comparison of Data ❏

The data collected about different alternatives have to be compared, to determine which is a better one. The parameters for comparison may be many. There could be a lot of technical information in terms of collaboration, specifications about semi-conductors and antenna, audio output, etc. One may have data through observation, appearance and trial performances. One may have data given by knowledgeable persons on reliability, frequency and nature of complaints. Not all this data is recorded, measurable or even factually correct. Most of it is in the form of impressions. An earlier client's satisfaction is not enough evidence to establish adequacy for a new client. Neither the problems nor the needs of two clients are identical.

The data, normally, would cover a variety of aspects. Not all products would score similarly on all aspects. Each product may score high on some, not all, of these aspects, The relative weightage of each of these aspects would vary. It is not easy to determine how all these weightages would combine into one final decision. In the case of a consultant, how does one choose from varying qualifications, experiences, costs, recommendations and impressions?

❏ Evaluation ❏

At the stage of evaluation, the personal preferences and predilections play a major role. A TV set is rarely bought on the strength of technical data. Probably, most owners may know nothing about the technical specifications of the set. Even if they read the operating manual, they may not understand the significance of the data therein. To many, the external appearances matter. To many others, the performance noticed in the showroom, (sharpness of image, brightness of colours, etc.) matter more than anything else. Some will be influenced by the brand name. Some may be impressed by the promise of the 'service' by the salesman. All of them will ask a lot of questions about the competing brands. Yet, in the final decision, the dominating factor may be one or two, as referred to above.

Even while making major decisions for armaments for defence, or aircraft for airlines, or equipment for projects, or computer systems for offices, the choice may be narrowed down to 2 or 3 options, on the basis of rational comparisons of specific economic and technical data; but, after that, the final choice is made on the basis of the personal preferences of the dominant individual or dominant group in the system. The choice may be made on preferences for shapes, one's emotional attachment to US based products, or presumption of problem-free quality and reliability of Japanese products, or the opportunity to visit countries of one's choice, or proximity of a close acquaintance at the other end, or response to the behaviour of the negotiating personnel. While Indian Airlines was considering the purchase of aircraft to replace the aging fleet of Boeing 737s, Prime Minister Rajiv Gandhi chose the Airbus 320, after he visited the Paris Air Show. He was impressed with the latest fly-by-wire technology. A person less 'modern' in outlook may not have done so. When J.R.D. Tata approved of Darbari Seth's proposals with regard to the setting up of the Tata Chemicals, against the opinion of the other members of the Board of the Tata Sons, the same personal factor was in evidence

Evaluations have to be made on the basis of criteria. Criteria for evaluation are chosen by the buyer himself. The price may be an important criterion for some, but not for all. Lower costs of operation may be found to be favourable with some. Intrinsic worth may be the criterion for some, while external appearances may also be an important criterion for some others. The choice of criteria is a personal matter. The logic behind such choices have no universal acceptance. Thus, the process of choice is not a rational one. It is not irrational either. The rationality is unique to each person, his situation and his needs.

❑ *Perceptions* ❑

The concept of perceptions is very significant in understanding customer behaviour. When one looks at the sunset and says it is 'beautiful' or admires the screen dialogue of his favourite hero, he is expressing his personal reaction to an external event. The beauty is not in the sunset, but in his mind. Another person may look at the same sunset and not get excited. Another may see the same sunset and remain quite depressed at the impending darkness. The powerful dialogues in a film may seem to someone else as ' ranting', a lot of meaningless noise.

What one 'sees' is not what is there outside to be seen. We do not react to all the stimuli that we receive from the outside. As one goes along the road, one does not see all that there is to be seen. The stimuli are selected. Each person makes his selection differently.

One responds to the selected stimuli differently. We form opinions of people from their appearances. If we find a young man walking behind a young girl, we attribute meanings thereto in our unique ways. We do so, on the basis of what we 'know' from past experience of similar situations. We shout at a subordinate who questions our decision, while we calmly explain the decision when another subordinate asks the same question. This is because the 'question' is attributed to meaning 'challenge' or 'insubordination' in one case and 'clarification' in the other, based on memories about the respective subordinate's past behaviour. When one does not believe in the validity of traditional Indian teachings, then introduction of the study of 'Vedic' lessons, Vedic mathematics, yoga etc., is described as 'indoctrination'.

In other words, the stimuli from outside, as visuals or as sound, interact with our beliefs, values, needs, etc. The meaning or significance of the stimuli emerges from that interaction. It is organised within our minds, in terms of our own logic, created by ourselves from our past. What we really see or perceive is what our mind interprets of the reality outside. What is real to us is not exactly the reality outside, but our interpretation or perception of the same. We may not feel happy with the tone of the waiter and we will say that the waiter was rude, as if that rudeness was a fact. It is not a fact. It is how we saw it, our perception.

Perception is a visual phenomenon. We see a stick in water as bent from the level of the water. Looking out from our train to another train in the adjacent platform, we may feel that our train is moving, a perception which is often corrected only by looking at a static object outside. The drawings below are examples. In one, the two lines between the arrowheads are of the same length, but may not appear to be so. In the other the black circle is the same size in both configurations, although one of them may appear bigger. The background or adjacent data tend to prevent us from seeing the reality.

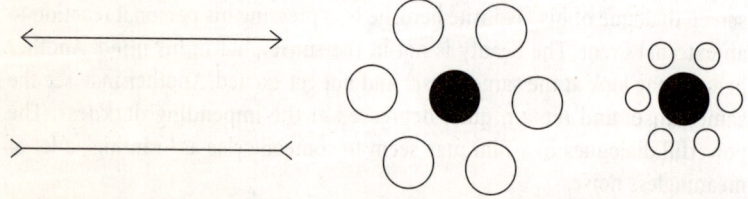

Perception is also a cognitive phenomenon, influencing our observations and judgements. We look at the face and behaviours of a stranger and form opinions about his personality and character. We perceive all politicians as corrupt and untrustworthy, the honest one being an exception. The perception may be an accurate understanding of the reality. It may also not be. The extent to which the reality differs from the perception, may be referred to as perceptual error. A number of factors causes perceptual errors. Some of them are:

- Role or status of other person. We look down or look up to some kinds of people.
- Occupation. Our jobs give unique points of view differently from others. Government servants, for example, may see all propriety in terms of procedures and rules, while business people see procedures and rules as red tape, improper and to be avoided.
- Physical features including dress.
- Body language viz., postures, gestures, facial expressions, tone of voice, loudness, pitch, that convey messages.
- Incomplete reception of, and/or attention to, all the available symbols and data.
- Stereotyping whereby we attribute positive or negative characteristics on the basis of generalised categorisations, like sex (lady drivers are careless), community (some are aggressive and some are mild), position (managers vs union leaders), etc.
- Halo effect, by which one single positive or negative factor forcefully eclipses all other characteristics. The polished behaviour of a person may generate favourable impressions that blind us to his attempts to cheat.
- Projection, which is the tendency to project our feelings, motivations or characteristics on to the other person. This may result in noticing undesirable traits in others that one fails to recognise in oneself.

It is because of differences in perception that people

- do not see facts/data the same way,
- are not objective about observations and judgments,
- argue,
- become prejudiced or biased,
- have preconceived notions.

Even newspapers, which are expected to be objective in reporting news, are not immune from the distortions through perceptions, as would be seen from the facts in the box in the next page.

Perceptions influence the nature of relationships between persons and towards organisations that such persons are deemed to be part of. We like, dislike, suspect, trust, rely, avoid, admire, respect, etc., because of our perceptions of the others.

Reporting on the proceedings of the Executive of the Bharatiya Janata Party at Bangalore, the headlines of *The Times of India* dated 4 January 1998 read 'Hardliners prevail at BJP meeting. Softpedal attacks on Christians. Oppose opening up of insurance sector'. *The Economic Times* of the same date, reporting the same news, had the headlines reading 'Meet backs P.M. Shuns attack on Christians. RSS told to stay away from State governance'.

Perception is a function not merely of the persons concerned, but also of situations or circumstances in which the events occurred. While making decisions, our understanding of the situation, the costs and rewards, etc., are all influenced by perceptions.

Perception is not an explicit process. The reception, selection and evaluation of the many sensory stimuli may occur below the threshold of consciousness. The perceptual process, being internal to oneself, cannot be directly observed, but may be inferred from observable behaviour.

Conflicts at interpersonal or inter-group levels, are created, and resolved, because of, and through, perceptual influences. One person's truth may be a lie to another. What is rational and reasonable to one, may be 'madness' to another. What one sees as 'facts' may be seen by others as either 'conjecture' or even 'figment of a fertile imagination'.

❑ *Strokes* ❑

Another useful concept to understand consumer behaviour in the context of services, is that of strokes, taken from the constructs of Transactional Analysis. Physical stroking is done by passing one's hand gently over the back of the other. Children calm down when stroked by the mother. Pets like to be stroked. Even adults in discomfort, distress or agony feel comforted, when someone establishes physical contact, through touch of hands, a pat on the back, or an embrace.

Physical stroking provides comfort. It is a message of caring, of recognition, of concern. Everyone is hungry for recognition and caring. A word of comfort or of praise, an enquiry of welfare, a nod of recognition, an assignment of importance, a smile, a wink, being called by name (instead of by a token number), all constitute strokes. Though not physical, these strokes provide great satisfaction.

People want strokes. They want positive strokes which maybe in the form of compliments, appreciation, praise—references to one's worth. Negative strokes like scoldings, rebukes, criticism and denial also have messages of recognition, but refer to one's lack of worth. *Negative strokes are preferred to absence of strokes.* Those who are ignored, not receiving any strokes, may sense being neglected and resort to behaviours that invite strokes, positive if possible, negative otherwise. 'Cantankerous' persons are those who got no strokes and are inviting negative strokes.

A waiter who argues, provides a negative stroke. A chatty barber may be giving a negative stroke, if the customer interprets the chattiness as an unwarranted assumption of familiarity, not recognising the difference in status. Not everybody likes to be 'familiar' with servants. Well trained waiters in high-class restaurants, will wait at a distance, unobtrusive, but sensitive to the needs at the table. If he overhears the conversation at the table, he does not let it be known. If he has any comments to make, he will do so only on being invited to do so. A curt enquiry, whether you have written down the telephone number while acknowledging receipt of a courier delivery, could be a negative stroke. A cashier throwing the money across the counter, the salesman frowning while pulling out clothes from the shelf, the storekeeper cutting down your indent for supplies, the accounts clerk who bluntly refuses to understand your urgency for the payment, all provide negative strokes.

❑ *Buying Services* ❑

In the case of goods, a lot of hard data can be available about the specifications and performance capability of the available alternatives, to enable one to make a buying decision. Even then, the buying decision is influenced by a lot of personal preferences and predilections which are subjective responses to the product features. In the case of services, there are no specifications, no hard data. The product features are intangible, not capable of precise description, not measurable, non-specific. The choice from alternatives may tend to rely on

- external physical attributes (observable tangibles),
- reputation (as read or heard),
- experience on an earlier occasion.

External physical attributes are very important as an influence in making buying decisions of services. Like the dress one wears while going for an interview, they create initial impressions, not necessarily valid. One would prefer to enter a restaurant or theatre or clinic which looks to be decent, clean and well lit. One may avoid a restaurant, where the waiters are shabbily dressed or the lighting 'seedy'. One may prefer a retail shop which has a good display, attractive decor, smart looking sales personnel, and/or adequate space. External appearances create impressions about the likely price levels and quality of the stocks. One may prefer a garage which looks to be well equipped, to one which operates from the road side. On the other hand, one may also choose the road side garage, hoping that the attention would be immediate.

Reputation about the quality of the service is a major influence in buying decisions. Reputation is what one has heard people say. It is the nearest equivalent to sampling of goods; a tasting before actually buying. Reputation is more powerful than the external attributes in influencing choice. People may travel long distances to buy from places with good reputations, even if the external physical appearances are not adequate. A road side garage with a good reputation will be preferred to a posh garage with a poor reputation. The preference for 'foreign' goods applies to services as well. Consultants from abroad are often chosen only because of their reputations. Doctors with full calendars, offering appointments a year or so ahead, have good reputations. Public sector organisations do not have good reputations and are therefore not preferred, if a private sector alternative is available.

Experience is what one has got on a previous occasion. If one's experience has been satisfactory, one tends to seek the same again, instead of going to a new place and risking unsatisfactory service. On the contrary, if the experience has not been satisfactory, the tendency will be to avoid that experience. Then reputation will have no influence. One's experience is more powerful than reputation, which is only hearsay of another's experience. If one has no experience, then reputation will be the influencing factor. If even reputation is not available, as when one has gone to a new town, then external appearances become the major influence. This is not a very reliable indicator. Therefore, even in such situations, one tries to find out the reputation by asking the taxi driver or the hotel manager or available acquaintances.

❏ *Satisfactions Vs Expectations* ❏

When one buys a service, there is an expectation of the nature, level and quality of the service. These expectations are based on

- what one experienced the previous time,
- what one needs now,
- what one has heard from others or seen in advertisements or the external appurtenances, or been made to believe by the salesman.

When going to the hospital, one's expectations will vary according to whether one is going there

- to call on a friend who is admitted there as a patient,
- to assist a friend who is admitted there as a patient,
- to have a check-up,
- for a childbirth,
- for treatment of a major disease.

In each case, the frame of mind is different. In one case, it is anxiety and fear, while in another case it is joyous expectations. A third may be concerned with medical outcomes only at a marginal level. Each of these persons will experience the same behaviour (of the hospital staff) differently.

The service is experienced after the purchase. The experience is not the same as the actual service rendered. The experience is a perception of the actual service rendered. If the perception of experience is better than the expectation, the service is evaluated as satisfactory. If the perception of experience is worse than the expectation, the service is evaluated as unsatisfactory. Thus, *for the same level of service rendered, some customers may be very satisfied and some others very unsatisfied depending on (a) the perception of experience; and (b) the expectations.*

When the service as experienced, is more than the expectations, there is satisfaction. For example, when one believes that a delay of one hour is to be expected with a particular airline—this used to be the case with the Indian Airlines in the 1980s—and finds that the actual delay is 30 minutes, there is a sense of relief and satisfaction. At the same time, a delay of 15 minutes in the case of an airline like Singapore Airlines, reputed for its punctuality, will be dissatisfying.

If one goes to a government office, ready for a long queue and cumbersome procedures and finds that there is no queue, there is satisfaction and a perception of quick service. On the contrary, if one goes to a foreign bank in the hope of immediate attention and finds that he has to wait because the staff is busy or that he has to go to different desks, there is a perception of inefficiency and dissatisfaction. The more the service exceeds the expectations, the more satisfying will be the experience. The experience, at any time, becomes the expectation for the next time. Thus the level of service will have to continuously improve in order to maintain satisfaction levels. In a hotel, for example, when a guest calls the room service or reception, he would be happy to get an immediate response to the call and acceptance of the instruction. However, when in a hotel, the response to the call is accompanied by an identification of the caller by name, the satisfaction is much greater. After that, on a subsequent occasion, if the personal identification by name does not happen, there will be dissatisfaction.

Therefore, service providers should strive to

- keep down expectations,
- keep promises,
- enhance perceptions of experience.

Keeping Down Expectations: Sales persons, while converting prospects to customers, promise the ultimate. Services are rendered by operational personnel, who may not be aware of what had been promised or are unable to perform at that level, for some reason. The experience is less than expectations and therefore, there is dissatisfaction. The sales persons may blame the operational personnel for inefficiency. The latter blame the sales for being ignorant of operational realities and making false promises.

When a post office has three counters equipped with computers and with the board 'multipurpose' in front of them, instead of the usual separate counters for registration, money orders, savings, etc., there is an expectation of speedier service and less waiting time. However, when only two of these counters are working, because of shortage of staff, the delivery is less than expected and the waiting becomes more burdensome, even if, on the average, the work is done faster.

Better be humble and modest before the service. However, try to perform in an excellent manner during service. If you are targeted to complete a transaction in 10 minutes, convey a requirement of 15 minutes. Indian practices are, in fact, contrary. Schedules are often not kept and excuses are liberally made for delays. The tailor who says that 'Only the buttons have to be stitched', the doctor who takes you in two hours after the appointed time, the counters that do not open on schedule, the show which begins an hour after the time you are requested to 'be in your seats without fail', the bridal couple that keeps the guests unattended and hungry for hours, the 'live' telecast which turns out to be a recorded version of a 2-hour old event, the industrial project that has time and cost overruns, the programmes that are always behind on targets, are all examples of raised and unfulfilled expectations causing dissatisfaction.

Prepare customers for the problems they may face so that, when it happens, it is not unexpected. Don't offer 'latest' movies on the video bus. It is better to announce that both the video and the air conditioning may fail. If the bank announces that it may take 30 minutes to issue a demand draft, and it is actually issued in 15 minutes, there is greater satisfaction, even if that could really have been done within 10 minutes. The next time around, however, the expectation will be 15 minutes, despite the 30 minutes notice. Therefore, the work will have to be organised to maintain the 15 minutes routine, improving on that if possible. If, on any day, it may not happen, it is better to let the customer know that there will be a delay that day. Give him the reasons. If there is turbulence ahead of the flight, do not just switch on the 'Fasten Seat Belts' sign, but also let people know that the plane may be tossed around. Regulatory authorities like the SEBI insist on the public being told about the risk factors. Many people look at such insistence on transparency, as an unnecessary and unavoidable intrusion and conform at the minimal possible level, conveying very little. Transparency may be threatening in the short term and distancing people, but is, to the extent that it informs correctly, very satisfying to the consumer and builds strong relationships in the long term.

Keeping Promises: Do not claim or advertise more than what can be delivered. Publicity and promotional efforts tend to make claims and make promises. If the actual performance does not match the claim, the service will be found wanting for this reason alone. For example, the cabin crew announced on a flight that passengers could refer to the inflight magazine 'placed in the seat pockets', and do the shopping on board the aircraft. In fact, no magazines were available in the seat pockets. A copy of the magazine was obtained and a listed item asked for which was not in stock. Dissatisfaction was created by making promises and raising expectations, which could not be fulfilled.

All public sector banks display notices showing time limits for various operations like updating passbooks and clearing outstation cheques. These are promises and are to be kept regardless of 'rush' or 'absenteeism'. The LIC's Own-Your-Home Loan Scheme was advertised as if anyone could get a loan and own a house. When people contacted the offices, the requirements and procedures were found to be outside the reach of many salaried persons. The assistance was available only if one already had some financial assets. The tax department's advertisements offering assistance to complete tax formalities are far more attractive than the reality. All ads tend to announce 'hassle-free', 'unmitigated pleasure' and so on. Making the service really so, needs effort. Similarly, direct mailers from banks suggest that credit cards will be available for the asking, but this is usually not so.

Not doing what is promised is far more dissatisfying than not doing as per customer expectations, because the promise then turns out to be a lie and is seen as an attempt to deceive, to cheat and to manipulate. Nobody likes to be manipulated. This seems to be happening increasingly in India in the early 2000s. For example, what many new 'clubs' offer in their brochures are neither available at all nor as per the time schedules. The offer of Reliance Infocomm to shareholders of 'Reliance' that the initial payments (of Rs 500) would be waived, was not honoured by many of their agents. Credit cards, issued 'free' to relatives of existing holders, are later found to be 'add-on's, subject to the same combined limit. One reason, perhaps, is that much of the marketing work is contracted out and these agents, wanting to show business, are not concerned with the long-term interests of the primary service provider.

Enhance Perceptions of Experience: Customers may not notice the services rendered well, but they will notice the one thing that is not done well—errors and failures. For example, a cockroach in a hotel room is noticed. The absence of any, is not a matter for notice. Uninterrupted water supply is not taken note of. If the water or electric supply stops, there is a furore. The ability of the BEST (Mumbai's city bus service) to cope with the burgeoning population, in numbers and spread along new colonies in remote areas, is rarely mentioned. The odd misbehaviour of a conductor is a matter of agitation. The hospital may have produced the best medical care, but if the sweeper did not give the patient due deference in the morning, there is a bad experience. The entire 13 days conducted tour may have gone through without a hitch, but if at any time, a guide had shouted at a member of the touring party, or had been missing when required, that one incident would rankle.

The case in the box below is one of differing perceptions causing anxiety where assurance was sought to be given.

For many years, the MTNL Bombay, had been advising subscribers to use the Dynamic STD locking facility, on their telephones. By dialling a set of numbers, of the subscriber's choice, the telephone could be barred to

- all outgoing calls (nobody can use it) or
- all STD/ISD calls only (local calls can be made) or
- all ISD calls only (local + STD calls can be made).

The lock could be opened and closed at will.
The facility had been advertised in the press and intimated individually to subscribers in nicely printed pamphlets. To many, this was an easy and safe remedy to the problem of unauthorised tapping of telephone lines.

In March 1993, subscribers got letters as follows from the local exchanges.

Dear Subscriber,

At present, your telephone no. _____ is having STD facility which includes ISD i.e., International Subscriber Dialling facility also. In case you feel that ISD facility is not required or very rarely required, you may let us know so that we can withdraw only the ISD facility. Occassional requirement of international calls can be easily met from our Demand International Trunk Booking Service - Tele No. 150. This is to safeguard your line from any possible unauthorised use for international calls.

We expect a confirmation for retention of ISD from you as early as possible and in case we do not hear anything from you by 13th April we will presume that you are not keen on ISD facility and the same will be disconnected with effect from 15th April 1993.

For any further clarifications, you may kindly contact the undersigned on telephone no.

P.S. I am sure that you are aware of Dynamic STD locking facility, details of which are available on Page No. XXVIII of Telephone Directory 1992.

Many of the calls received by the Divisional Engineer enquired about the effectiveness of the dynamic locking facility.

If anything is being done exceptionally well, it is useful to draw the customer's attention to it and let him know the effort that has gone behind that particular result. His attention can be drawn to specific features of one's product design. This can be done while engaging the customer in conversation. Such conversations will also help in finding out his perceptions about experiences and the errors he may have noticed. Do something special to a customer; something that he may value, but others may not need. Let him know that it was specially arranged for him. Ask him for his choice of songs and let the band play the choices dedicating them to the guests.

Asking guests to nominate employees for the best behaviour, is one way to focus on the positive. A small pamphlet can be given saying what they could look forward to. A visit to a museum or an exhibition is a wonderful experience, if the features of the exhibits are explained by someone knowledgeable. Otherwise, one just walks through a collection of unique exhibits with no appreciation of what one saw. Cruising along the Thekkady lake (Kerala) can be an entirely different experience if someone in the boat can point out the rare birds and animals and explain their habits and peculiarities. When the staff in some popular places continuously urge you to move on, regardless of one's need to stop and browse, the stroking is negative and the experience unsatisfactory. Popularity, in the sense of attracting large crowds, may be good commercially for an exhibition, but is not good service for those who want to savour the experience in a leisurely manner.

At a remote station, the 80 outgoing passengers did not flare up on hearing that the aircraft was not landing that evening, despite the inconvenience of cancelled appointments and a day of forced idleness. This was because many of them had heard the radio conversation in the control room and knew exactly what the problem was. In the case of insurance, surveyors and garages strongly influence the customer's perception of service. When the garage overstates the jobs and the costs and the surveyor tries to cut them down, the surveyor is perceived as a representative of the insurance company, trying to deprive the customer of his legitimate dues.

❏ *Significant Needs* ❏

Studies have shown that there are certain needs of customers which, if satisfied, heighten the perception of 'good' service. They are:

- positive strokes or recognition,
- accurate information,
- assurance of quality,
- reliability or credibility,
- ease of access.

Recognition: The importance of strokes or recognition has already been referred to earlier. This factor is most critical. If satisfaction of this need is provided fully, several other defects in service will either remain unnoticed or will be excused. *There can never be a perception of good service from a person who senses that he has been ignored. In fact, such a person will find a defect even if there were really none.*

The opportunity to ignore or to recognise, exists at every point in the process of service delivery and at every point of contact the customer has with the service provider. Telephone operators, receptionists, watchmen, bellboys, liftmen, nurses, messengers, sweepers, ushers, cashiers, counter clerks and chauffeurs are all points of contact, and can influence the sense of recognition and provide positive strokes.

Recognition does not mean that there has to be prior familiarity with the person. The receptionist in a hotel can address a person by name. He can tell the porter, 'Please take Mr X to Room No. 203' instead of 'Please take the guest ...' or worse, an abrupt ' Take him to ...' The telephone operator who recognises your voice, the waiter who remembers your last visit to the restaurant, the *panwalla* who starts preparing your favourite *paan* as soon as he sees you approach, are all perceived as highly efficient. The reverse is true of one who asks you to repeat your name, or is busy doing something else, while you are waiting to speak to him.

Recognition means that the contact point accepts the customer as a valued person and indicates a readiness to satisfy his needs. The opening of a door, the earnest attention, the helping attitude, the attempt to find and provide information asked for, the understanding of the enquiry or demand being made, all constitute recognition and are very satisfying. When the other person listens or even smiles, there is recognition. The printed matter in most service centres does not suggest helpful attitudes. The notices in parks and museums, the printed matter on airline and railway tickets, the conditions of laundry or couriers, do not provide any happiness to the customer. *None of them promise any service. Almost all of them warn the customer of what he is not entitled to do or to demand. They threaten him with consequences for one thing or another.* Even the person who checks the number on the tag on your baggage as you walk out of an airport, can make it pleasant, if he smiles and does not give an impression that he is there to catch you deliberately stealing someone else's bag.

An eminent doctor dealing with cancer patients was very thorough in examination, business-like in writing down and explaining clear instructions, but very curt in responding to questions from the patients or their relatives about the condition of the disease, side effects of proposed treatment, etc. He was justified, because he was always hard-pressed for time, with long queues of patients, and the questions were, in his opinion, generally puerile. He also believed that people neglected their health and came to him only when the conditions had become grave. Despite his professional competence as a specialist, he did not recognise that patients had the need to speak to the doctor and so he ignored their queries. That was dissatisfying. Anxieties were not allayed, and many patients tended to avoid him. Those who continued with him, and there were many, had preferred the excellence of his medical care and ignored the lack of recognition. People who provide services and who do not want to lose customers and want to increase the size of their markets, cannot afford to rely on the excellence of their core product, as heavily as this doctor used to do.

When the enquiry clerk does not listen to the customer's question carefully, or brusquely asks him to wait, or wonders why he cannot be patient, or throws the ticket or change on the table, he is ignoring the customer. When someone gives you advice which you do not need, on a matter on which you think you are alright; when the repairer tells you that the trouble had been created by your not following the instructions properly; when the president of a meeting introduces you by the wrong name; when one is contradicted while making a assertive statement; when the sales person seems reluctant to show the available choices; when someone fails to keep his appointment and does not intimate earlier or apologise later; when someone tries to manipulate your behaviour, there is non-recognition and dissatisfaction. When a hotel remembers that on an earlier visit you had liked a particular room and that you had asked for an extra pillow, there is excellent recognition. Similarly, if a chemist remembers the medicines you regularly buy and lets you know, or keeps aside for you, as soon as stocks (normally scarce) arrive, he recognises you. If a departmental store, has noted that you buy items for children's use and advises you on new products of that variety, there is recognition. The barber who knows your preferred style, the gymnasium attendant who is almost 'waiting for you to arrive', the cashier who sees you coming in and starts counting the pension and the librarian who has kept the latest arrival for you, are all providing satisfaction through recognition.

Recognition is strong when there is understanding of the customer, when the service provider is sensitive to the specific requirements of the customer. Very often the customer's requirements are sought to be fitted into the systems or the routines of the management. Good understanding may require flexibility in systems and operating procedures. There is very poor understanding when the response to a specific request is, 'Sorry, sir. Our rules do not permit'. A hospital discharging a patient on a Sunday morning, asking for cash payment of Rs 30,000 and refusing to accept a cheque or settlement on Monday, shows little understanding. Another hospital in the same situation informed the patient on Saturday morning as to the approximate amount of the bill to be paid on Sunday.

Recognition is poor when the response is one that questions the integrity and bona fides of the customer. The stories in the box below are examples of poor 'recognition'.

Someone (Mr A) received a telephone call one morning from a representative of a new club which had just been opened. The caller said that Mr A had been identified by a computer according to the profile for membership of the club and that he, the caller, would like an appointment. Mr A had heard about this

Dr Nair was a retired surgeon who had held important positions in India and abroad. He was invited by a university to be on the panel of examiners for considering the award of the post graduate degree in neurosurgery. On receipt of the invitation, he booked his tickets by air availing of the senior citizen's concession for the onward flight and the apex concessions for the return journey. The apex fares could not be availed for the onward journey because the time gap between the date of booking and date of travel was less than the prescribed number of days. When he presented the bill to the university, with the copy of the air ticket counterfoils, he was told that he was making a claim for the Business class to which he was not entitled and that therefore he would not be paid the full claim. Nair had to write a stiff letter and the Vice Chancellor had to intervene, before he got his reimbursement.

In the second case, Bimla collected some cash from the ATM in a crowded market place and went to buy something in the neighbouring store. The store said that the Rs 500 note with her was not genuine. That she had just withdrawn it from the ATM, made no difference to the situation. So she went to the bank, which was nearby and asked them to check. The bank confirmed that the note was a fake, but refused to admit that it could have come from the ATM. After lengthy arguments, a senior officer intervened and asked that the numbers of the notes placed in the ATM be checked. The number tallied and she was given a replacement.

club and h ad thought that it had the potential of becoming a very prestigious one. He was delighted and fixed an appointment for the next morning. He waited but nobody turned up. There was no contact thereafter. The high level of recognition provided by the call, made the disappointment much greater and practically made him hostile to the club. Not keeping an appointment without an apology, is not non-recognition. It is much worse. It is derecognition.

The phrase, 'You have been specially selected ...' etc., is part of the direct marketing techniques that are being extensively followed by companies. The sense of recognition which this conveys, when heard for the first time, vanishes totally when it is heard repeatedly. Technology has also made it possible for letters to incorporate the addressee's name within the body of the letter as if it has been specially prepared for him. This continues to satisfy even for the umpteenth time despite being mechanical. People who work mechanically do not satisfy. The telephone call which wakes you up from your afternoon rest, to offer a personal loan, shows poor recognition. The telephone company or bank which engages agents to collect arrears, through threats of muscle, is showing very little recognition, particularly when the agent is not told that there is a dispute about the bill. Many 'reputed' service providers resort to such third party intervention.

The Karnataka Bank in Mumbai, changed their weekly holiday to Mondays, making Sundays half days and Saturdays full working days. A customer who did not visit the bank everyday, came to know about this change only when he went to the bank on a Monday morning with an urgent job to do. He was told the next day that the information was advertised in the press and put up on notices in the branch premises. He thought the bank could have posted a notice to all its customers, probably at less cost than the press advertisement. A personal communication would have been a message of recognition, while an announcement in the press is non-personal and therefore without recognition.

The audit function generally develops an adversarial relationship with other operational departments mainly because, while finding faults with operational matters and decisions, there is lack of recognition. A more empathetic approach will enhance recognition and generate more acceptance and better effectiveness. Interpersonal relationships sour mainly because what is called as one's 'ego', which is nothing more than one's sense of self-importance, prevents recognition of the other.

The story in the box is an example of how wrong information can create a lot of problems unnecessarily. *One of the services a customer needs is correct information about the services on offer.* Consultants thrive because, with the knowledge they possess, they serve this need. They advise on purchase of technology, insurance, financing arrangements, market trends, computer systems, etc. They also advise on choice of spouses and careers.

A survey in the UK disclosed that one of the reasons for the poor image of the insurance companies was that the insurance agents were not knowledgeable. Even in a retail store, the prospective buyer expects knowledgeable and correct responses to his questions on the comparative advantages of alternatives. He is wary of someone who is perceived as not knowledgeable and perhaps trying to push his favourite wares. A salesman who is casual about the responses, or suggests that the questions are not pertinent, is effectively driving the customer away from the store. Several finance companies assign newly recruited clerks

Accurate Information

The three morning flights scheduled to leave Mumbai for Delhi at 6.30, 8.00 and 9.30 were all delayed due to fog in Delhi. The first two were rescheduled for 9.00 a.m. in the hope that, by then, the weather would show improvement. At 8.30 a.m. the passengers were asked to proceed for security check and await the departure call. An announcement at 8.50, requested passengers on the second flight, who were waiting in the lounge on the ground level, to board the aircraft. Those booked for the first flight, waiting on the first floor lounge, heard this announcement. Anticipating a similar announcement for them, they moved gradually to the gate. The movement of the staff through the aerobridge and to the telephones, gave the impression that the aircraft was ready for take off, but the gate was not opening. At about 9.15, one of those persons was asked the reasons for the delay. He said that they would be boarding 'within five minutes'. At 9.30, another traffic assistant also said 'within five minutes'. The passengers naturally became restive. When another assistant passed by and gave the same answer, the passengers screamed at him and the airline with words which, to say the least, were unbecoming of the status of the passengers. The content of the abuses were that they were not doing their duty and that the delay was avoidable. Within another five minutes, the passengers were asked to board the aircraft. When all were seated, the pilot came on the system and said that the weather in Delhi was still bad, the visibility being only a 100 metres, that the next report was expected at 10.15, (nearly 30 minutes to go), and that breakfast would be served on board. On enquiry with the airhostess, the passengers were told that the second flight was also boarding only then. This incident could have been avoided if the state of the weather and the expected delays had been announced periodically, The announcement of boarding the second flight was also misleading. The traffic assistants themselves, perhaps, did not know the real situation, when they said 'five minutes'.

to call up potential customers offering finance for cars or household durables. Unaware of anything beyond the standard introductory lines, they are unable to answer any question. Some try to get smart and provide answers that prove to be wrong. The inaccurate information as well as the lack of recognition implicit in this exchange, are very dissatisfying. Accurate information is particularly important in the financial services, where on the basis of advice received, long term commitments are made. Errors could ruin futures.

Accurate information is expected. So, when it is received there is no great satisfaction; but when it is not, there is great dissatisfaction. The error in information is usually discovered later, when correction may not be possible. Regrets do not adequately compensate for the inconvenience. This is so, even when the matter is a simple one like checking arrival time or a visitor being told that you are not in the hotel, while you are there waiting for him. Sometimes, the wrong information may have serious financial and long-term stakes. Decisions involving millions, are made as immediate responses to data (relating to money markets or political developments or corporate performances) that is carried on satellite channels. Failures in this respect occur, because of human factors (indifference, insensitivity, ignorance, lethargy, lack of priority, pressure of other routines) or mechanical, electrical or systems factors. None of these reasons will mitigate the seriousness of the failures.

Assurance of Quality: Quality, to the manufacturer, is defined in technical terms, made up of tangible, measurable factors, things that he puts into the product. Quality to the customer is in terms of those intangible needs for which he buys the product, things that he gets out of the product. The aluminium engine in the Maruti Esteem car or the direct fuel injection system of the Santro or the technology that separately cools the four compartments of a BPL refrigerator, are less important to the user than the comfort and trouble-free performance he likes to have. The company's computerised, on-line billing system may be quality to the company, but to the customer, it is the clarity, the description of charges and the accuracy of the bill that matters. In a computerised system, the cashier may not be able to sort out a challenge from the customer pointing to error, like the promised discount not having been adjusted. If a courier flies his own aircraft to carry mail, that is of no interest to the user of that service. The number of gateways owned by the Internet Service Provider and the capacity of 200 gigabits per second of his fibreoptic carriers, is less important to the user than the ease with which he gets his connections, without frequent interruptions. Different restaurants with varied exotic cuisines may be quality to the hotelier, but not to the customer looking for a cosy place providing clean food to his taste. Many small hotels, with just about 20 or 30 rooms, managed, say by an owner couple, offering homely comforts and a family atmosphere, have become popular in India and abroad. Certain segments of travellers judge quality not by the comfort of the bus or the lodging places en route, but by the opportunity to spend enough time at each of the holy shrines on the schedule. Many people shy away from events, not because of the costs involved, but to avoid being hustled by the ushers and security guards and the traffic jams that precede and follow. Quality of educational institutions and courses may be determined in terms of placement offers (students do so) or by the results in examinations (teachers do so), or by the extent of learning and character building that happens. These are not necessarily related. What to an insurance office is unavoidable routine, can be traumatic to the claimant.

Despite such variations in the criteria and perceptions of quality, the customer has a clear expectation and if he gets satisfaction, quality exists. He wants to be assured that quality will be available every time. He goes to the same garage, the same laundry, the same hair cutting saloon, the same grocer, the same departmental store, the same doctor, the same tailor, the same astrologer, the same courier, the same group's plays, with the expectations that the same level of service will be consistently available. The emphasis is on consistency of that quality which the customer is looking forward to; not a specific level of quality *per se* which differs from individual to individual.

Reliability or Credibility refers to trustworthiness. Services are bought before they are experienced. There is a certain amount of trust that the service bought will be of the expected level. If that does not happen, there is serious lack of satisfaction. If a salesman says he will replace the equipment if anything goes wrong, or send somebody out for repairs within half an hour, will it in fact be done? Many transactions are entered into and commitments made, on the basis of assurances and promises. Reliability deals with the extent of comfort one has, that the promise will indeed be redeemed. Reducing the promise into writing, even as a legal document, does not improve reliability. *When reliability exists, there may be no need for documentation.*

Customers do not usually buy used secondhand materials, except expensive durables like houses, cars and furniture. Even if used material is bought, there is an attempt to replace the old with new upholstery, paint, curtains, tyres, etc. In the case of services however, many of the materials 'purchased' are used, like the crockery and cutlery in the restaurant, seats in transportation, equipments in gymnasia, all the tangibles in hotels and hospitals. If evidence of prior usage remains in the materials, the satisfaction and credibility are low. Stained linen, unmade beds, unwashed toilets, tattered carpets, torn cushions, fused bulbs, unemptied ashtrays and wet towels, are examples of items that convey messages of indifference and lack of credibility.

An insurance agent who keeps the prospect's concerns in mind, without bothering about the advantage to him therefrom; the computer system that does not fail; the operator who wakes you up as requested; the nursing staff being indeed considerate; all contribute to enhance the institution's image and reputation on credibility. The insurance agent who is nowhere near the prospect when the claim arises; the tour operator who denies responsibility for making arrangements for the tour party stranded in a foreign city, due to cancelled air services; the marketing agency that defaults on weekly payments due as per the agreement; the extras that are added on to final bills due to taxes or other factors, without this possibility having been indicated earlier; all add to the erosion of an institution's credibility.

Candour is the best way to get credibility. In the networked world, information will have to be transparent. The boundaries of what may be considered 'private' are narrowing. The right to information is overtaking the right to privacy. Everyone professes a preference for transparency, though few practise it.

Ease of Access: The service has to be easily accessible. Locations, telephone connections, hours of operation, adequacy of staff and other facilities, make for ease of access. Waiting is the opposite of easy access. Waiting is not avoidable, particularly if the service is good and the demand for it is high. If there is to be long wait, access is difficult. The telephone system is the main medium meant to improve the ease of access. That is how the fax, Internet, e-mail, LANs, etc. function. (Boxes 1 and 2 at the end of this chapter contain some principles relating to waiting and usage of telephones). The cellular phone enables instant accessibility in a large number of situations, but not always, because the cellular is made non-operational sometimes. A doctor who is on the move can improve his accessibility even without a pager or a cellular phone, if he could be in touch with his home or the secretary in the clinic at regular intervals of say, an hour or so, and call back those who have asked for him. Or else, he may have an assistant on duty, who could be contacted for urgent consultation till the doctor becomes available.

The story in the following box is an example of how a system developed to make access easy, can in fact make it difficult.

When a customer of the State Bank of India pressed 10,000 on the ATM machine of that bank in another town, the message flashed 'Please state the amount in multiples of 100'. He thought that he had made a mistake and carefully punched 10,000 again. He got the same message. Unexpectedly, an employee of the bank was in the ATM cabin, doing some repairs. He noticed the perplexed look and said 'Try 5,000'. The response of the ATM was the same. He then said, 'Try 4,000'. This was done and the ATM released the cash. He went through the same process again and got another 4000 and again 2000. Many reasons were given for this, but clearly the ATM was not programmed to be customer friendly.

The Automobile Association offers emergency breakdown services. 'Help is just a telephone call away', they say, and the telephone number is on the membership card. Access is easy. Credit cards organisations claim that the service is 'round the clock' and 'round the world'. Even if the card happens to be lost, there would be a replacement within 24 hours or so, wherever you may be. However, to honour this assurance, the specified telephones have to be attended to round the clock. At a much lower level of complexity, the railways and the airlines provide, on a 24-hour basis, information relating to arrivals and departures. The automatic recorded system handles more enquiries simultaneously, but is updated only at intervals and cannot be interacted with, if the recording is not clear. The manual system works slower but is more up-to-date.

Access is not easy, if one has to search for (*a*) the office to be contacted; (*b*) the people who will take the responsibility for action. Very often, everybody knows what is not his job, but does not help with a clear direction about where to go or what to do. Access to the repair service (airconditioners, refrigerators) can be made easier if

- address and telephone numbers of service/repair centres are written on a panel stuck to the equipment itself,
- the first contact takes down details and sends messages to relevant action stations for attention, like the 198 number in telephone services.

When goods are sent by railway wagons, they are required to be cleared within a specified time after arrival at the destination, failing which demurrage is charged. The consignee wants to know about the arrival of goods, not merely to avoid demurrage, but because he needs them. Often, this information is not obtained either on the telephone or personally. One may be directed from one table to another. Access is not easy.

Whether for the Internet or otherwise, if the telephone does not connect soon, access is difficult. As you are surfing the Internet or taking note of valuable information, the connection snaps and you have to start all over again. There is dissatisfaction to the point of annoyance. This is a problem of access.

An Indian businessman travelling in the US, found his hotel room burgled one evening. The hotel manager arranged for the replacement of the damaged bag and the clothes and then got him to sign the insurance papers, authorising the hotel manager to collect the claim amount when admitted. The hotel made it clear to the businessman that the replacement was not subject to the decision on the insurance claim. Access was very easy.

Another Indian businessman travelling abroad needed hospitalisation. He had taken an insurance policy in India, which covered medical attention while abroad. He had been given certain telephone numbers to be contacted for help, if needed. The persons manning the telephones promised to authorise the local hospital to treat him. The hospital did not get the authorisation and the businessman had to pay the bills himself. The access in this case was quite difficult. Some explanations were given to him later, but no apology or explanations, or even compensations, can make up for the failure of service. When there is no access, there is no question of reliability or quality.

A government office is a provider of service, enabling the smooth running of society. The service is provided by the enactment of laws and the administration thereof. The common man requires access to these services. However, access to the service becomes difficult because (a) there is inadequate familiarity with the laws; (b) the offices are not located at convenient places; (c) there are complicated routines to follow; and (d) it consumes a lot of time because there are too many people demanding service. That is a situation when consultants emerge. They make it easy for a price.

Access is better if there are less

- forms to fill,
- people to meet,
- distances to travel,
- time to get results,
- procedures and routines,
- steps from beginning to end,
- laws to understand.

❏ *The 10 Factors* ❏

Parasuraman et al. (1985) have identified 10 factors that significantly influence perceptions of quality in service. These are, Responsiveness, Competence, Courtesy, Credibility, Sensitivity, Access, Security, Appearances, Reliability and Communication. The first five factors are reflected in the behaviour of the person who, on behalf of the organisation, is in contact with the customer.

- *Responsiveness* refers to the willingness to serve. A responsive person is willing and happy to serve the customer and has the customer's interests at heart. This is observed not only from what he does or says, but also from his body language, particularly his eyes and face. He is prompt and ready. He does not find the first available excuse to say 'No'. He does not think that the customer's request is without justification or that any lapse on the part of the customer needs to be pointed out to him, as a 'lesson' to be taught to him. Responsiveness comes from concern for the customer, a genuine interest in him, his comfort and his needs. Responsiveness can be tested by asking the cashier for change. This factor does not arise, when the service is provided through automation. The story in the box below is an example of poor responsiveness.

A person who had deposits worth about Rs 900,000, went to the bank (a multinational) to collect the TDS certificates, required to file the income tax returns. The clerk at the counter refused to give the certificates because 'They had already been sent earlier'. The depositor's statements that, even if sent earlier, they were not available and that they were required urgently, made no difference. The clerk said that he would have difficulty in tracing the details. The depositor pointed out that the computer in front of him should make the job of tracing simple, but to no effect. After 20 minutes of heated arguments the supervisor sensed a problem and came over. He asked the clerk to give the duplicate copies, which was done in less than a minute. The deposits were withdrawn the next day.

- *Competence* refers to the level of knowledge and skill of the person in contact. If the person in contact is observed to be inadequately informed on matters relating to the service and the company policies in that regard, or is seen to be fumbling, repeatedly referring to someone else, or trying to hide his ignorance, there is dissatisfaction. This amounts to lack of recognition of the customer. Not everybody can know everything about everything. However, if the person concerned, aware of his ignorance on a particular matter, is quick to obtain the correct information and satisfy the customer, he is competent. The body language of a competent person, will reflect experience.

- *Courtesy* refers to politeness and respect shown during the interaction. One does not need to be servile while being courteous. It is possible to be quite assertive stating a different point of view and yet be courteous. While disagreeing with another, it is not necessary to declare that 'I dont agree' or 'You are wrong'. One can deny the other's request without being discourteous.

- *Credibility* refers to the trustworthiness of the person in contact. The question asked while evaluating credibility is, 'Does he mean what he says?' In assessing competence, the question is 'Does he know what he says he knows?'

- *Sensitivity* refers to the ability of individuals to recognise and understand the customer's feelings and needs. Sensitive persons do not hurt others. They become aware of the feelings and needs of others, even if they are not explicit about them. They read body language well. Sensitivity is almost the same as Empathy. One may be sensitive (aware), but not responsive, not willing to do. Some may be responsive, but not sensitive. They need to be explicitly asked for help. Both responsiveness and sensitivity are important for a perception of good service. An assistant in a book store, who is watching the books or journals being picked by the customer and is ready with the amount to pay as soon as he reaches the counter, is being sensitive.

This story highlights issues relating to sensitivity, ease of access and accurate information.

Bookings

The National Training Organisation (NTO) located in Mumbai, organises training programmes for senior managers in the industry. These programmes are of durations varying between three to 10 days and are conducted in hotels in different cities and are normally attended by 25 to 30 participants.

Mr Wagle, a faculty member in the NTO, was planning a three-day workshop programme. On 10 November, Mr Wagle telephoned the Mumbai offices of two well-known hotel groups. The conversations were as recorded below:

Hotel Group A

Wagle	:	(to telephone operator) I am calling from NTO.
TO	:	Yes, sir
Wagle	:	I want some information about your hotel in Hyderabad.
TO	:	I will connect you to reservations, sir. Please hold on.
Wagle	:	Okay.
A Voice	:	Reservations. Can I help you?
Wagle	:	I want to make an enquiry about your hotel in Hyderabad.
Voice	:	Yes, sir.
Wagle	:	What are the rates for single and double rooms?
Voice	:	900/- for single, sir and 1200/- for a double room.
Wagle	:	I want the rate including morning tea, breakfast, lunch and dinner and two additional teas?
Voice	:	Is it for a conference, sir ?
Wagle	:	Yes.
Voice	:	Then please hold on, sir, I will connect you to the right person.
Wagle	:	Okay.
Voice No. 2	:	Can I help you ?
Wagle	:	I want to know the rates in your hotel in Hyderabad.
Voice	:	Who is speaking, sir ?
Wagle	:	My name is Wagle from NTO.
Voice	:	Yes, I know you Mr Wagle. I had come to you for some business earlier. Are you planning a conference?
Wagle	:	Yes.
Voice	:	When ?
Wagle	:	28th or 30th of January next.
Voice	:	How many people?
Wagle	:	About 30.

Voice	: Will they stay in single or double rooms?
Wagle	: That will depend on the rates. That is why I am making enquiries.
Voice	: I have to find out from Hyderabad about the availability of rooms and the conference hall on these dates. That is why I want to tell them and find out the rates. January is a busy month in Hyderabad.
Wagle	: The dates are adjustable if the conference room is a problem for these dates. But I suppose you will have no difficulty finding 30 odd rooms, 2 months ahead.
Voice	: You see, we do not control the reservations here. If the dates are adjustable, as you say, I will get in touch with Hyderabad and get back to you in the afternoon about the rates.
Wagle	: Give it to me, including taxes and conference hall—everything.
Voice	: Yes Sir.

Hotel Group B

Wagle	: (To telephone operator) I am calling from NTO.
TO	: Yes, sir
Wagle	: I want some information about your hotel in Hyderabad.
TO	: Please hold on, sir. I will connect you to the right person.
A Voice	: Can I help you, sir?
Wagle	: I want to know the rates for your hotel in Hyderabad.
Voice	: How many people, sir?
Wagle	: About 30.
Voice	: Is it a conference, sir?
Wagle	: Yes.
Voice	: When will it be, sir ?
Wagle	: 28th or 30th of January next.
Voice	: The rates will be 850/- for a single room and 1300/- for a double, all inclusive.

Wagle	:	Bed tea, breakfast, lunch, dinner and two conference teas included?
Voice	:	Yes sir, all included.
Wagle	:	Can the booking be made now?
Voice	:	I would like to confirm from Hyderabad that they have no problem. There should be none. I shall call you back in the afternoon, sir. Would it be 30 single rooms, sir?
Wagle	:	I think so.
Voice	:	I will get back to you in the afternoon, sir.

- *Access* has been dealt with earlier. Access is reflected in location of facility, hours and speed of operation, waiting periods, etc. Proximity is not determined in physical distances. Electronic systems have cut down distances and time.
- *Security* refers to the extent of safety, privacy, confidentiality, etc. Again the security sought is not only for physical possessions, but also for reputations, information and business data. Security has implications in terms of ergonomics (effects on body), asset effectiveness, response in emergency, workplace safety, etc.
- *Appearance* has also been dealt with earlier. Pleasant surroundings, affecting the senses, heighten the pleasure of experience.
- *Reliability* refers to the consistency of performance. An experience raises expectations. If the subsequent experience does not conform to the expectations, there is an adverse experience. The reputation will be damaged. Consistency of performance comes from the control on processes that deliver the service at levels that are predetermined.
- *Communication* refers to the extent to which the customer is being informed on matters relevant to the service. This is related to accurate information, which is a significant want of customers.

❑ *Moments of Truth* ❑

A moment of truth is the moment when a customer comes into contact with the organisation. At every point of contact, he experiences the service and makes an evaluation about it being good or bad. That is the moment which creates the satisfaction or otherwise. That is the moment when a problem may occur. If a problem does not occur and the moment passes off as expected, there is no dissatisfaction. That is also the moment when the experience could be very different than what was expected, creating a perception of intense delight and expression of 'Wow'. That is the defining moment of the reality.

A telephone instrument in the premises is not service. The moment of truth is when one begins to use it. If at that time it works and the connection is made well, there is nothing to be happy about. It functioned as expected, but if one hears a couple of beep and a voice saying that the line is temporarily disconnected for non-payment of the bill, there is dissatisfaction. In the efforts that will follow, to either find the bill and pay it or to establish that the bill had been paid and the disconnection not justified, every event, like the response to the telephone, the number of persons to speak to, the wait, questions to answer, extent of listening and understanding, the promises made and the implementation of the promises, is a moment of truth. While using a cellular phone, if suddenly the signals fade away, one would start thinking whether the choice was the right one. That would be a moment of truth.

In relation to a restaurant, the moments of truth may be

- (While making a reservation on the phone), the tone and words of the person who takes the call, the way he pronounces the name, the speed with which he confirms the reservation.
- (After reaching at the specified time), the recognition and acknowledgement of the reservation, speed with which the table is provided, the place where one has to wait, the odours around, the size and location of the table, the cleanliness of the cloth and the napkins, nature and level of the sounds around, the way the menu cards are brought and placed or given, the clarifications available while placing orders, quality of food (temperature, presentation, spiciness, taste, etc.) and the behaviours of the waiter (including gentleness, care and spillages) while serving food.

Every contact is a moment of truth, when a judgement is made about the service, the organisation and the people. Expectations are being revised at each of these moments and decisions made with regard to continuance of the contacts. Each moment affects the perception of the total experience. A series of moments of truth constitute a cycle of service. If one were to identify each moment and the corresponding cycles, the understanding of and response to customer requirements would improve. Each of these moments is within the control of an employee of the restaurant. These employees, whose behaviours define the moments of truth, effectively determine the quality of the total service.

❏ *Complaints* ❏

Dissatisfied customers do not always complain. 75 per cent of them or more stop using the service and go over to the competition. A study of customers switching patronage showed that the reasons for the switch were

- moving out of town (3 per cent),
- personal friendship (5 per cent),
- cheaper outlets (9 per cent),
- unhappy with product (14 per cent),
- unhappy with behaviour (68 per cent).

Those who make complaints expect understanding first, then redress. You can hear angry customers saying 'I don't want it. I can do without it. But I want you to understand that this is not the way to treat me' or words to that effect. They do not like to be pushed around with 'Please report to ...'. etc. Attempts to dismiss the complaint through defensive explanations, causes more dissatisfaction. Such attempts create perceptions of not caring. Asking him to put down in writing, a procedure normally attributed to bureaucratic adherence to paper work, may create perceptions of lack of seriousness,

Customers like to know that the management had taken the complaint seriously. Rarely does a complainant seek punishment of individual employees, unless there has been deliberate rude behaviour. Complaints are, more often than not, caused by lapses in systems. If the complainant is informed that the system had been rectified subsequent to the complaint, and he is thanked for making that happen, there is immense satisfaction. If the information is conveyed by a senior person there is greater satisfaction. Response by telephone is better than response by a letter.

Effective managers have recognised that complaints by customers constitute worthwhile feedback on the operations. If nobody complains, it is not good news. It may be very bad news. Customers may have given up all hope of improvement. Therefore, attempts are made to seek out complaints, to find out what was not up to expectations. This feedback helps the management to know what the expectations are, and to appropriately upgrade product features. However small, a grievance removed, is effectively, enhanced quality. For example, a garage was not aware that car owners disliked the dust and grease marks on cars that awaited delivery after repairs. The correction required was to park repaired cars out of sight and bring them out only after cleaning them. Another garage had the habit of washing the car just before being handed over to the owner and wiping it clean, just as it was being handed over. That effectively was a communication of 'We care'.

Box 1

Some Principles About Waiting

1. Satisfaction (or dissatisfaction) during waiting, carry over to the experience of the real service for which the customer is waiting.
2. Make reservations, so that the arrival of customers to receive service, may keep pace with the readiness to render service.
3. Even after making reservations, waiting may become unavoidable, because either the earlier client takes more than the expected time or there may be an 'urgent' matter needing priority. Dissatisfaction increases as the actual wait (as perceived) exceeds the expected waiting period. To reduce dissatisfactions, therefore, increase the expectation of actual wait.
4. If customers have to wait, let them know how much time they may have to wait. Do not underestimate the likely period of waiting.
5. Make waiting comfortable. Provide adequate sitting space, fan, reading material, etc. These are tangible indications of concern for the customer and influence perceptions of the service to follow. On the contrary, if these facilities are lacking, the perception is one of lack of concern.
6. Unoccupied time seems longer than occupied time. Let waiting customers have something to do. These need not be related to the service being provided. Restaurants provide astrologers, portrait painters, mehndi artistes etc., to keep waiting customers busy. Literature, magazines, fishes and birds, TV sets, serving tea/coffee, etc., are other options available to keep people busy. People like to browse through pictures.
7. Shorter queues seem to move faster and reduce the perception of waiting, compared to longer queues, which, in fact, may be moving faster. A larger number of counters to receive bills and payments help.
8. Moving queues seem faster. If a service requires multiple operations like while checking in (verify ticket, weigh baggage, collect excess fare, issue tags, issue boarding card,

check passport, customs, etc.), it can be organised in two ways. One is to have all the operations at one point and have many such points. The second is to have the queues move from one point to another for each operation. Even if the total time may be the same in both cases, the second method may seem to be more satisfying because of a quicker progression through the queue.

9. Pre-process waits seem longer than in-process waits. The main servicing may begin after some time. However, if some of the preliminaries can be done during the waiting period, the perception may be more favourable. Some of the possibilities during waiting periods are

- taking orders in restaurants
- recording case history, checking weight, blood pressure, etc., in doctor's clinics
- collecting biodata, certificates etc., in interview halls
- issuing tickets before the bus arrives
- answering enquiries, by staff moving about near the queues

10. Anxiety makes the wait seem longer. A wait outside the operation theatre where a relative is undergoing surgery, always seems eternal. When one is in a hurry, the bus seems to be unusually late.

11. The other queue always seems to move faster. All others seem to get better, quicker attention, even if they came in later, in restaurants, doctor's clinics, reservation counters, etc. Provide assurance and comfort to correct these perceptions.

12. Unexplained waits seem longer than explained waits. It helps to know why one is required to wait and what is being done to reduce that time. Ignorance increases anxiety. Let the waiting patients know what is keeping the doctor away at the scheduled time. Let the waiting relatives know how the operation is progressing. Otherwise, they will interrupt and interpret (wrongly) the movements in and out of the operation theatre. When the aircraft is hovering around the airport without landing, when there is no announcement

for boarding well past the scheduled time for departure, when the claim check is not being delivered on the promised date, let the persons know the real reasons. 'Technical reasons', 'Under consideration', are not good enough reasons. 'Undercarriage is not coming down', 'Pilot has not arrived', 'File is not traceable', are real reasons. Hiding these facts do neither relieve nor avoid anxiety. In a small airport, in inclement weather, the passengers were standing around the wireless set and listening to the conversation between the duty officer and the headquarters. Being in the know, there was little agitation.

13. Uncertain waits seem longer than finite waits. Those who come early, wait contentedly till the appointed time, but get restless afterwards.

14. Unfair waits seem longer than equitable waits. Those who wait at suburban stations are always agitated. They push, they rush and tempers are invariably lost. However, those who wait at bus stops in queues are more relaxed. There is order there and a perception of fairness. If queue jumping is permitted, then there is a perception of unfairness till the reason for that is made clear and seen as justified. A receptionist ignoring those in front of her to attend to a telephone enquiry, is not seen as being fair. It is always better to segregate telephone enquiries from personal enquiries, if there is a heavy load on either. A restaurant that changes priority in queues according to the size of the group, matching with table size, is not seen to be equitable, although it is meeting the needs of the restaurant.

15. The more valuable the service, the more the readiness to wait. Patients will wait without a murmur, if the case is serious and the doctor is a highly regarded specialist, but would murmur for even a 15-minute wait at the chemist. The waiting of a few minutes after landing is more burdensome than the 10-hour long flight. The waiting for the bill after a dinner, seems always to be too long.

16. Solo waits seem longer than group waits. A group is active and has something to do. Waiting patients, unknown to each other, share their experiences. If the flight is delayed, waiting

passengers begin to interact, with some comments about the airline. The sharing makes the wait bearable.

17. Some of these ideas apply even for waits on the telephone, waiting for the right connection or information to come through. Nobody likes to listen to the music for too long. The operator should be able to monitor long waits and inform the callers as to the reasons for the delay (explain).

Box 2

On the Use of the Telephone

Be Aware that

City telephone systems are heavily loaded. People have to try several times to get a connection.

Electronic exchanges are programmed to disconnect automatically if no voice travels through the lines for specified time limits (usually 20 seconds). The line is also disconnected if the call is not answered within the specified time limit. If these happen, the caller has to start all over again.

The person calling may be from his mobile phone, costing several times more, or from another city or even another country. He pays according to the duration of the call. Even local calls are metered and charged extra, if the duration of the call exceeds certain limits.

Therefore

1. Pick up the telephone as soon as it rings. A measure of efficiency, accepted by many organisations, is that the response should be within four rings or five to six seconds.

2. Do not pick up the phone unless you are ready to speak. If you pick and say 'Please hold on' and become busy else-where, the caller is paying for the waiting. An interim acknowledgement, pending detailed attention later, is alright in correspondence, but not on the telephone.

3. Identify yourself or your organisation, the way it is usually known, as soon as you pick up the phone. Otherwise, the caller has to ask and confirm that he has got the right

connection and that may take up a few seconds. These seconds cost.

4. Whatever you say, articulate clearly and slowly. Fast speech sounds garbled in electronic systems. It helps to keep the mouthpiece a little away from, and not too close, to the mouth.

5. In long distance calls, the sound takes time to travel. After you speak, wait for a couple of seconds for the other person's response to reach you. Speak only after the other person has finished. If you try to cut in for any reason, it will not be effective, because he will hear you only after some time and during that time he would be continuing to speak and you do not hear it. Both of you would miss what the other had said.

6. Make sure that in your absence, someone designated, like your secretary or peon, answers the phone. A phone unattended is a communication of indifference. An unauthorised person picking up the phone and saying that he does not know anything about your whereabouts, is an insult to everyone concerned.

7. Callers expect that those who respond to the phone should answer their queries. Try to be helpful by

   • providing the information asked for
   • getting the right persons to answer the queries
   • transferring the call to the right person and/or
   • giving correct advice on how he can get what he wants

8. If the call is coming through the operator, delay in answering the phone prevents the operator from doing something else. The operator's efficiency depends on you.

Telephone operators should

1. Keep the list of persons and departments (locations and extension numbers) handy and updated.
2. Put through the connection immediately.
3. After putting through the connection, check that the person being called has lifted the phone. If not, find out why and keep the caller informed as to what is happening. Also ask whether he would like to wait or whether he would like to

leave a message. This show of concern for the caller is a matter of recognition.

4. If messages are taken, pass them on promptly. It is always better to do so directly.

5. Avoid being abrupt. Cultivate a polite friendly voice and tone. People are quick to notice rudeness among telephone operators, more than among others, probably because the rest of the body language is missing.

5 MARKETING OF SERVICES

❑ *Objectives of Marketing* ❑

Marketing is concerned with the study of needs, desires and habits of customers, asking questions like what people buy, when they buy, why they buy, how much they buy at a time or over a period, at what price, how often, from where, etc. The answers to these questions will help the producer to decide what to produce, how much and when and also how to make them available to buyers, in what sizes and at what locations.

Marketing concepts are developed on the basis that the customer is at the centre of all organisational activities. To win and keep a customer is the purpose of an organisation's existence. This is so not only for business organisations, but even for governments and social service organisations. Otherwise they would not be able to achieve their objectives and would not remain relevant. If people do not understand and accept the concept of the family planning programme, and the facilities made available for its implementation, the money spent on the programme would be wasteful. This happened in the early days.

The producer makes decisions with regard to procurement and use of resources, to produce and to sell. The resources are processed through practices relating to personnel, finance, production, materials, ancillaries, vendors, etc. The consumer makes decisions with regard to the purchase of goods and services. *Marketing looks at the decision processes of the customer and the decision processes of the organisation and tries to bring these two decision processes as complimentary to each other, in an exchange transaction that is free and beneficial to both.*

If there is no exchange, there is no marketing. If the exchange is by compulsion, then also there is no marketing. Marketing is relevant only when customers have a choice, not only between two alternatives that serve the same need (competition), but also the choice of 'To buy or not to buy'. An organisation, to be successful, has to create and produce and deliver goods and services, that customers value and want, at prices which are affordable and relatively attractive, in relation to the perceived value.

When it is said that there is no marketing if there is no exchange or if there is compulsion, it would appear that in a state controlled economy, or in a monopolistic situation or in conditions of scarcity, marketing has no role. People will buy whatever is on offer as they have practically no choice. Even a monopoly has to generate revenue. Revenue will not increase through increased production, if the existence of the product is not known, if the need for the product is not felt, if the price is not considered appropriate, or if the product is not available at convenient places. Even if a product is needed, it will not be wanted if there are doubts about its useability or if access to it is not easy.

When Liquid Petroleum Gas (LPG) was made available to households in the late 1950s, there was no rush to buy them in the Indian metros. People were not sure about the advantages as well as the risks involved. The CNN channel was available in India long before the Gulf War of 1991 boosted demand for it from households. One of the several reasons why the family planning programmes floundered in the early years, was that the facilities were not available at convenient places.

❏ *Marketing Adds Value* ❏

The linkage between the various processes and activities producing the output, and the customer's benefit is the marketing activity. Thus, marketing tries to match a company's human, financial and physical resources with the needs and wants of customers, by means of a product and the whole cluster of attributes associated with it, creating it and delivering it in ways that are convenient to the customer. The customer is therefore at the core. Marketing helps to

- add value by finding a better match between product and needs,
- reduce wastages, which would otherwise occur, if product is not needed or if production does not match demand (needs and wants),
- improve effectiveness of communication through better targeting of messages,
- cut costs through more effective distribution arrangements,
- improve better understanding between producer and customer.

An owner of a marriage hall can make money, by renting it out for marriages. For the marriage function, the person hiring it out also requires a decorator, a caterer, a pundit (for the rituals) and so on. If the hall owner can make arrangements for these also, as part of a single package, he is lightening the burden of the hirer. The value of the total service, is now enhanced and will provide greater satisfaction.

❏ Marketing of Ideas ❏

Marketing has relevance beyond the sale of goods and services. People do not buy the tangible goods produced. They, in fact, buy *only ideas or concepts*. When a person looks at a picture of a beautiful film star with the Lux soap, he buys the beauty associated with it. LPG has value because there is convenience, ease of operation, cleanliness. These are not in the LPG cylinder, but are in the minds of the user. When the user realises that he can have these without any problems, at prices which seem reasonable to him, there is value for money and he makes the purchase. When the income tax payer understands from the various statements of the government that the VDIS (of 1997) will give him safety and mental peace at a price (30 per cent), which he considers alright, then he will buy the scheme and make a voluntary disclosure. The family planning programmes of the government were trying to make citizens buy the concept of both the happiness of the family through reduced numbers and the baseless nature of the prevalent fears relating to various methods of birth control. If such buying of ideas did not occur, the family planning programmes would have made no progress. A candidate standing for an election, is in effect 'marketed' to the electorate, making them 'buy' the concept that his victory is good for the constituency or country. The posters and the meetings and the door to door campaigns, and the literature, all project him as 'value' for the voter. A marketing orientation helps to improve the 'buying' rate of ideas, which governments or social reformers or campaigners of any kind, choose to pursue.

❏ Marketing Orientation ❏

A marketing orientation implies

- recognition that conduct of an organisation's activities must revolve around the long- term interests of the customers,

- onward looking responsive attitudes to events in the external environment,
- understanding of the balance between the need to earn profit from existing assets and an equal need to service future profits (long-term growth),
- a positive innovative attitude to conduct exchange transactions.

As against the marketing orientation, there are three other orientations. One is the product orientation which is the same as the mousetrap fallacy that states that if you have a good mousetrap, people will queue up to buy it. In fact this does not happen. Some effort has to be made to carry the message about the mousetrap to houses that have mice. If there are no mice anywhere, there will be no queue. Some people may prefer slightly lesser quality mousetraps, if it is cheaper. There will be further problems if someone develops an idea that gets rid of mice without traps, using perhaps, sounds or odours.

The second orientation aims to improve profits by reducing costs of materials and production. Profits will improve through reduced costs, only if revenues are generated. Revenues are provided by customers who buy. It cannot be assumed that reduced costs will produce cheaper products of the same quality. It also cannot be assumed that customers would prefer cheaper goods. They may prefer costlier goods, if they see appropriate value therein. That is the reason for imported goods being preferred, even when the same brands are made in India, examples being Dove soap and Scotch whiskey. Price matters, but not always.

The third orientation laces emphasis on large production capacities and large turnovers. The assumption is that increased production will lead to bigger markets and lower costs. Large turnovers require attempts to attract large numbers of customers. That is what marketing helps to do, but it will not happen automatically. Otherwise the first orientation would have been valid. It is also not true that larger markets, turnover or production, will always reduce costs per unit. It depends on the nature of the market and the product.

❑ *Marketing and Selling* ❑

Before the emergence of marketing concepts, producers attempted to sell whatever they produced through

- advertising and publicity, informing and persuading the prospective buyer,
- promotion (like offering gifts for every purchase),
- price manipulation, to tempt the customer to buy,
- personal salesmanship.

Marketing orientation recognises the usefulness of all the above activities. It asserts however, that these are not enough by themselves and that there could be a wastage. The market is a collective of persons of diverse characteristics. The total could be divided into fairly homogeneous (in relation to needs, habits, status, etc.) groups of persons to form different markets. Each of the different markets, called segments, have distinct characteristics, which could be used to advantage, more effectively

- designing and developing the product—i.e., what benefits to provide,
- determining the price,
- deciding on the distribution system—how to make the product available to the customer,
- planning the promotion, media, message etc.—what to say, how and where.

Each of the above, can add value to the product. If done scientifically, the buying decisions can be positively influenced. If done haphazardly, value is not added, the expected results are not realised and there is a waste of resources. *While selling focusses on the producer selling in the market, marketing focusses on the customer buying the product.* Some of the differences between selling and buying are listed below

	Selling	Marketing
Focus on needs and interests of	Seller	Buyer
Approach	Push products to buyer	Make buyer pull for products
Review/profits through	Sales volume	Value satisfaction
Product development depends on	Producer's resources	Customers' needs
Product	Precedes sales	Follows marketing
Packaging	To contain/protect	To add value/appeal also
Price	Determined by cost	Determines cost
Distribution functions, storage transportation, etc.	Seen as extension of product	Seen as related to customer satisfaction
Position	Selling subordinate to production	Marketing is central
Relevance of customer	Little, after sale is completed.	Important throughout

❏ *Market Segmentation* ❏

The most important task of a marketeer is to know his market. The word 'market' refers to the collective of existing and prospective customers. The total collective may not be customers for any marketeer. If there are 1000 offices in a locality, all the 1000 offices may be customers for pencils and writing paper, but not all of them would be customers for special papers used in computers, faxes or drawing boards. *One has to know which portion or segment of the total market, is one's market.* The concept of segmentation deals with the ways of dividing the total market into meaningful parts, so that marketing activities may be focussed on the chosen target segment.

The customer for a hotel is generally one who has to stay outside his usual residence, while travelling on business or otherwise. Customers include also

- users of the halls to conduct official business like seminars, workshops, conferences,
- users of the halls for personal celebrations, like birthdays, marriages,
- users of the space in the shopping arcades to conduct their own business
- users of the restaurants,
- users of the rooms as offices, on a long-term or short-term basis (to conduct selection interviews),
- users of the business centre for secretarial or commercial assistance,
- users of other facilities like health clubs, swimming pools.

These users are using different services on offer. All these users differ, in respect of occupations, ages, lifestyles, economic positions, aspirations or any other criterion one may use to identify and describe individuals. However, there would be similarities between users of a health club, a business centre, a restaurant and so on. In other words, there would be similarities between users of the same service, but not between users of different services. By identifying these similarities, one might be able to group individuals into separate collectives that would represent customers for each of these services. Each such collective relevant for a service, is a segment of the total market. The total market consists of the customers of all the services of all types of hotels.

A segment is a discrete, identifiable, viable and appropriate part of the total market, having common characteristics of purpose, needs, motivations, benefits and behaviour distinctively different from another segment. For example, people of the same age are likely to have the same thoughts, having grown up during the same periods. The patriotic fervour of those who were young during the freedom struggle, may not be shared by those born in the 1970s. The values of these two generations would differ considerably in terms of lavishness of expenditures, lifestyles, food habits, concern for others, religiousness, material possessions, corruption and so on. Differences such as these, are referred to as the 'generation gap' in common parlance and 'age cohorts' in jargon. Thus, if people are differentiated on the basis of age, there could be a certain commonness among the groups so formed.

Segmentation is usually done on one or more of the following characteristics:

- geographic like region, district, density of population, climate, urban/ rural,
- demographic like family size, age, religion, sex, income, occupation, language, education,
- psychographic like value systems, lifestyles, personality types,
- behavioural (related to buying) like volumes, frequency, delivery requirements, decision-making practices.

Segmentation will provide data on

- customer profile,
- end users vs intermediaries,
- loyalty to product or to outlet or to manufacturer,
- relative buying size,
- preferences in configuration of product,
- experiences with competition.

❑ *Target Market* ❑

No marketeer is likely to be able to cater to the entire market. Even a public service like the government or the municipality directs each of its multifarious services/activities to separate segments of the population. Government hospitals aim to serve patients who are distinctly different from patients who would prefer posh hospitals like Appollo in Madras or Hindujas in Mumbai. The reasons for such choices are not necessarily the availability of medical expertise. Government hospitals normally have the services of professors of medical colleges, who are academically accomplished and teach others. They also have wide experience as there is more variety of patients in government hospitals.

A municipal department concerned with roads and traffic will be serving customers of different kinds like taxi operators, rickshaw drivers, private car owners, fleet owners, transporters, pedestrians and hawkers, all of whom have different needs and expectations. These are different segments. Developers, single tenement owners, professional architects and shanty residents are different kinds of customers and therefore, different segments of the market, for the town planning department.

Some hotels look upon big conventions (1000 participants at a time with smaller rooms for concurrent sessions) as a major business opportunity. The customers would be professional associations or big companies. The approach to these will be through business and professional journals, not TV ads. The prices will always have to be negotiated. The business will come only if convention-related secretarial, presentation, reporting, recording etc., facilities are provided. There is also need to be able to cater to big numbers in quick time and also provide support, if need be, in organising outings, cultural programmes etc. Those who do not have the resources to manage these requirements, will not offer this business, even if they have the space.

After the market is segmented, the marketeer studies the unique characteristics of the particular segment or segments to which he would like to cater. This is the target market for him and all his strategies will have to be developed keeping in mind the unique characteristics of the target market. Services have to be specifically organised to meet the needs of the particular segment of the market which avails of that service. Or else there could be dissatisfaction. The special features of the service being rendered, including the process of delivery, must be specifically tuned to meet the needs and expectations of the target segment. A target segment helps to focus one's marketing efforts very sharply. If the hotel's target market is the domestic tourist in the religious circuit, there would be no point in advertising in foreign magazines or providing exotic foreign cuisine in the restaurant.

A target market is chosen after considering the marketeer's objectives and resources. What one can do well, decides the target market. Also, the chosen target market decides what one has to do well. A target segment is perceived to be accessible, sizeable and profitable. There has to be specialisation and excellence in specific services and that will depend on, as well as decide, the target market. Among couriers, one handles only garments to the US, while another handles only diamonds between Surat and Mumbai.

There can be more than one target segment. If there is more than one segment as the target, the two would have to be looked at as separate businesses, requiring organisation of delivery systems differently. It is difficult to provide for the luxury of discerning customers simultaneously with the spartan needs of the budget traveller and the orthodox requirements of the ultra religious. Recently, the Mughal Sheraton Hotel in Agra, has found that hosting a meeting of the alumni of Doon School of Dehra Dun, can be good business. A four day meet for the class of a particular year turned out to be a lot of fun with inter-division competition and league matches. The hotel in a hill resort, which organised tournaments for school children had targeted more than one segment. *Separate target segments of complimentary seasonality, help to even out the demand-supply imbalances.*

A narrow target market is called a *niche market.* It enables one to become familiar with the unique demands of that segment and develop skills appropriate to those needs. Consultants specialise in niche markets. Sports goods dealers may have niche markets, catering to the requirements of specific games. Niche marketeers have the advantage of having mastered the relevant technology and the practices. A doctor who specialises in sports medicine, has developed a niche market.

❏ The Marketing Mix ❏

Marketing concepts had been developed originally in the context of tangible consumer goods. The main elements of a marketing programme are conceptualised in terms of the 4 Ps, which stand for Product, Price, Place and Promotion. It is by making adjustments or changes in one or more of these 4 Ps that the attractiveness to the customer would be strengthened. These four elements are known as the marketing mix, since the marketeer can mix these in different ways for maximum effectiveness in terms of customer satisfaction, like a chef mixes the same ingredients in different ways to achieve high levels of culinary satisfaction.

Product includes name, design, features, quality, operational ease, packaging, warranties, appearance, range and size. It also includes, pre-sale and post-sale services like training, repairs, maintenance, replacements. An earlier chapter in this book deals with aspects of the product contributing to satisfactions.

Price includes concessions on basic price, discounts, rebates, credits, instalment facilities and delivery terms.

Place includes retail outlets, wholesalers, transportation, warehousing, inventory levels, and order-processing procedures, that are ways of reaching the product to the customer.

Promotion includes advertising, publicity, media choices, messages, frequency of exposure, public relations, campaigns, sales promotion, point-of-purchase (POP) displays, merchandising, which communicate to the customer the availability of the product.

In the case of services, three additional Ps have been added to the marketing mix. These are People, Process and Physical Factors. Services are performed by people. People therefore, constitute an integral part of the service product. The process of performing the service corresponds to the process of production of goods. However, in the service business, the process is in operation at the time of consumption by the customer. The concept of Inseparability discussed in Chapter 2 is relevant here. It is part of the process of production. The way the process is managed affects the satisfaction experienced by the customer. Process, like people, is an integral part of the service product.

Services are bought and rendered mostly in the premises of the service producer. This may also happen in the customers' premises, though rarely. The physical surroundings of the service provider's premises, the sounds, the decor, the colours, the artefacts, the layout, all add to satisfaction. This is not the same as the concept of Place referred to earlier. This refers to the tangibles in the physical space, where service is accessed and is available.

Each of the elements in the marketing mix is important. Each has an influence on the customer. None of them can be ignored. The marketeer has a choice of concentrating on one element more than on another, to create the necessary distinctive impact on the market.

○ *Price* ○

Price has several nomenclatures in the service business. One buys a *ticket* for a cinema, pays *fees* to a professional, *charges* to a beautician, *fare* to an airline, *freight* to a cargo transporter, *honorarium* to a speaker, *commission* to an agent, *dues* to the union, *interest* to a banker, *premium* to an insurer, *rent* to the landlord, *salary* to an employee, *tariff* to the electricity company, *toll* to the road builder and *taxes* for public service. All these are prices for services rendered.

People often buy without knowing the price. When one goes to a hotel or a hospital, the price list is not checked beforehand. Affordability is determined on the basis of the images one holds about the place (see the section on Positioning below). The actual costs in a hospital may be known only well after admission (there have been cases where the actual bills at the time of discharge far exceeded the costs estimated at the time of admission to the hospital). When a car or a stereo system is to be repaired, estimates are not taken from different repairers. Some people buy because the service is expensive. These are people who do not want anything 'cheap'. Repeat purchases do not often depend on price. The concept of products being 'expensive' or 'cheap' are perceptions. An opinion from an eminent solicitor at a fees of Rs 100,000, could perhaps be had from a relatively lesser known solicitor at a fraction of that price. However, the former is more satisfying, because there is a perception of higher value, coming 'from a more experienced person'. Good marketing can raise perceptions of value and make price less significant. In such cases, a price cut may not only not attract customers from competition, but may also drive away existing customers, suspecting a drop in quality.

The price of a service is not related to the cost of producing that service. The cost of production of service is difficult to know in the case of a consultant or an entertainer. The mental effort put in by him to relate pieces of general information, into a specialised repertoire cannot be measured, either in time or in money. However, even if it can be known, as in the case of a film, the value of the product is not related to the cost. Hindi films produced with multistarrers and billions of rupees flop, while Malayalam films produced at less than half those prices are hits, regionally and internationally. The price of a service is not related to the time it takes to provide the service. Quality of service has nothing to do with the time utilised, unlike physical labour. Experts may provide the service in lesser time, yet levy a higher price than the lesser experienced. The 'inputs' that create an advertisement copy, the vision for a strategy and the insights that solve a problem, are neither measurable nor easy to put a value on. The car mechanic, who corrected a fault with just one turn of a screw, charged Rs 100 out of which, he explained, Rs 90 was for knowing which screw to turn and how much to turn.

When a customer pays a certain amount of money for a service, the 'value' obtained is calculated in terms of time, energy and psychological satisfactions. That is why the price may appear to be steep in absolute terms, but reasonable under the circumstances. A taxi driver, who agrees to take you home when you arrive at the railway station on the day of a *bandh*, is thanked regardless of what he charges. The extent of sales varying according to the price charged, called price elasticity, depends on the alternatives available, size of price, perceived value, cost of switching and difficulties of comparison. The last three are particularly important in the case of services.

The price of a service may vary according to

- season (higher during peak seasons of high demand),
- location (municipal taxes and seats in theatres vary in this manner),
- frequency of use (concessions to those who are regular patrons, season tickets on railways),
- volume (prices going down with volume, in bulk purchases or price going up with volume as in electricity and telephone tariff),
- collectives and groups (sports teams, holiday groups, school children on study tours),

- purpose of use, distinguished by social desirability or otherwise (priority lending in banks, cheaper electricity for farmers, subsidies, etc.),
- status of user (hospital charges vary according to income of patient's family).

The service remaining the same, the price varies according to the circumstances of the customer. This is called differential pricing. Prices may also be determined in order to influence the demand for the service. In this case the price is varied, upward or downward, for specific reasons like

- promotional, by way of discount, to attract prospects to try out new offers,
- to reduce purchases—either to reduce the rush for the offer or to reduce waste (telephone and electricity),
- to avoid undesirable segments of customers.

The last two practices are called 'diversionary' pricing. Prices may include guarantees offering partial or full refund if service does not correspond to the promise made. Some contracts have such clauses. The courier service, speedpost offers it, if the delivery is not done within the specified period. Some book stores allow refunds if the books are returned within say, seven days. In services, prices may also be 'discrete', following no rule. It may also be negotiated.

Prices may include or exclude related services like

- airport transfer, breakfast, in hotel tariffs,
- food, in conducted tours or hospitals,
- insurance and freight, in trade,
- electricity and water charges, in rent,
- free calls, in telephone and cellular services,
- stopovers and conducted tours en route in air travel,
- payment plans, deposits etc. in cellular phones and leasing.

Cellular phones aiming at volumes in business, offered in the beginning, discounted charges for airtime and free handsets, making for low entry costs with minimum credit verification. When this led to bad debts and low average recurring revenues per subscriber, they adjusted prices to consolidate the customer base. Non-users were required to pay higher rates. Volumes gave way to value. Mobile 1 Asia (M1) had the same experience in Singapore. To meet the competition of Singapore Telecom, it offered free trials and cheap package deals and cut rates by 30 per cent. However, ultimately, they had to invest in upgrading services, better quality batteries, better sound quality inside cars, more base stations, etc. Price reductions do not build markets.

Prices are normally published showing permissible variations in case of a range of services like hotels, tours, utilities, railways and airlines. In many cases, price is also negotiated with individual customers, even if there is a published tariff. Comparisons between prices of competitors would be valid only if the inclusions and exclusions are known. Advertisements offering car loans at 9 per cent or at even 0 per cent, are meant to mislead. The 'conditions apply' note must be looked at carefully.

Sometimes prices are charged and paid in advance before the services are rendered. Examples are consultancy, construction, hospitals. Sometimes, prices are payable only after completion of satisfactory service. Property brokers and placement agencies collect their dues after the recommendations are accepted and the transactions completed. There is no charge for the intermediate activities, if the transaction is not completed. This is so also in the case of insurance agents who get their commissions only after completion of policy, but not for the efforts of prospecting and selling. Finance companies charge 'processing fees' for considering the request for loans. These are prices.

The considerations in fixing prices are not always economic, like return of capital or break even point. In the case of services, sometimes social considerations prevail, charging more for the neglect of hygiene or less for environment care. Industries going into undeveloped districts are given concessions in power tariffs and sales taxes. Socially relevant cinema may be exempt from entertainment taxes. All these are in the nature of reduction of prices.

Sometimes charges are based on the affordability of the consumer. These happen in a number of social activities like medical care, hospitals, educational institutions, administration of justice, local transport, etc. The parties availing of these services do not pay fully for the cost of the services. There is hidden subsidy, unlike the subsidy in fertilisers or kerosene.

O *Place* O

Place, in the case of services, relates to the access and delivery procedures. These are in some ways integral to the product (of service) itself. In the case of insurance, claims procedures, including speed of survey and loss assessment, are effectively elements of distribution. When the railways made it possible to make reservations from multiple points across the city and that too, for journeys originating from elsewhere, access was being made easier. When a pathologist comes to the residence of a patient to collect samples, that is part of distribution. When a bank transaction is made possible through computer linkages, the account holder may be a resident in another city or country. The access and service becomes instant. The National Stock Exchange and the depositories have also made dealings and transfers much easier in the capital market. The Internet has made distribution of information across the world, easier than picking up a file from one's cupboard. Ease of Access is determined by the distribution system. When the State Bank of India, the ICICI bank and the HDFC bank agreed to share their ATM networks, it is the factor of place that is enhancing the customer's convenience.

Distribution has the following purposes or functions:

- provide access, making it possible to avail of what is on offer,
- provide information about availability, terms and conditions, usage, procedures,
- provide advice and purchase assistance (enquiries),
- arrange entitlement through reservations (cinema and restaurant bookings),
- receive and transmit revenue to principal (collection centres for bills of utilities),
- provide ancillary service like credit collection, storage (refunds and left luggage facilities),
- assist in complaints processing,
- become a source of market intelligence (feedback),
- supplement promotional activities.

The characteristics of services makes it difficult for any service business to have many outlets. However, McDonalds kiosks are in every part of the world. The Solomon B. Guggenheim Museum of Manhattan, has managed to extend its services to other parts of the world. Instead of the traditional travelling show, it has franchised its services with outposts at Bilbao in Spain and Berlin in Germany, which are in fact sister museums. It finds that local firms are keen to sponsor these outposts. The Amex car loans are distributed through nine district sales associations, non-manufacturing dealers (brokers) and three authorised manufacturing dealers, just as in India also, car loans are distributed directly, through manufacturers, through dealers and sometimes also through banks. Max Touch, faced with the problem of heavy outstandings, opened collection centres at places near suburban railway stations (in Mumbai), where people generally congregate. This, it is said, helped bring down their outstandings from 52 to 26 days.

The retail business, which is the distribution network for others, is a service business, providing information about and access to products. More than 95 per cent of the retail business is in the unorganised sector, with space of as little as 500 square feet. There is likely to be a retail outlet within five minutes walking distance from any household, even in villages. Retailing is also a big business. The organised retailers are found mainly in the cities. Teleshopping and retailing at home like Amways and Tupperware, are examples of effective innovations in the retail service, taking the distribution to where the customer is. *Chain stores constitute distribution of the retail outlet itself.* Big chains with many outlets in the same city is common in foreign markets and is becoming the trend in India, particularly Bangalore, Chennai and Hyderabad. Some of them are big with more than a 100,000 sq.ft of floor space. Industrial houses like ITC, Hindustan Levers, RPG and Tatas are entering the retail business with their own brands. A study by A.T. Kearney shows that India is seen as the fifth most attractive emerging market in the world.

The shopping mall is another development in the retail business. Such malls, where there are a number of outlets under one roof, are common in the developed countries, but are new in India. The first mall was Crossroads in Mumbai, which came up in 1999. It is expected that there may be more than 25 malls in Mumbai and perhaps, more than 200 in the country by 2005, offering over 400 million sq.ft of space. The shopping experience is affected by the ambience in the malls, outside the shop itself. Therefore, mall managements and operations are becoming service businesses themselves, providing signages, directions, cleanliness, lifts, security, crowd control, etc. The customers, in this context, are the shops and the shoppers and also the other visitors to the mall. Crossroads, even after four years, is a tourist attraction in Mumbai.

O *Promotion* O

Promotion refers to communication. It aims to

- inform prospective customers about product or producer,
- inform existing customers about new product features, price offers, new channels,
- generate interest in offers,
- persuade prospective customers to try the product (first purchase),
- persuade existing customers to continue use of product (repeat purchase).

Promotion tries to improve attitude and receptivity, to eliminate misconceptions. If A is the total market, B is the portion that is aware of the product, C is the portion that has tried the product and D is the portion that has tried and is satisfied, promotion tries to improve the ratios B/A, C/B and D/C.

Promotion is done through a mix of

- advertisements, which are paid for and are non-personal forms of presentations in the printed or electronic media, including posters, hoardings, banners, stickers, exhibitions, stalls, direct mail, giveaways,
- publicity, which is communication, usually impersonal and carried by the media, seemingly emanating from sources other than the marketeer,
- public relations (PR),
- personal selling and
- sales promotion.

Advertisements may be visual (having pictures), audio (as on the radio), static (as in print media and hoardings) or moving (as on TV and cinemas), having national reach or limited local reach, aimed specifically to target groups through general or speciality magazines and journals dealing with medical, fashion, sports, business and finance matters. Effectiveness of advertisements would depend upon the match between the profile of the readers or viewers of the media chosen, with the profile of the target market. The messages must also be consistent with the social norms, practices and culture of the target population. For example, a strategy that is developed to communicate about AIDS, keeping in mind the gay population of the USA will be totally inappropriate while addressing ladies in Chennai.

The number of people likely to see a message, is referred to as the 'reach'. The cost of the advertisement has to be calculated in terms of total cost paid to the media divided by the reach. Options available are infinite, but to remember is the adage, 'Don't sell a mile wide and an inch deep'. Messages that evoke fear and anxiety are less effective than messages that evoke hope and compassion.

Big advertisements are not necessarily more effective than small ones. Long copy works, but not if it is pompous or rambling. If the first 50 words can sustain the interest of the reader, the interest seldom falls for the next 100 words. Credibility improves when the messages are simple. Even the most profound ideas are simple in the basics.

Communication through advertisements in the media traditionally, aimed for maximum reach. With the availability of the Internet as a vehicle for commerce, the concept of reach has given way to the concept of 'richness', which measures

- Bandwidth: which is the amount of information that can be moved in a given time,
- Depth of customisation: which is the extent to which the message can be personalised,
- Interactivity: enabling dialogue.

Richness increases considerably through the Internet. The message in the bulletin board does not perish as in the printed press or on the TV. It stays till the viewer finds it. Perishability is low. It facilitates responses to enquiries or required clarifications. It can be interactive and also updated. It overcomes the limitations of proximity. It can reach across the world.

Publicity is more credible than advertisements, because the message is seen as originating from the medium itself, as a news item or report. The tools of publicity are:

- press releases issued to the members of the press (including TV news channels),
- press conferences, where facts are stated and questions are answered,
- conducted visits, to familiarise the media with the facilities and arrangements set up,
- presentations, where details of offers are provided to the media and intermediaries,
- informal briefings, providing material, on a selective basis to some members enabling them to write on the product or the offers,
- sponsored articles.

The press will carry the news, if the activities and messages are seen to be interesting, timely, accurate and of interest to the readers. Awards for excellence, given by outside agencies like industry associations or trade journals, for hotels and airlines, constitute news and also effective publicity.

In the case of services, the most effective form of publicity is word of mouth. This happens when a person familiar with the product or service, endorses it to another, personally. Such an endorsement, when not made at the behest of the marketeer, is credible. An endorsement made in an advertisement, is made at the behest of the marketeer and is therefore, not very credible. Thus, satisfied customers, who speak to others, are the most powerful form of publicity. This is how, doctors, lawyers and consultants widen their range of clients. The credibility varies according to the person endorsing. Arranged in descending order of credibility, are the following sources

- immediate family,
- personal friends,
- professional colleagues,
- independent commentators,
- retailer's representatives,
- producer's representatives.

It is *good strategy to make customers talk of satisfactions.* They should be encouraged to talk. They can be given objects or materials that are giveaways or mementos (pens, keychains, paperweights, brochures, pictures, etc.,) and can be passed on. Their attention should be drawn to the elements of the service and the conveniences. They are not likely to notice everything that is well done. Contacts with them should be maintained, even after their contact as customers may have, for the time being, ended. This can be done by sending them

- bulletins, mentioning new facilities, innovations and improvisations that add value,
- greetings, gifts, souvenirs,
- invitations for special events.

Those who may help in word of mouth publicity should be carefully targeted. Opinion leaders are important to this strategy. Opinion leaders are persons whose opinions are respected by a large number of people and include columnists, parish priests, teachers, village elders, professionals, etc. When Shabana Azmi is seen hugging a child suffering from AIDS or a Thai minister drinks Coca Cola from the same glass as an AIDS patient, the communication is effective that AIDS patients do not have to be isolated by society.

Awards given by professional and other recognised bodies constitute excellent publicity. The Mena House Oberoi hotel, Cairo, was nominated in December 1998 for the prestigious Pinnacle award, which is given to hotels for their service, cuisine, business and meeting facilities, recreational facilities and social consciousness, as evaluated by guests. Airlines are also similarly rated and awarded internationally. Newspaper ratings on educational institutions, motor cars, restaurants, etc. are credible communications.

Public Relations refers to the deliberate, planned and sustained efforts made with a view to establish and maintain mutually beneficial relationships between an organisation and its publics. PR is based on the recognition that without the active support from the publics, the organisation will have difficulty to carry on and grow. PR seeks to shift the public from

- hostility towards understanding,
- prejudice to acceptance,
- apathy to interest,
- ignorance to knowledge.

Publics are many. All stakeholders are publics. In a sense, employees are also publics. PR efforts have to be directed at key personnel. It is difficult to evaluate the effectiveness of the PR because the target is the mind sets of people and therefore, both intangible and non-measurable.

PR tools include

- all the tools of publicity,
- journals/newsletters,
- sponsorship of sports and other activities,
- special drives,
- interest group meetings.

Personal Selling is part of the promotion mix. This is because advertisements and other non-personal communications are not adequate to persuade customers to make choices. The information required to make choice decisions is more than what is available at cognitive levels. There is more anxiety while purchasing services than while purchasing goods, because the nature of the purchase is not clearly known till after the purchase. The acceptance of the loan scheme offered by the different agencies does not depend only on the rate of interest or the EMI. There are questions, sometimes difficult to articulate, and fears as to 'what would happen if...' which need, not merely answers, but credible answers. The reports about finance companies employing heavy handed methods to recover from defaulters does not help the mind to be at ease. Only a personal interaction can help in this situation. Even after personal interaction with the salesman who calls on the customer, doubts may persist about the nature and quality of service and integrity of the producer.

A service being intangible presents a lot of uncertainties to the prospect. If the salesman is perceived as non-professional or incredible, the uncertainties increase. Salesmen should be seen as reliable and friendly and well meaning by the customer. They should emphasise conveniences, but not ignore to mention precautions necessary in usage. Effective salesmen understand and empathise with the customers. They are more acceptable to the customers. And they also make demands on the organisation on behalf of their customers.

Effective salesmen meet customers after the sales are made. They do so to

- obtain feedback about the experience and satisfactions after buying,
- strengthen the perceptions about the purchase made,
- provide reassurance, if there are any doubts about the wisdom of the decision to purchase,
- obtain further contacts (prospects) as referrals,
- talk about new products and achievements of the organisation, as a PR effort,
- intensify sales campaigns in specific segments/areas.

The salesman has to be sure that the reality as experienced by the customer corresponded to what he promised during the sale. This becomes necessary because the service is rendered by some one else and standardisation is difficult. In the case of some services like cinema, beauty and laundry, the feedback can be received as the service is being rendered. However, in the case of services like healthcare, repair, couriers, training, conventions, the feedback can be received only much later. When salesmen send clients for conferences or tours to other destinations, the salesman cannot get feedback except through personal contact soon after the experience. The salesman's credibility itself could be at stake. The direct feedback so obtained is also important for the top management of the organisation as they would not otherwise be in touch with what is going on at the customer contact points, unless of course, there are complaints.

Sales promotion attempts to overcome hesitations about buying, and to induce the prospect to buy. It is a slight push that is made through the offer of

- bonus,
- additional services not normally available,
- price discounts, coupons, rebates,
- instalment payment facilities,
- contests and prizes,
- gifts.

These are made available only for short specified periods. Bonus offers may take the form of three for the price of two, concessional or free tickets for spouses, trade-in at attractive prices and free check-ups. Contests may not become popular if there are too many at a time or the required level of skill is negligible. Gifts have strong appeals. Even a tea spoon is enough. Children tempted with a ballpoint pen can be persuaded to put pressure on their elders to conform to certain behaviours. Those who do outdoor publicity in rural areas find that a contest gets the entire village involved.

❑ Merchandising ❑

The display and appearances at the point of sale (POS), also called the POP, is effective communication. Physical facility is the first communication to a prospective customer in the service industry. If there are ten shops in a street, stocking refrigerators or Vimal suitings, the customer unfamiliar with the shops will enter those which appeal to him in external appearances. From that, he forms an opinion as to which one will

- have a bigger range to choose from,
- have the latest stocks,
- quote reasonable prices,
- have the right answers to one's questions,
- give proper advice,
- keep promises on warranties,
- be prompt to respond if there is a problem.

The physical facilities create expectations of quality of service. The ambience influences the expectation as well as the experience. The attractiveness of the facade, the decor, the colour of the wood or laminates on the counters, the fitting of the glasses, the lighting, the uniforms (of staff), the cleanliness, the scents, the colours, the music, displays and the sense of space, make the customer feel more (or less) favourably inclined. The enjoyment of a cinema is affected by the stuffiness of the atmosphere, the noise of the fans, the pests on the floors, the stench in the toilets and so on. This is similar to making judgements on the basis of the external appearances of the person. Though not altogether valid, such judgements are made as first impressions and do influence responses, till other more valid data is generated. If the physical facilities in government offices improve, the satisfactions of service may not improve greatly, but the irritations would be less.

Merchandising includes also the promotion of other products by displaying literature or samples of those products, which may be related to the business of the outlet or to the owner of the outlet. The display should add to the attractiveness of the outlet as well as be of interest to customers coming to that POP or POS.

❏ *Process* ❏

The delivery system is the process by which the service is rendered. Strictly, the processes are of four kinds. One is the management process, that looks at the control of documents and records, as well as the functions of planning, accounting, protection of patents and trade marks, compliance with regulations, safety, security, etc. The second is the resource process, dealing with people including training, information, infrastructure, work environment, etc. The third area is the product, including contracts review, product development, purchasing, packaging, logistics and handling of orders. The fourth area relates to assessments, testing, handling complaints, corrective actions, audit, etc. All of these impact the customer, some directly and some indirectly.

The story in the box below shows how the process badly handled, can totally spoil the PR effort of the management.

The Access Forms

On Thursday morning aboard Flight IC 185 from Mumbai to Delhi, I saw in the inflight magazine, *Swagat*, a letter dated May 1998, from the Chairman and Managing Director addressed 'Dear Passenger', announcing a new programme called ACCESS, requesting feedback on the new ACCESS forms available on the aircraft, and promising that the Deputy Managing Director would make every effort to act on the suggestions, 'to the best of our ability'.

I asked the airhostess for the ACCESS form. She did not understand what I was asking for. I showed her the letter in *Swagat*. She read through it, went back to check from the seniors, and returned after five minutes to say that the forms were not available on board.

On Saturday, while checking in for Flight IC 405 at Palam airport, I saw strings of leaflets with the words ACCESS, hanging across all the counters. These were hiding the boards indicating the flight numbers and destinations being handled by each counter. The form was now available. On the flight, I saw the press announcement from the airlines, saying that this programme was launched on Friday. The catchy slogan was, 'Tell us about your flight today and change the way you fly tomorrow'.

The form had 18 questions, to be responded to, by tickmarks on 'Yes'/'No' or 'Good'/'Satisfactory'/'Poor' or 'Courteous'/ 'Indifferent'/'Rude' options. Compared to the feedback forms in use till then and available on all flights, the difference seemed to be the addition of more questions. I did not get a feeling that the management was more serious this time. The words 'to the best of our ability' in the Chairman's letter looked like an apology in anticipation, like anticipatory bail.

I had the following experiences in the two flights and could not convey them in the prescribed columns, because the questions were not appropriate to cover these. Neither was the space for additional comments adequate.

1. While serving breakfast, the airhostess said that the non-vegetarian dishes were over at the 3rd row itself (I was in Row 19) and that I could have only vegetarian food. As I was eating, I heard the airhostess behind me, who had started from the rear end, offering non-vegetarian breakfast. When I asked how she had the supplies while the one in front did not have, she looked quite surprised and showed me that she had surplus. A little while later, when I had almost finished, the earlier airhostess came back saying that she had managed to get a non-vegetarian tray from the Executive class and that I could have a further helping.
2. While waiting in the long queue, for checking in on Saturday, one of the staff said that passengers with only hand baggage, could go to another counter that had just opened. I went and was checked in, but the process of checking in was interrupted by a friend of the counter clerk wanting to, and being allowed to, check in with his baggage for the hold.
3. There were no hand baggage tags at the counter. They had to be asked for and were brought from the Executive class counter, after the second request.
4. The tables in front of seats 20C and 18C (I could see them), could not be closed easily as the cloth was coming in between. The cloth had torn from pressures exercised earlier, making it still more difficult.

❑ *Market Research* ❑

For proper planning of marketing activities, it is necessary to identify the various characteristics of the market. The process of collecting information about the market and its characteristics is the field of market research. Data is systematically gathered, analysed and evaluated, providing the basis for marketing decisions.

Market research may be undertaken to answer specific questions or to generate general information, to be used in due time. Market research may be about

- market size, to show size, spread and growth of market in terms of customers, volume, revenue, shares of competition, economic conditions,

- consumers, to know profiles of consumers, their awareness levels, habits, preferences, expectations, perceptions, both quantitatively and qualitatively,
- products and price to know acceptability of products, their features, technology involved, price sensitivity, packaging,
- promotion and sales research to know consumer reactions to alternate concepts and media, sales force effectiveness, promotions,
- distribution, availability of facilities for stocking, outlets and shelf space availability, merchandising possibilities,
- evaluation and performance monitoring, looking at extent of customer satisfaction.

Data produced from market research is to be used for decisions on marketing strategies. The data will be used only if relevant to the decision maker for the kind of decisions he is faced with. Geographical and demographic characteristics may appear to be easy to know and relevant for segmentation. However, it is not so always. For example, the purchase of overseas medical insurance providing for medical expenses if taken ill during travel overseas, is made through agencies who make the travel arrangements. Therefore, the geographical locations of travellers (actual consumers) becomes irrelevant. If the courier services are availed of mainly by business houses and commercial establishments, characteristics like age, sex, are not relevant, but data relating to the decision makers may be relevant.

❏ *Research Methodology* ❏

The market is so large and scattered that it is impossible to do a complete study of it. *Market research depends on techniques of sampling.* It is not possible to be sure that the sample is truly representative of the whole, but a properly chosen methodology can improve the representative character of the sample.

A lot of data can be collected through desk research, looking at records containing reports like sales reports, trade information and press cuttings. Various free services provide information over the telephone without any charge. But they ask questions before providing the required information. They are collecting data about the 'market'. Customers at shops, visitors at fairs, temples, shopping malls, etc., can be interviewed. Controlled experiments, looking at responses to simulated situations and asking people to respond to carefully prepared questions, help to explore perceptions and attitudes to life, to work or to the world. Buying and usage patterns can be observed.

Some of the studies may provide quantitative data and some qualitative. While designing products for the Indian market, car manufacturers and fast-food owners like McDonalds, did qualitative research to find out their tastes and needs. Some studies are done on a continuous basis. Some can only be done periodically. When studies are done at regular intervals, trends and changes will become known. The Census is the biggest study of the market done periodically, every ten years.

The manner in which research is designed and conducted determines its reliability. Research findings often form the basis of corporate decisions, of long-term implications. Techniques of sampling, constructing questionnaires and other instruments have been developed after much study. These are used in opinion polls and prediction of election results. Different techniques would be necessary for different purposes. For example, advertisers wanting to know the audience profiles of different TV programmes or channels are still working on the ways to improve the reliability of what are called TRP ratings, that indicate popularity, and influence advertisement decisions.

In the case of quantitative data, the numbers tend to give the study an illusion of objectivity and reliability. The numbers coming out of a study, depend also on the questions asked, the way they are asked, the nature of the data used, the weightage given to the different data, etc., and therefore cannot be assumed to be saying everything there is to know. To carry out a proper interpretation and evaluation, it is necessary to know how the numbers have been generated as well as have insights into the context, nature of operations, etc. One must have insights to make valid evaluations, as will be seen from the box below.

A downtime of 25 per cent may mean that the machine breaks down too often or that repair personnel take too long to attend to breakdowns. A manager taking over a hotel, improved the occupancy ratio of rooms overnight by simply treating every fraction of a day as one. A study of the Indian Institute of Science in 1996 showed that poverty levels had dropped six to seven percentage points between 1987 and 1994, while the Planning Commission had, around the same time, working on the same methodology, calculated the same to be only two points. The specific reason for a product not being patronised is not quantifiable. The preference for a particular colour among four may be because a fifth colour had not been offered as a choice. In a factory from which goods are sent out everyday in about

300 lorries working round the clock, a study showed that the time spent by the lorries within the factory premises ranged from 90 minutes to seven hours in some cases. The scrutiny of loading procedures turned out to be futile as the longer durations were found to be because the drivers had parked their vehicles in the compound and gone to sleep.

In the case of services, the data to be collected and evaluated is more abstract and qualitative than in the case of tangible consumer goods. It is relatively easier to elicit responses by showing samples of goods and the way they perform, than to elicit responses to services which cannot be guaranteed to perform as per samples experienced. Second, it is not easy to articulate satisfactions and expectations. They are often not in the realm of conscious rationality. How does one explain the impressions created by a movie, except to say whether it was liked or not? This answer is not adequate to decide what movies would be generally acceptable to an audience. The 'liking' of a film or of the manners of an attendant, is not because of any identifiable details. It is the totality that a person reacts to. That too, he does in his context. The liking is not rational, in the sense that others will also find it so. It is also not irrational.

The experience is total. It is difficult to isolate and identify particular aspects that make that experience pleasant or otherwise. If a specific element is identified as critical to the experience, the identification may have been made for a number of unrelated reasons. One's irritation at the breakfast table may be because of the waiter's behaviour, or because the coffee was cold, or the oatmeal was poor in consistency, or due to the offensive behaviour of the couple at the corner, or the pressures of the morning's appointment, or because of the late hours of the previous night, or perhaps even because the music was loud. What is the acceptable delay when the patient calls for a nurse? How much more insurance will be bought if the premium is reduced by 5 per cent or 10 per cent? What will be the effect of a change in the gymnasium's timings? What will happen if drivers are withdrawn from senior officers entitled to cars as perks? These are difficult questions to answer. The data is not related to measurable, objective phenomena.

Capturing qualitative data needs very sophisticated and sensitive instruments. Some of the methods adopted are:

- use of focus groups, specially invited to discuss and express themselves,
- individual interviews where the person met is encouraged to talk freely,
- trade off or forced choice questions to determine relative values.

Responses to an academic study are not the same as in real life, because the latter is affective and the former is cognitive. People often do what they say they do not, do not do what they say they do, or do not admit what they do. Almost everyone would say that they would take an accident victim on the road to the nearest hospital and not easily admit that they fear consequent harassment from the police. Every manager agrees that it is important to develop a second line of succession, but very few spend the time or effort for that. They have a number of valid reasons to justify what they are actually doing. They are quick to rationalise behaviour.

Expertise in research design can be hired, but insights into the subject being researched cannot as this from experience. There is need for expertise and insights to interpret and evaluate. These insights should be used both to design the study and to interpret the data. *Inadequate experience cause misleading interpretations and incorrect decisions.*

In the business of services, unlike in the business of goods, 90 per cent of the personnel are in touch with the customers. When one is in touch with the customer, he is in direct contact with the explicit comments and the implicit body language of the customer. Both provide invaluable data about the customer's experiences, expectations and satisfactions. Contact personnel can be trained to be sensitive to such comments and body language and feed the data to specific points in the marketing department. *This data is more authentic and more complete than what a research study, based on samples and questionnaires, can find.*

❑ *Marketing Organisation* ❑

The structure of a marketing organisation depends on the marketing objectives and marketing tasks to be performed. The organisation is created by creating various positions, called roles, in an hierarchy. These roles clarify who will perform what tasks, who is responsible for what results, the authority vested in each role and the relationship between roles.

The tasks to be performed by a marketing organisation relate to

- market research,
- collecting information about the happenings in the market on a continuous basis,
- monitoring customer satisfaction levels,
- advertising, promotion and publicity,
- arrangements for distribution outlets, warehousing, etc.,
- selling.

Not all organisations are big enough to perform all these tasks with their own personnel. Some of these tasks can be entrusted to specialist organisations who undertake to do such tasks on behalf of the primary marketeers. There are agencies in Mumbai which undertake to promote and sell hotels in other parts of India. Advertisement agencies are geared to take care of promotional activities, including PR, on behalf of those who do not have their own specialist staff. Major selling agents make their sales force and network of outlets available for other products, in India as well as abroad. Exporters with established linkages abroad, make these facilities available to those who are new in exports.

Sometimes, the relationship between the marketing organisation and the principal producer is more intimate than one of agent and principal. When Spencers of Chennai or Akbarallys of Mumbai, or Shopper's Stop undertakes to market a product, be it a hotel or a household appliance or a financial instrument, they ensure that the service which the customer gets from the principal producer will be of a satisfactory level. The product of a newcomer to the industry will find easier acceptance from the market, when retailed through these outlets.

❑ *Marketing Strategies* ❑

Strategic planning for marketing would cover all marketing activities including

- setting marketing objectives based on scanning of the environment for opportunities and internal assessment of strengths,
- formulating marketing targets and programmes,
- formulating detailed activities to execute the programmes, covering promotion, advertising, etc.,
- monitoring events as they occur, both internal and external, and evaluating them with reference to plan,
- determining costs, revenues and margins,
- ensuring coordination between different departments.

Planning begins with information about the environment, obtained through market research and other sources. This information has to be analysed to determine legal, political, fiscal, social, economic trends and then related to one's own situation. Opportunities to be exploited have to be identified and then objectives and tasks determined.

○ *Opportunities* ○

Opportunities would be seen if one were to define one's business in the broadest possible terms. The example often quoted is that the railways sees more opportunity if it recognises that it is in the business of transportation. The post office is in the business of communication. If an insurance company sees itself as in the business of financial services, it will find ways of integrating other attractive financial instruments with insurance and strengthen its competitiveness. If the restaurateur sees his business as food, he might extend it to varieties of cuisine or increase the number of outlets he owns. If he sees his business as one of hospitality, he can extend it to lodging, to entertainment, to travel, to air catering and to casinos, which are all elements of hospitality. A CEO of a cement company said that he was in the business of mining and materials handling. The port that he developed for transporting the cement to the coastal towns, had to be regularly expanded to handle different requirements and he realised that the port could be a business by itself, offering its facilities to others. The opportunities were plenty.

Another way to find opportunities is to see what values may be added to existing products. One may have gold cards and platinum cards in the credit card business; embassy suites in hotels offering free access to health clubs etc.; different classes in airlines with inflight facilities, checking-in conveniences, priority luggage handling; special categories (for speed or safety or because of volumes) in couriers; clubs for exclusive showing of outstanding films; rooms in restaurants with exclusive monogrammed crockery and cutlery; library membership with first right for new additions. The possibilities are unlimited, as the elements constituting value are unlimited.

O *Threats* O

Realistically, one must also become aware of the threats revealed by the scanning of the environment. If opportunities have to be exploited, threats have to be warded off or contained. Threats may come from any of the factors in the environment. Threats from technology and competition are particularly difficult to be noticed on time. With advancements in digital photography, shops which developed exposed films and prepared negatives and prints may go out of business. Even traditional cameras and photostudios may disappear.

O *Strengths/Weaknesses* O

It is also necessary to carefully examine one's strengths. While opportunities and threats are in the external environment, strengths and weaknesses are within the organisation. One needs strengths to exploit opportunities and ward off threats. Weaknesses are handicaps which impede effective action. Both strengths and weaknesses may be political (ability to lobby with powers that be), financial, technological or organisationai, which includes people (employees, suppliers) and marketing (distribution network, customer loyalty, brand equity, etc.). Weaknesses can be overcome, but take time. Strategic planning can be effective only if the assessment of strengths and weaknesses are realistic. *One must know what one can do and what one cannot do, both as individuals and as an organisation.*

Studies indicate that the environment for business in 2003 is vastly different from what it might have been some 20 years ago. Perhaps, these changes may intensify in the years to come. The changes, to which strategists have to adjust, are of the following kinds:

- Cash flows which used to be steady and even, are now subject to violent fluctuations.
- One cannot be only in the metropolitan rich markets. The new markets which are developing, are sparsely populated and geographically spread out.
- The number of services are multiplying. Competition is intensifying.
- Instead of multiple shops for offering different services, the trend is towards one stop businesses, one window outlets.
- Instead of narrow and well defined industry structures, there is convergence.
- The margins game is giving way to the volumes game.
- Face-to-face transactions are giving way to remote linked channels.
- The demand is for 'instantaneous' service. Customers do not like to wait.

O *Strategy* O

Marketing strategy includes the determination of

- marketing objectives,
- target segments,
- marketing mix,
- product mix,
- anticipation of and preparation for uncontrollable variables.

Objectives are end results and provide direction for action as well as bases for control and coordination. They should therefore, be specific, measurable and timebound. To want to improve one's business is too vague and general. This would become increasingly specific as one states the extent of improvement to be aimed at (20 per cent), the market in which the increase is to be made (Punjab), the kind of improvement (in numbers, volume, revenue, penetration), the period during which the improvement must occur. The 3-M company in the US is said to have the objective that 20 per cent of its annual revenues has to come from new products. Such details help in resource allocation as well as in verification of progress.

When one has more than one product, separate objectives can be laid down for each one of these products. A university may have separate products, in the form of different courses, at different levels and also correspondence courses, being offerred within the country or abroad. The Indian Institute of Science, Bangalore has specialisations in 42 subjects as diverse as aerospace, biophysics, and structural chemistry. It offers in each of these disciplines: (*a*) doctoral programmes; (*b*) research; (*c*) developing products for industry including new drugs, diagnostics and vaccines; (*d*) consultation for power projects, civil construction and ecology. Effectively there are over 100 products.

Large organisations, for the purposes of developing strategy, may conceptualise that each product is a separate business and give it a distinct operational identity with specific objectives. A travel agency can have separate targets for revenue from: (*a*) inland travel bookings; (*b*) international air bookings; (*c*) commissions from hotels; (*d*) tours to Europe; (*e*) tours to Asia; (*f*) tours to Africa; (*g*) tours into India; and (*h*) incidental services like insurance sales or passport facilitation. Each hotel in a group can be a separate business. Within a hotel, each restaurant can be looked upon as a separate business to lay down its own objectives of costs and revenue. It will then have to work out its strategies and try to make profits. The R&D department, when looked upon as a separate business unit, seeks to make itself relevant to the environment, selling its expertise for a price.

A financial services company may be providing services to individuals, Indian corporates, foreign companies operating in India and non-resident Indians (NRIs). These are different segments and the related work would differ in terms of volume, complexity, margins etc. It is possible also to differentiate between different kinds of services, to look at each one of them as separate businesses and to examine what objectives and strategies would be appropriate for each one of these. An engineering company treated its R&D department as a separate business, earning its revenues from the various product divisions who were their customers, requiring analysis of and solutions to their problems. The divisions had the freedom to go elsewhere for their requirements.

Strategies have to be

- clear and identifiable,
- fully exploiting environmental opportunities,

- consistent with corporate skills and resources,
- within acceptable risk limits,
- stimulating organisational effort and commitment.

Each organisation has to choose its own strategy. Some may want to remain market leaders setting high standards of business offer and going further before others catch up. They would be positioning themselves as unequalled and beyond compare. Among couriers, Fedex and DHL are of this category. In India, among educational institutions, the IIMs and IITs are leaders in their respective fields.

Some others would want to confront the market leaders and occupy an equally competitive position. This is a strategy of confrontation and attack, saying one has better features than the other, highlighting one's merits and the other's demerits, sometimes directly and sometimes indirectly. This happens in the business of motor cars, household electronics, soft drinks, computers and between the leading newspapers in a city. Hospitals try to do this by poaching on doctors and preventing their consultants from practising elsewhere.

Some may prefer to avoid the more popular segments of the market and make offers of a kind not usually available in the market, a speciality offer. These may be small niches and not of general interest, perhaps without very heavy volumes, but with good margins. This is called the niche marketing strategy. An Indian courier, which was among the earliest in the Indian market, had cornered the business of handling share certificates.

Some may be quite happy with the existing position in the market and would be trying to protect its territory, preventing others from making inroads. Public sector institutions used to do this when faced with competition for the first time. This is a defensive strategy, emphasising on the past and strengthening customer loyalties.

Strategy development is the responsibility of the top management, because it lays down the manner in which the organisation's resources are to be applied. In a service industry, corporate strategy dealing with the achievement of internal and external goals, cannot be separated from marketing strategy, which deals with effectiveness in the market place. This is so because the process of manufacturing, distribution, delivery, etc., are inseparable in services.

❏ *Programmes and Activities* ❏

Marketing programmes and activities are sequences of actions which have to be undertaken to realise the strategies and to achieve the objectives. These will include:

- *Sales* including setting up the sales force, training them on the offers and sales techniques, laying down territorial or other targets and monitoring their work.
- *Distribution* meaning deciding on ways by which customers can access the offers as well as laying down the systems that deliver the promises.
- *Advertising* and promotion, executing campaigns, keeping in touch and so on.
- *Research* leading to segmentation, targeting and product development.

Three important factors to be taken care of in marketing planning are:

1. *Consistency* There has to be a logical and useful fit between all the elements of the mix, for example, not to sell high quality products through low quality outlets.
2. *Integration* Focussing on active harmonious linkage among elements of the mix, for example, heavy advertisement harmonises with high price through brand differentiation.
3. *Leverage* Each element should be used to best advantage in support of the total mix, for example, price promotion is to be used if product is price sensitive, not packaging or heavy advertisements.

❏ *Product Lifecycle* ❏

Every product has a lifecycle, just like every living being has a lifecycle. The lifecycle consists of:

- birth or introduction,
- growth or development,
- maturity,
- decline and death.

These stages represent the degree of attractiveness of the product in the market.

At the first stage, the product is new, unknown, untested. Not many people buy. Gradually, through intense promotional efforts as well as through customers who may have tried it, the product may gain popularity. Sales volume will increase steadily. This is the stage of growth. The third stage is when the product has become well known and is accepted in the market, the demand is steady and high and earnings are quite satisfactory. Promotional efforts are minimal, mainly in the nature of reminders. After some time, the demand may begin to fall, either because better substitutes are available or because consumer tastes and styles have changed.

The compounder in a chemist shop, who used to mix medicines (in the 1950s) as prescribed by the doctor, has become redundant because of ready made formulations. The computer is still at the growth stage with newer and newer applications. Microwave ovens and washing machines are still at the first stage in India. They are not very widely used even now, although knowledge about their utility is spreading. Irani restaurants, available at every corner in Mumbai's commercial district in the 1950s and 1960s are on the decline. Fast food restaurants are in the growth stage. Pubs were in the birth stage in Mumbai in the early 1990s, but have now reached their maturity stage. Internet is in the growth stage. The capital market and related businesses are just about getting into the maturity stage.

In the birth/introduction stage, both investment and promotion costs are high without adequate returns. The business may even be making losses. The returns improve during growth and maturity stages. The marketeer will have to spend heavily in demonstrations, samplings, displays, concessions, etc., in the first two stages, hoping to recover fully during maturity.

When a product is in the decline stage, there are two options. One is to cut losses and kill the product. If it has not already paid for itself, the product was just bad. The second option is to revitalise the product growth by

- adding new features that may enhance its attractiveness and value,
- emphasising new uses for it,
- finding new markets/users.

Burnol was being sold for a long time as a specific for burns. Later, it was sold as a general antiseptic. The market picked up. Milkmaid, which used to be sold as a milk substitute is now seen as a useful dessert ingredient. When video cassettes and satellite TV became popular in the late 1980s, the cinema theatre was moving into the declining stage. Several theatres closed down and commercial complexes came up where theatres once stood. The decline of the cinema theatre was arrested due to more sophisticated sound tracks and grander spectacular visuals, which the TV screen was not able to capture fully. In some places, the cinema is becoming part of a bigger entertainment venue offering total value for a family for an evening or day. Tourist destinations like the Ajanta/ Ellora caves, may 'grow' further through added attractions like theme parks or replications of historical and archeological sites, providing both educational and experiential value.

These four stages are not of uniform length. Some products, even of reputed firms have died soon after birth, not growing at all. Some products never seem to decline, remaining for ever, as it were, in the consumer's favour. Colgate toothpaste is one such example. The Taj group of hotels is another. The poor performance of a product in the market place may be due to

- product features not meeting the needs of the consumers,
- customers not accepting the product despite some commendable features,
- ineffective marketing causing poor awareness and/or poor availability.

Spencers had a group of hotels in Bangalore, Chennai and Ooty. Very popular at one time (maturity stage), they declined in the mid-1970s. Losses were being incurred. The Taj group took these hotels on long lease, changed the furnishings and decor, redefined the target segment and marketed it aggressively. These hotels are now back on the maturity stage. At Ooty for example, the target segment was shifted from rich businessmen in the south, escaping from the hot weather of the plains, for rest and relaxation in the cool climate of the hills, to the business executives from the rest of India, to whom a holiday meant a different surrounding but not necessarily totally cut off from official responsibilities. They were relatively young, with children, from cities, needing facilities for games, and enjoying a variety of cuisines. Therefore, the kitchen changed, rooms were given telephone connections, games and outings were organised. Bookings were made possible from all Taj offices. Clients of the Taj elsewhere became clients for the Savoy in Ooty.

The concept of the product lifecycle is useful in developing strategy. If the product has a significant share in a market that is growing, it would be wise to invest further in that product. If the product is not growing, but the market is growing, steps are to be taken to push or to add to its features and take advantage of the growth in the market. The implications of the different stages in the lifecycle are listed in the table on page 133.

❑ *Positioning* ❑

Another concept in marketing is positioning. It arises from the thesis that a product cannot be everything to everybody. Every person distinguishes between one product and another on the basis of some distinct characteristics and thus holds an image of the product in his mind. A Taj hotel denotes luxury beyond

	Introduction	Growth	Maturity	Decline
Product	Design and customer feedback key to success	Technical and performance differentiation	Superior quality established—less rapid changes	Little differentiation from competition
Marketing	High marketing costs Advertisement/ Sales ratio high	Advertisement/Sales ratio decreasing	Broadening segment Efforts to extend lifecycle	Low advertisement and other costs
Manufacture	Excess capacity. High production costs. Short runs	Under capacity. Shift to mass production	Some over capacity. Stable manufacturing process. Long production runs	Substantial over capacity
Distribution	Specialised channel	Mass channels	High physical distribution due to brand lines	Limited channels
Competition	Little	Many new entrants	Price competition	Fierce
Margins	High	High	Falling but stable	Low
Profits	Low	High	Lower	Low
Buyer behaviour	Inertia. Need convincing	Widening group	Mass market Repeat buying. Choosing among brands	Sophisticated buyers

the reach of ordinary people. To be a guest at the Taj, is indicative of high status. The Udipi restaurant is a cheap place. One does not go there to celebrate or to entertain a guest. A Subhash Ghai film has to be a spectacular like a Cecil B De'Mille film. Lifebuoy soap kills germs. Lux is a beauty soap. Godrej locks are safe. Tata products are quality products. BBC news is authentic. Doordarshan is not. *Femina* is a woman's magazine. A ration shop is a poor man's shop. These are all images in one's mind, which determine one's behaviour relative to that product. One would not like to be seen in a ration shop queue, for fear of being understood as belonging to the poorer class. A man may not like to be caught reading *Femina*.

These images are formed in the minds of people partly by their own direct experience, but it is not always that experience which is responsible for the images. People who have never travelled in an airline have distinct images about different airlines. The images are created by the marketing messages of the producer.

The images so created in the minds of the consumer through the marketing efforts is the 'position' of the product. The position influences the customer's inclinations to purchase. Certain restaurants have an image of being seedy. Certain theatres are known to show only pornographic movies. Certain other theatres are known to show only new movies or plays of high quality. The choice of a theatre without knowing which film or play is on, is made on the basis of such images.

A product may be positioned against a competing product or exclusively by itself. It can be positioned for men, or for youngsters or for senior citizens. Positioning has to be related to the target segment. Cadbury's chocolate which was for a long time positioned for children (two glasses of milk), attempted to expand the market by repositioning it as a 'fun' product.

Positioning is the objective and the outcome of the communication efforts in the marketing mix. Promotion is the main communication process, but price also communicates value and position. The outlet where the product is available also communicates. A premium product will not be sold in a *bidi* shop.

Competitive pressures can blur, even distort, the images in the mind of the consumer. For example, life insurance is essentially to cover the risks contingent on human life like, early death or retirement. In the minds of many, it is 'positioned' as an investment, the unique advantage being the savings on income and other taxes. This detracts from the real value of life insurance. It also redefines customers as those with tax liabilities and/or with surpluses to invest, and excludes a vast majority who do not have either tax liabilities or investible funds.

In the minds of the general public, a government office like the income tax office, rationing office or the police station is a place where you get harassed. People tend to avoid them and consequently neither comply with nor cooperate with the regulations these offices seek to administer. With some sustained marketing efforts, these adverse images can be modified. When the modification happens, customers would be willing to go to these offices. There could be then better compliance with the expectations under the law. There was some evidence of this happening towards the end of 1997 with the Voluntary Disclosure of Tax Liability scheme. Elaborate arrangements made in government hospitals and clinics for preventive healthcare, are not effectively utilised for many reasons, one of them being the positioning of the government and its products.

❑ *Branding* ❑

When the images about the features, characteristics, benefits etc., of a product are very strong in the mind of the consumer, a brand is created. The brand

- is associated with recognisable symbols like name, logos, designs, colours, jingles,
- creates awareness, familiarity, recognition,
- influences favourable action,
- gives confidence of quality, value and satisfaction,
- leads to customer loyalty and repeat buying.

Brands are created as a result of sustained promotion and adherence to standards that are claimed for the brand. *A brand exists only when it is associated with features and attributes that are distinctly different from other products in the same category.* Services can also be branded. Hertz (car hiring), Kidskemp and Shopper's Stop among retail stores, MTR (tiffin room in Bangalore) and China Garden among restaurants, Blue Dart and DHL among couriers, Cunard lines in shipping, Palace on Wheels in rail transportation, Appollo in hospitals, BBC and CNN in TV news, and Mastercard, are examples of brands in services. They hold distinct images in the minds of the public with regard to what they offer, what to expect from them, the quality of the service, whether they are reliable, whether they are expensive, and so on. All of them are identifiable by their distinct logos, the lettering used for the names, the colours in their logos, packaging and uniforms. One of the brands in restaurants is Hollywood Planet created by film stars like Sylvester Stallone, Arnold Schwarzenegger, Bruce Willis and Demi Moore. A similar Bollywood Planet was also planned in Mumbai by

Jackie Shroff and others. To dine there would place one in the same social orbit as the stars.

When a brand is created, there is less need to communicate product quality, features etc. The customer is already favourably inclined towards that brand and all that it represents. There is better customer loyalty, which means more steady business, less marketing costs, strong cash flows. A brand is also a defence against competitive inroads. There is no need for price wars, because the value addition in the brand cannot be matched by a similar product of a competitor. *While the manufacturer makes a product, the brand is what the customer buys.* That is how he identifies value. There are many well known Indian brands like Akbarally's, Amul, Aspro, Bombay Dyeing, BPL, Dalda, Godrej, Good Knight, Hero, Kwality, Lifebuoy, L&T, Maruti, MRF, Nirma, Nirulas, Pan Parag, Reliance, Sita Travels, Sunlight, Tatas, Times of India, TVS, Vimal and Wipro. Some of them are very old brands, like Amrutanjan balm (104 years) and Hamam soap (67 years).

A brand is based upon differentiated features. It has a legal title, can be patented and is subject to copyright and trademark protections. The brand is built over a period of sustained marketing efforts and, when established, has a value of its own. Brands are purchased and sold as if they are assets. Kraft was sold to Philip Morris for $13 billion, Kitkat and Polo to Nestle for $4.5 billion, Nabisco (biscuits) to BSN for $ 2.5 billion, Parle Products to Coca Cola for Rs 18 million, Transelectra to Godrej for Rs 8 million, Ciba Geigy (toothpaste and brushes) to Colgate for Rs 13 million. The Rolls-Royce car brand name (including the car marque) was bought by BMW of Germany at $ 66 million, although the motor car company had been bought earlier by Volkswagen.

Effective brand building requires sustained communication of differentiation at different levels. The Body Shop for example, dealing in cosmetics and skincare products, has the principle of preservation of the environment, and therefore opposes testing on animals, contributes to rain forest preservation, sets an example for recycling, arranges rallies to save the whales, assists development of alternative energy resources, lets the employees wear T shirts with social messages and uses only recycled paper. The Haagen Daas icecreams, entered the market at prices that were 30 per cent to 40 per cent higher despite economic recession, with the theme of thicker, creamier, ultimate experience in icecreams. The company opened posh icecream parlours in prominent affluent locations with heavy foot traffic, obtained placement in quality hotels and restaurants, provided branded freezers in retail stores, sponsored cultural events and got included in scripts of theatre. Hugo Boss clothiers sponsored Porsche in Formula-One car racing, symbolising exclusive image and international presence. The Benetton identity was youth, cultural diversity, racial harmony and world peace. In its campaign against AIDS, it showed an AIDS patient kissing a priest and baby's bottoms stamped HIV +ve. These alienated the target market. Though awareness improved, likeability reduced and retailers boycotted. When Nestle bought Burtoni, the 70-year old pasta company, it provided recipes for Italian cooking.

The communication about brands is not only through advertising, but also through the distribution outlets and the price. *This is described as the brandscape in the minds of the consumer,* which, similar to the landscape in which the land rests, constitutes the set of ideas or notions in the minds of the consumer, in which the brand rests. It is this brandscape that the brand manager has to take care of. The place where they meet the product, the environment of that place, the other elements at that place (people, crowd, space, noise, the 'clutter'), all add up to build the brandscape. It is an amalgam of images and impressions, all of which have to convey positive and consistent meanings.

Big brands become generic to their category, like Godrej, for steel cupboards and locks, Dalda for vegetable hydrogenated cooking oils, Kirloskar for pumps (in Africa). Their messages do not change, even if they need to be repositioned for growth. Boots' Burnol retained its original features, but added on. So also was Nestle's Milkmaid. Lifebuoy will continue to be the health protection soap.

No brand, however big, can afford to be complacent. It has to continuously monitor its strength and innovate. In 1997, the image of Parachute, the coconut oil from Marico, was sought to be changed, when it sensed that the place of oils in general was different in the lifestyles of the younger generation. The wholesome goodness of the coconut became the theme. Hamam soap has been repositioned, after 67 years, as a herbal skin care soap, with *tulsi, pudina, neem,* lime, etc., as its ingredients, targeting the housewife and children.

Service providers could aim at building up brands for their products. One strategy is to get associated with other brands in the same line of service, particularly if one does not have the financial strength or the size of operations to build a brand separately. The association may include technical collaboration or only royalty payments. Chapter 8 on Strategies discusses this subject further.

❑ *Relationship Marketing* ❑

One of the objectives of current marketing practices is building up relationships. This is based on the belief that it costs several times more to find a new customer than to retain an existing customer. A customer who leaves, is taking away the profit-making potential of the company. Therefore, it is argued, that it is worthwhile to try to retain existing customers, to build strong long-term relationships with them, so that they remain loyal. If there is a normal attrition of say, 25 per cent in customers, reducing that by 5 per cent can mean substantial savings by way of increased purchases, reduced operating costs, and more references. A study by the All India Management Association showed that among service firms, reducing customer defections by just 5 per cent boosted profits by 25 per cent to 35 per cent.

A popular story is that an aged couple, in the midst of a holiday tour, were handed over their boarding cards along with a greeting of 'Happy Anniversary'. The checking-in clerk had noticed from the frequent flyer data that that day was their wedding anniversary. This was a WOW experience and the couple never flew thereafter by any other airline. Relationship marketing, to be effective, requires such little gestures that mean a lot, but also require careful infrastructural support. The frequent flyer data in the files has to trigger the airline staff's attention to the significant fact. Otherwise, it is possible that such relevant facts may be overlooked. Several programmes can be organised to convey messages of 'We care for you'. Events like get-togethers, field visits, music concerts, movie or theatre shows, can be arranged depending on the tastes of the customers, which can be part of the data base. When relationship marketing becomes popular, events management services have a great opportunity.

Relationships of a long standing nature, are built on trust and confidence that one's interests are safe in the hands of the other. Attempts to exploit the other's compulsions mitigate against this principle. When a supplier refuses to take advantage of the customer's difficulties, customer's trust is created. Banks are traditionally referred to as saviours who offer umbrellas until such time as it really begins to rain. When a company is in some trouble, the badly needed understanding and accommodation from the bank would not be available. *Fair weather friends do not build lasting relationships.*

In Relationship marketing, also called Customer Relationship Management (CRM), every customer is seen as a segment of one. Not as one out of many of a kind to be dealt with as an average. This is the traditional Indian way of the neighbourhood grocer, the dhobi, the village doctor. The relationship is built on messages that convey to each of the customers, recognition, willingness to help, concern for the other and implicit trust. Modern technology makes it possible for even big organisations to operate on the basis of the segment of one. Mailers can be addressed to individuals as if they have been prepared specifically for each of them separately, with particulars relating to his preferred items and outlets. It is possible to retain the preferences and peculiarities of each customer and retrieve the information at any time, by any one who is in contact with the customer, thus providing personalised service.

The following box contains two examples.

In the music cassette industry, Gramco offers to give customers cassettes containing those songs which they like to hear. The additional price is willingly paid and the music company gets an authentic feedback on what the market preferences are like.

Nestle (France) provided rest stops on highways, where hostesses provided free food samples and disposable diapers for babies. More than 10,000 visits were recorded per year. Toll free telephones were provided for advice on nutritional matters. Both these together, provided data on 200,000 mothers. Birthday presents were sent to children. The market share shot up from 19 per cent to 43 per cent in seven years.

Relationship marketing requires that the provider keeps in touch with the customer even after the sale is over. There is a phenomenon called cognitive dissonance, which occurs because of doubts that arise after the purchase, about the correctness of the purchase decision. If the experience after purchase is not exactly as anticipated, the dissonance will be enhanced. In the case of services, where the purchase of service is accompanied by some anxiety, it is very necessary to be in touch, after the sale is over, to convey reassurance that the purchase was not a mistake, to avoid cognitive dissonance. Some studies show that this aspect is not taken care of. Sellers are more in touch with big buyers, not the smaller ones. Those engaged in after sales service, do not show enough concern for customer's needs as they do before purchase. For example, repairers visiting the premises of customers do not carry spares. In the case of computers, annual maintenance contracts are being given to third parties, not the ones from whom the purchase was made, in more than 50 per cent of the cases. The likelihood of cheaper maintenance costs may not be the only reason for the shift. The real reasons may lead also to word of mouth publicity that may be adverse to the service providers. The most successful insurance agents invariably have strong relationships with their clients. They find some reason to keep in touch, and as a result generate a treasure of referrals.

Relationships are based on closeness and trust. Local retailers have this advantage as their customer loyalties are strong. It is possible for them to source well-known products directly from the manufacturers and sell them under their own brands, thus displacing national brands with their own local brands. This is happening in the US and even in India. Schemes like frequent flyer programmes of airlines, or privilege cards for users of Appollo tyres enabling them to acquire music systems or concessional travel arrangements are sales promotional arrangements, not relationship marketing, because in these cases the service provider does not have knowledge of the individual customer's preferences. The International Hotels had a database of about 15 million customers in travel and non-travel areas, obtained from Allianz and generated 6,77,000 room nights worldwide in global mileage awards. Carlson had, in its headquarters, data from 5,300 travel locations in 140 countries about travel, leisure and hospitality customers.

The Strand Book Stall is a case of relationship marketing. The owner knew his clients and they included prominent names from all walks of life, like M.C. Chagla (Chief Justice of Bombay), Keshub Mahindra (industrialist), Aditya Birla (industrialist), Raja Ramanna (head of the Atomic Energy Commission), Salman Rushdie (author). He procured books for his clients. He read every book and told the clients about the new ones. He offered discounts. Results? He had sold 17,000 copies of the *Ascent of Man*, more than any other book shop in the world. He bought out from McGraw-Hill 1,000 copies of the *Encyclopedia on Science and Technology* (20 volumes each), sold them all at Rs 12,500 a set, with a margin of Rs 500 per set and made Rs 500,000 in four days. The slated price for the set was Rs 72,000 per set.

Relationships have to be built, not only with ultimate users, but with everyone in the value chain. Retailers and wholesalers used to be looked upon as 'costs' that eroded profits. They are now seen as partners, whose loyalties and commitments are important. However, the expectations from retailers and wholesalers may run contrary to those of the ultimate consumer. Will they invest to satisfy the end user? Primary producers may have to invest in retailer facilities for the sake of consumer satisfaction. This is possible only if the relationships are sound on a long-term basis.

The concept can also be extended to suppliers. Loyal committed suppliers can save a company extensively through lower inspection, inventory and documentation costs. This objective is significantly more important in the current and future days because the Internet has expanded the market place beyond all known boundaries of space and limitations of time, and the consumer is becoming aware of, as well as close to, alternative markets. It is the service elements in the transaction—the intangibles—that build the relationship.

Relationships also have to be built with suppliers and vendors, investing for them and helping them with technology if necessary, which alone will ensure consistent quality in supplies. Otherwise the practice of looking for the cheapest tender every six months or one year, can turn out to be expensive in inspection costs and non-adherence to specified schedules. Car manufacturers, wanting to make their facilities in India the hub for their global businesses, are building relationships with steel manufacturers to determine and develop the right kind of steel, required for the prescribed levels of safety.

O *Caution* O

The objective of relationship marketing is to retain the existing customers. The methods adopted should in no way create impressions that some customers are lesser in importance or value than some others. The practice of 'frequent flyers' in the airline business and similar loyalty programmes elsewhere, may give some customers a benefit and advantage. It should be obvious that the benefit is earned and conferred. The meaning is that every customer understands that he can also earn it. Otherwise, the programme will have the opposite effect.

6 ATTAINING HIGH QUALITY

❑ Why Quality ❑

As mentioned in Chapter 1, entry barriers are minimal in the service business. The way to beat competition is to acquire product differentiation, which is reflected in quality. The better the quality, the more delighted is the customer. Business after business is learning that 'delighting the customer' means

- fewer customers lost,
- less time and money spent putting things right for dissatisfied customers,
- less time and money spent on advertising and marketing to find new customers,
- less use of costly discounts and offers to attract new customers,
- more time to devote to anticipating and meeting the needs of the best customers,
- free (word of mouth) publicity from the satisfied customers.

The 'Keys' to service quality are three:

1. Customer. It is necessary to become aware of his expectations and experience, using insight, feedback, complaints and formal market research.
2. People management. Appropriate leadership that makes people skilled and empowered, sensitive to problems and customer oriented, with ability to build work teams.
3. Processes. To be reviewed constantly for improving effectiveness, in terms of results achieved as well as speed, accuracy and costs.

Product features (service elements) are similar among competitors. All couriers collect letters and deliver them within 24 hours. Funeral parlours provide a range of coffins and hearses and also arrange for the service and rituals.

Tour operators all go to the same places and provide almost the same facilities, often even the same guides. All insurance companies provide almost the same benefits. All banks give loans with very little difference in interest rates or other terms. These are the tangibles of product features, which are not distinguished as different in the same business. Every innovation can be duplicated. Technologies are not exclusive. The crucial distinguishing characteristics that distinguish one business from another are the quality of the service and the manner in which it is delivered. One bank becomes different from another because of the speed and lack of hassles in processing. What provides competitive distinctiveness is the behaviour, the sincerity of the people, the considerations shown and the responsiveness, etc., factors that were referred to in Chapter 4 as factors relevant to customer satisfaction.

Quality is the value added offering that provides a more satisfying experience, which makes the customer come back for more of the same pleasurable experience. Quality is essential to build long-term loyalty. It helps to gain a larger market share in the face of competition. It alone helps in the word-of-mouth publicity. It takes effort to achieve and is never an accident. It needs strategy.

The basic assumptions of a service provider have to be

- Quality service brings in customers and generates profits.
- Quality is to be maintained, whatever it takes.
- Quality means 'willing to walk that extra mile' for the customer's sake.
- Quality can always be improved upon.
- Quality is provided by people.
- Quality is provided not only in the front line, but also in the back office.

Poor quality becomes the norm when the following assumptions prevail:

- One can never be perfect.
- To err is human.
- Employees are not interested.
- Quality is expensive.
- We cannot afford.
- Customers want price cuts, not quality.
- May work elsewhere, but not in our country/company/industry.
- Nothing much can be done with politicians and trade unions around.
- Our complaints department is good enough to take care of customer satisfaction.

❑ *What is Quality* ❑

Quality is what the customer says it is. It is not what the provider says it is. Good service is not when you smile at the customer, but when the customer smiles at you. If a class does not find the teacher interesting, the teacher is 'bad'. If the audience does not patronise the film, it is 'bad'. It does not matter what the inputs from the provider are. The teacher may have indeed dealt with the latest developments on the subject, not easily available to the students. The film may have been a big-budget one with extravagant sets, top star cast, relevant story theme, etc. These are technical details relating to inputs. Inputs do not determine quality. The quality of the spinach dish does not depend on whether it has been cooked according to the specifications laid down by the master chefs. Even if it passes the test of the most accomplished epicure, to the child who spits it out, the quality is poor. A manufacturer who thought that he had the right measures of carpet foam backing, molecular weight distribution, particle size conformity, per cent of unirelated monomer and adhesive strength, was surprised that the user rejected the supplies because they did not pass his roller test, which is, spinning an office chair on it 3000 times.

Jim Kelley, CEO of UPS, in a speech, said 'We have 12 mainframes capable of computing 5 billion bits of information every second. We have 90000 PCs, 80000 hand held computers to record driver deliveries, the nation's largest private network and the world's largest BD2 database, designed for package tracking and other customer shipping information. To give you an idea of how valuable information has become to our company, that data base actually has more storage capacity than the repositories of the US Census Bureau'. This impressive infrastructure is of no consequence to a person, if the delivery of his package is delayed.

Quality is measured by the extent of satisfaction of the customer. There is no other measure. The more satisfied the customer is, the better the quality. Quality in service is not tangible. It is not measurable. It is an experience. It is the perception of an experience. It is how the customer reacts or responds to what the service provider has done to him. When the nurse responds to the patient's call within a minute, this is 'fast' or 'slow' depending on how urgently the patient needed her. The measure of one minute may be too long sometimes leading to the patient repeating the call and even shouting for the nurse. Quality of service is the difference between expectation and the perceived experience. This has been explained in Chapter 4 under the section Satisfaction versus Experience. Every failure to perform, brings down quality.

There is unlikely to be a perception of quality, unless there is quality in fact. If there is no courtesy in fact, there cannot be a perception of courtesy. Quality in fact and in perception interact multiplicatively, not in addition. If one is zero, the resultant is zero. Providers have to focus on the 'facts' that are likely to produce favourable perceptions. These are the elements of service. Providers have also to be aware that the 'facts' are not adequate guarantees of satisfactions. The elements of service are like the design of a product being manufactured. The concern for quality begins from there. Technical considerations like weight, strength and safety features matter. Equally important are non-technical factors like styling, appearance, beauty, colours and ease of operations and maintenance. In the case of services, the non-technical, psychological factors have to continue throughout the production or delivery system, till the consumer receives it.

Internal efficiencies, in terms of better resource utilisation and/or productivity, may improve the quality of the process or of the system, but not necessarily the quality of the service. A service rendered in a very short time may be appreciated in an Udipi hotel, but not so in a five-star restaurant, where the requirement is to spend some time together. A doctor who is able to come to a quick diagnosis, without elaborate examination, without asking many questions and without allowing the patient to narrate the full history, may be perceived as doing a rush job—'so that he can dispose of many patients and make a lot of money'.

The Mumbai Port Trust was planning to invest Rs 9.9 billion for replacement of submarine pipes and modernisation of jetties. This investment had been cleared by and was supported to the extent of nearly $100 million, by the Asian Development Bank. This expenditure will not constitute improvement in the quality of the port services, if vessels continue to wait for days for a berth and more than a day for a turnaround. Hospitals provided with the latest equipment do not necessarily provide satisfactory healthcare. That depends on how the equipments are used and on the way in which the patients are dealt with.

❑ *Levels of Quality* ❑

Robert Galvin, Chairman of the Executive Committee of Motorola Inc., says that there are four levels of acceptable service—'Good', 'Very Good', 'Near Perfect' and 'WOW'. John Humble, management consultant from the UK, uses the word 'Delight' for WOW. Both Delight and WOW occur when the experience is far beyond all expectations.

Experiences that cause dissatisfaction are usually talked about. Experiences that cause satisfactions are usually not talked about. They are taken for granted.

However, when there is a WOW experience, it is not forgotten. It is talked about. One expects courtesy and attention in a hotel. If these are missing, there is dissatisfaction. However, there is no significant satisfaction, when courtesy is noticed. If the manager of the hotel calls you up as soon as you enter the room and welcomes you—that could be beyond expectation. That may be remembered, but still not a WOW. However, if that evening, the band plays a birthday song, because that is your birthday, that would be a WOW.

To be told that there is no reservation for you at the check-in counter of the airlines is bad. To be welcomed, as if they were waiting for you instead of a 'NEXT', is good. To be received as soon as you enter the main gate and to be conducted through the formalities, would be a WOW. To be left listening to music on the telephone, without knowing whether the person you are calling for is available or not, is bad. To be told that the particular person is not available and that you could leave a message, is better. To be handed over a new book in the library, because the librarian knows your taste, is WOW.

WOW comes essentially out of recognition, which is special, not routine. Not all services provide opportunities for WOW levels of service. Further, an experience is WOW only the first time. It is expected the second time and if not received then, causes dissatisfaction. A person ordering food for home delivery had just mentioned his name, when the person at the other end mentioned the address for delivery and asked for confirmation. That was a WOW experience. However, the next time he orders, if he is asked for his address, he would be unhappy.

❑ *Costs of Quality* ❑

Concerns with productivity seek reduction in costs. In manufacturing, any reduction in costs of processes, is invisible to the ultimate consumer. However, in the service business, reduction in staff will immediately reflect on the services being rendered, because the service is 'manufactured' in the presence of the consumer. When the outlet of an internationally renowned fast-food company, eliminated the small plastic cup (costing perhaps a few paise) in which sauce was served with the burger, the customers did not like the alternative of having to tear the sachet of sauce and pouring it on the plate because the sauce often spurted out.

The people element in the delivery of service is significant. The reductions, if any, in personnel are visible to the consumer and may create perceptions of curtailment in service quality. *Better productivity is not necessarily better quality.*

Reduction in inputs, leading to readjustment of work schedules and systems may cause stresses on employees for many reasons, like unfamiliarity with new systems, additional work loads, adjustment to new colleagues and so on. These stresses could impact directly on customer service. This in turn, will lead to complaints and grievances, adding to stresses. It is a vicious spiral.

Cost reductions are possible through cuts in inputs as well as through increases in turnover. In the case of manufacturing, when volume sales increase, there is reduction in indirect costs per unit of production. In services, the major costs are indirect, not direct, in the sense that the infrastructure put in place (capacity to perform) does not change with actual turnover. The factor of Perishability arises out of this fact. If the capacity is less and higher volumes are undertaken, the performance will turn out to be less than the promise. Like the courier who got large volumes of business, but did not have the capacity in the delivery system. The infrastructure is the delivery system. Cost reduction therefore, in services, may be similar to cutting raw material costs and expecting production to remain high in quantity and in quality.

Government establishments suffer enormously in quality, because the standard formulae for economy seems to be to

- regulate the induction of new personnel, regardless of growth in business or number of exits,
- centralise purchases or withdraw powers, ostensibly to regulate waste.

It is assumed that when powers are withdrawn to higher levels, sanctions will be slow in coming and lower levels will learn to manage with less. That is the prescribed route to economy. In fact however, this leads to increased costs. Behaviourally, lower levels try to beat the system through exaggerated demands and surplus inventory. There are other costs in terms of lost opportunity and service quality. A restaurant cannot function on the sincerity and energy of the captain alone, if he does not have support to lay the table, serve the dishes, remove used plates and so on. Even if he takes the strain for sometime, he will quit if the prospects for early relief are not visible. Even before he quits, the customers would have quit. The problems of the restaurant will accentuate. The morale of the staff will fall. Poor morale and good service do not go together. It is a similar case with hospitals that remain without essential instruments, medicines and staff, because sanctions are being processed. While this is true of the government, private organisations are not free from this problem. *Sharper focus on costs should not blur the focus on customers.*

The costs of achieving, sustaining and improving quality are classified into four main groups:

1. *Prevention*: costs of investigating and planning for prevention of failure, systems reviews, testing and controls, training of personnel.
2. *Appraisal* or *Inspection:* costs of assessing quality achieved, monitoring, testing, feedback.
3. *Internal Failure:* costs of correction, redoing, scrap etc., when failure occurs before customer contact.
4. *External Failure*: costs of failure after customer contact, compensation, warranties, penalties, losses, recalls, claims, including loss of customers.

Spending money on appraisals will not help much in services, unlike in manufactured goods, because of the factor of Inseparability. There is also no internal failure. The customer would experience the bad service as soon as it is rendered. The main focus should be on prevention, as these costs will have a positive pay-off. The policy in services has to be 'Right the first time'. *It takes more time and effort to detect and correct an error than to avoid it.* This is true in accounting, cooking, manufacturing and in service operations. The adage 'prevention is better than cure' is applicable in business as much as in the other aspects of life.

There is effective cost reduction if defects, accidents and breakdowns (errors) come down to zero. All cost initiatives should have a direct impact on customer satisfaction, product quality, brand equity and shareholder value. Cost reductions and better effectiveness occur mostly in purchases, inventory, cycles and lead times. These are all services.

❏ *Measuring Costs* ❏

While attempting to measure costs, they should be analysed according to the nature of the department, function, product, causes, suppliers, equipment, people, etc. Many costs are incurred for the benefit of several activities. For example, administrative, data processing and accounts costs have to be allocated to all operating departments. Traditional practices used to allocate these common overheads on the basis of criteria like the number of people engaged, or revenues generated by each product. These are ad hoc allocations and do not recognise the actual contribution that each cost makes towards that activity. Techniques like Activity Based Costing (ABC) seek to understand the exact relationship between the costs and activities or operations, so that values can be determined more realistically. The costs of reservation are the same regardless of the class for which the ticket is issued and therefore, have to be allocated towards the costs of different classes only on the basis of number of tickets sold. However, the salaries of the travelling staff on the train or of maintenance of coaches cannot be done on that basis. The cost per ticket in first class is higher and there are fewer passengers per coach. The basis of cost allocation will determine the accuracy of focus on the relationships between activities and also identify the areas where improvements or economies are possible.

Measurement of costs is most useful when indirect costs, as the proportions of direct costs are rising rapidly. That is when serious questions will have to be asked about the markets to be in, the markets to be out of, the right kind of product mix, the features and benefits that need to be added or curtailed, the relative competitiveness of products and so on.

For systematic control of quality, Frank Price, in his book *Right First Time*, suggests

- no measurement without recording,
- no recording without analysis,
- no analysis without action.

The concepts of value analysis can be applied in studying and improving quality and costs in service operations. Each person can be asked to state briefly (in a few words), what he is doing (function). Prepare charts as in the example below, for a hospital.

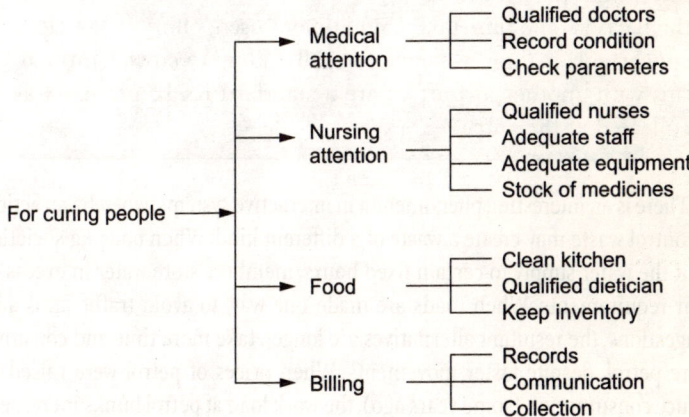

As you go right, you get answers to the question 'How?'. As you go left, you get answers to the question 'Why?'. Functions are rated according to importance and reliability from the perspective of the customer. Costs are determined. Ideas can then be generated through techniques of creative thinking, on how to perform the function differently, for better customer value and/or at a lower cost. The questions to ask could be of the following nature:

- What is the purpose of the job?
- Who is benefitted by it?
- Does the work achieve what it is intended to achieve?
- Is there duplication?
- Is it avoidable?
- Can jobs be combined?
- Is there another way of doing it while achieving the same purpose?

The example in the following box illustrate the points given above.

> At an airport, cars coming out of the car park had to stop at the barrier, hand over the entry slip, pay the charges, collect a computer-generated receipt, wait for the barrier to be lifted and then drive out. The barrier was then closed for dealing with the next vehicle. The time taken, on an average, is 30 seconds per car. The charge is Rs 10 per car, unless the duration of parking is more than four hours. The attendant has to stretch to collect the slip, punch the computer keys, stretch to hand over the receipt, press the release button, twist his body to see whether the car has passed the barrier and then press the button to close the barrier. The time taken, equipment used, effort of the clerk concerned, stationery, salary, etc., all add up to costs. Compare this with another airport where a standard Rs 10 per car was collected at the entry.

There is an interesting phenomenon in interactive systems, whereby an action to control waste may create a waste of a different kind. When housing societies limit the water supply to certain fixed hours, members store water in excess of their requirements. When roads are made 'one way' to avoid traffic jams and congestions, the resultant alternatives are longer, take more time and consume more petrol, despite faster movements. When prices of petrol were raised to reduce consumption (some years ago), the work load at petrol bunks increased, because vehicles came in more frequently to take in lesser quantities at a time. When a bank decided that the cheques for clearance would not be acknowledged over the counter, but must be dropped in a box, the frequency of updating pass books increased. Customers wanted to ensure that credits had been made.

Costs are often given as an excuse for neglecting quality. 'It costs too much' is normally considered a valid finality, without asking, 'How much is too much' and in relation to what is the 'too much'. High quality and low costs are compatible. The Japanese have proved it. Achieving quality may be expensive, but bad quality could be even more so. It has been estimated that up to 30 per cent of manufacturing costs could be saved by doing it right the first time. Repairs are said to cost 15 to 30 cents of every sales dollar in the USA and 5 cents in Japan. (Data of 1991). A study by Mckinsey & Co. (1984) showed that companies produce at least 30 per cent of their products at above average quality, for average or below average costs. If bad quality causes damage and there are compensation or liability claims, the costs can be pretty stiff. Insurance covers may not provide full relief. Courts in the US are liberal in awarding penalties, compensation and damages. The Indian consumer courts have also begun to take a serious view of defective service.

The example of Sundaram Clayton is given in the following box.

Sundaram Clayton Limited, which won the Deming Prize in 1998 is said to make 'supplies of products of right quality at the right time and at the right place', have excellent practices in 'housekeeping, keeping machines and shopfloor clean, 100 per cent exactness, mistake proofing techniques, minimal in-process inventory, negligible warranty claims, reduction of new products development time by half, and continuously rejecting the status quo'.

Who can figure out the costs of a dissatisfied customer? In insurance, the front end costs of placing business in the books is high. A policy discontinued early means that the initial costs have not been recovered. Loss of customers due to poor service can rapidly erode the bottom line. Even in other businesses, the cost of finding a new customer is several times higher than retaining an existing one. The difference represents the costs or gains of quality.

The story below is meant to show that it is easy to go overboard when working on costs.

Shetty ran a small restaurant in a busy street of the town. He stocked packets of peanuts on the shelf above his cash counter. An expert asked Shetty whether he knew how much it cost him to keep those packets on the shelf and whether he was then making a profit. Shetty thought that it cost him nothing. The expert then pointed out to him that the costs included the cost of the rack on which the packets were kept, rent, electricity, taxes, decoration and salaries of the restaurant, plus the cost of washing, security, etc. 'The more you sell, the more the allocation of overhead costs', Shetty was told. Shetty threw his stock of peanuts out of the door.

❑ *Elements of Quality* ❑

Managing service quality requires attention to a number of related issues, like techniques to define and measure customer satisfaction, benchmarking service quality, setting and achieving service standards, obtaining and evaluating customer feedback, handling of complaints, diagnosing service delivery problems, serving internal customers, empowering staff and using work teams to reinforce quality.

A product is the outcome of a process. This is so in services also. The process is functional, interactive. The process has systems, technology and people. Outcomes, systems, technology and people, all contribute to quality. In the case of a garage, the outcome is the repair job. If this is done well and the vehicle is rid of defects, the service is good. If the owner of the vehicle is present while the repair is being done, what he sees of the mechanic's behaviour affects the 'experience' of service. He forms impressions about the earnestness and competence of the mechanic. If he sees the vehicle remaining unattended for a long time, he may think that the people are indifferent and that there is unnecessary delay. If he sees them hammering a part crudely, to make it fit, he could feel upset. The billing and payment procedures form a part of the service. Any one of these can have a dominating influence on the total experience, whatever be the quality of the repair.

The Malcolm Baldrige awards for excellence, instituted by the US government in 1987, evaluate organisations on the following seven factors:

- Leadership: which looks at the way senior executives guide the organisation and how the organisation addresses its responsibilities to the public as a good corporate citizen.
- Strategic Planning: which looks at how it sets strategic direction and key action plans.
- Customer and Market focus: which looks at how it determines requirements and expectations of customers and how it acquires, satisfies and retains customers.

- Information analysis: also called measurement, analysis and knowledge management, which looks at the management and analysis and improvement of data and information to support key organisational processes and performance management systems.
- Human Resource Focus: which looks at how the workforce is enabled to develop its full potential and how the workforce is aligned to organisational objectives.
- Process Management: which looks at how the key production and delivery and support processes are designed, managed and improved.
- Business Results: which looks at the performance and improvement in key business areas, customer satisfaction, financial and market place performance.

Of these, the last is the final outcome of the other six intervening causal variables. Further, in evaluating the factors, improvement is emphasised. No organisation can rest on its laurels.

❑ *The Five Gaps to Manage* ❑

There are five critical gaps that may occur, which affect the quality of service. Strategies to enhance quality must focus on ways to reduce these five gaps.

Gap 1 called the knowledge gap, is the difference between the management's perception of customer's expectation (MCE) and the customer's expectations (CEE). This gap can be bridged through a better understanding of the customer. Surveys, feedback, complaints, etc., help.

Gap 2 called the standards gap, is the difference between MCE and the product benefits as designed (DPB). DPB includes the parameters of delivery systems. This gap may occur while translating intended benefits into systems. The gap arises because of constraints, limited resources or inaccurate evaluation of the systems' capability. The gap can be reduced through a regular audit of the system.

Gap 3 called the delivery gap, is the difference between DPB and the actual product benefits as delivered (APB). This happens because of incompatibility between different parts of the systems, modifications made during operations, errors during delivery of service or skills and attitudes of those delivering the service. This gap can be bridged through middle managers, supervision, communication, control systems, training, etc.

Gap 4 called the communications gap, is the difference between APB and the communication of service benefits (CPB). This gap may differ from *Gap 3* because of the unique factors present at the time of delivery of service. Specific mention of, and drawing attention to, aspects of the service by the provider or by other users, cause differences in perceptions. It is said that a cardboard box dealer, who never missed a delivery schedule for years, added in his invoices a 'performance index' column in bold letters, listing the date of delivery as required and as performed. His business took off.

Gap 5 called the service gap, is between the customer's perception of actual experience (CAE) and CEE. When CAE is better than CEE, quality is good. One common reason for this gap is the hype created by the marketing people (affecting CEE), which is not matched by the delivery systems (people and processes). Marketing and operations must be synchronised.

It is to be assumed that these gaps always exist. Only then will one keep looking for them. If unattended, the gaps will widen. When noticed, the gap can be bridged. The correction may be in product design, process, equipments or in people.

The responsibility to manage quality is at the top management level. This is so, despite the fact that quality is determined at the lowest level of operations, where service is made and delivered. Often, there is a tendency to say that quality has to be managed by 'those at the front'. It cannot be. Although the error takes place 'at the front', more than 80 per cent of errors are due to systems which only top management can change. Even for the remaining 20 per cent or less that are caused by people at contact points, the management must take the responsibility to train them specifically for their respective jobs and build an appropriate culture of quality in service. When the waiter in a five-star hotel does not see that the table does not have cutlery, or that the glasses are empty, or that the dish on the buffet table does not have a serving spoon, it very often is a deficiency of training and not of the waiter's attitude. It is not enough to clothe a newcomer in uniform and tell him to look after the diners. The steward who keeps talking to the waiters, while the restaurant is full, is also not well-trained. Many firms provide more training to entry level personnel than to middle management. *Training has to be viewed as investment in quality.*

The story in the box can be used as a short case to study the existence of and the requisite responses to gaps.

❏ *Keep Customers Out* ❏

In the case of goods, quality is experienced only while using the product, not in the process that makes the product. If the customer had access to the process and saw how cleanly or dirtily the product was made, much of the gloss and

A group of two families, went on a visit to a well-known sea-side resort for a day's outing. As soon as they arrived at 10 a.m. at the launch jetty, they were welcomed and informed that the boat would arrive within 10 minutes to take them to the hotel. On reaching the hotel after a 15-minute boat ride through verdant landscapes, during which the boatman gave a running commentary on the birds, vegetation and lifestyles of the neighbourhood, they checked the lunch menu and placed the order for service at 1 p.m. The resort was exceptionally beautiful. Many cottages were built on floating rafts. They decided to spend some time at the pool side. The bar was located inside the pool and there were stools inside the bar as well as in the water around the bar. Beer was ordered by the men who were sitting under the shade. It did not come for nearly 45 minutes. One of them called out to the bartender to find out what was happening. He went to the main hotel, and came back with two glasses of beer. He had a bill with him for two bottles of beer. The quantity did not seem right and he was asked to explain. He finally admitted that some beer had spilled while he was pouring it into the glass. After some time he was asked to bring another bottle of beer. As he started pouring, it was obvious that more beer was going to be spilt. He was scolded for being clumsy. On further enquiry, it transpired that he was a student in a hotel management school 40 miles away and had been deputed to this hotel, along with five others, for practical training for six months. He had been here for three months already along with other freshers. Nobody had told them about how to do their work.

glitter of the final product would be lost. In the case of services, the customer is very much part of the process. One way in which the provider of the service can avoid the dissatisfaction arising out of process factors, is to keep the customers out of the process. If they witness an argument among the staff about the proper response to a query, they would lose faith in the reliability of the system. They need not see how long the cheque or document, waits on any table for a signature. Do not let them into the kitchen where food is being prepared. They need not see that the ice cubes are being picked up by hand. Doctors avoid 'outsiders' when they handle serious emergencies, or even when they consult among themselves. Clients are not generally part of the strategy planning process of lawyers. Quite a few elements of the process can be disturbing. The direct telecast of legislative proceedings is partly responsible for the increasing disappointment with the political systems. If we were not aware of the process (what was happening), the disgust may have been less.

The scope for keeping customers out, depends on the extent to which the customer's presence is required. Laundry, couriers, repairs, advertising, warehousing, banking, insurance and market research, are services in which scope exists for keeping the customers out. Wherever the customer's physical presence can be avoided, avoid it. He can be brought in after the final outcome is ready. Wherever his physical presence cannot be avoided, see whether his mental presence can be avoided. Doctors who operate, ask their patients to look the other way. A barber does this through continuous chit-chat. Insurance companies use agents and surveyors as buffers.

Avoidance of customers from the process has to be balanced with his need to know—the factor of being informed or communication. When the outcome is satisfactory, this does not pose a problem. However, if the outcome is not satisfactory, the need for communication will surface strongly. Explanations are sought only in the event of failure. People want to know what is going on, only when the train is not moving for a long time, or the queue is not moving at all, or the patient in the doctor's clinic has been in for too long, or when the increment/promotion list is delayed, or when the examination results are not released on the due date. The way the Unit Trust of India invested its funds was not a matter of public concern till the news broke that the US64 did not have adequate reserves.

❏ Use of Equipment ❏

The use of equipment in the process helps to maintain consistency in output. Many services can be mechanised. The railways and airlines have installed machines to respond to standard enquiries about arrivals and departures. Telephone exchanges in offices are automatic and interactive. Computers are used extensively. Both medical practitioners and astrologers use them. Printers judge precision of colour through computers. Ships and other carriers, including courier services, track, sort and stock, through the use of computers. Beauty salons and movie makers rely heavily on computer graphics. Many decisions and controls on logistics are taken care of by computers. We might see, in the future, computer applications in our daily life, so far unknown.

Equipment is expected to function true to specifications and as programmed. Errors can enter into the systems, for technical or human reasons. An error, if not noticed and corrected immediately, may be the cause of major and repeated errors. A malfunctioning equipment is more annoying than a malfunctioning person. When the tape gives at 11 a.m., information recorded at 2 a.m., about expected arrivals up to 8 a.m., one cannot even shout and ask it to find out what you want to know. A client of a bank wrote 22 times and got no reply. Another client wrote once and received 40 replies. A policyholder of the LIC got over 400 premium notices on a particular day, all for the same policy. Automated services do not correct malfunctions automatically. They need more constant audit.

❏ Moments of Truth ❏

The *moments of truth*, explained in chapter 4, are *critical for quality*. These are incidents or events which constitute service in the minds of the customer. These are basic building blocks of service, the small units of value delivered to the customer. If these moments are handled casually or insensitively, without seriousness, as if it is routine, there is a possible failure of service.

A series of moments of truth make a cycle of service. These moments may be attended to by different persons or departments of the organisation. However, the customer sees it as a single process. The big, total picture as seen by the customer and the big, total picture as seen by the provider have to match. If there is a mismatch, there are gaps, failures of service, dissatisfaction and loss of quality.

Managing moments of truth, requires attention to minor details. For example, a plumber called in to attend to a choked wash basin may

- walk in just when the householder is about to have lunch,
- walk all over the carpet while moving into the bathroom with feet that are not clean,
- ask for a wrench, because he did not bring his tools,
- go out and return after 30 minutes with the tools and more dirt on his feet,
- open the pipe and let a lot of murky sediment splash on the floor and the freshly painted walls,
- show you some of the sediment for your inspection, as if you had put it in there,
- refix the pipes, which, you notice, are not in proper alignment,
- hammer hard to get the alignment right.

Most of these have nothing to do with the technicalities of repairing a plumbing line. A plumbing service needs something more than technically competent plumbers. They have to be sensitive to the moments of truth, if the cycle of service has to be satisfying to the customer. There are several cycles of service which together make up the transaction of service. In this case, response to the call for repair and billing would be further cycles in the same transaction.

❑ *Error Free* ❑

In some services, there is some margin for error without causing permanent damage. The frown on a dissatisfied customer's face can be converted to a smile through remedial action and compensation. Replacing a defective item, is partly compensation. An apology is also acceptable. A discount (part refund) on the cost of that item is a tangible expression of regret. It is said that a caterer, on being told that the supplies for a birthday party did not reach on time, rushed additional supplies free of cost and added special gifts for the guests. The caterer thus conveyed the message of genuine regret and that he was serious about keeping his word.

The guarantee of money back, in the event of failure, is a statement of good intent. However, good intent is not good enough for all services. In some cases, the failure can cause irrevocable damage. It is assumed that a delay in a financial settlement can be compensated through the payment of interest. If marriage arrangements are fouled up because of the insurance money (loan or claim) being delayed, the loss is more than that of interest. Non-payment of retirement dues on time, prevented an employee from taking full advantage of tax rebate provisions. The resultant liability of higher tax was a loss which the employer could not reimburse.

There are services in which flaws just should not happen. They have to be 100 per cent perfect every time. There may never be a second chance to make a first impression. That is what Motorola claims it does. If a life-saving medicine is held up by a customs officer, unaware of the proper rules, no apology can undo the resultant damage. When a child is lost because it fell into a manhole left uncovered by the municipal workers, sanctions of generous grants do not compensate the parents. There is also no point in asking whose fault it was. That is something that should not have happened. In the case of insurance, if at the time of claim, it is discovered that what was thought to have been insured, is in fact not insured, or that there has been neglect of some important requirement, the claim will not be paid. It does not help to say sorry or even to refund the premium. If a doctor amputates the wrong leg, there is no compensation possible. An error of delayed delivery by a courier may mean a final blow to a person's career or other ambitions. The consumer courts have awarded heavy penalties on couriers, who delivered papers late and thereby damaged the chances of the user's employment abroad.

It is good management practice to strive for a 100 per cent fault-free service. There should be no tolerance for errors. Even a one per cent error, can mean as many as a 100 mistakes per day in a small branch of a bank. To the customer who is part of this 100, the failure is 100 per cent, not one per cent. A gynaecologist who mishandles a childbirth cannot console the disappointed parents, saying that it was a one in a million error. The financial news service which Reuters distributes worldwide and is depended upon by several treasurers, would cause major disasters if the data happened to have clerical errors. A hotel calculated that a one per cent error would mean that every day a guest would leave without paying, 20 orders of fried eggs would have human hair in it, 15 tables would have soiled linen, 250 plates would be broken, drinks of 40 guests would be mixed up and 20 guests would not get their laundry. One way to move in the direction of fault-free service, is to seek out data on every fault that may have occurred, document it, analyse causes thereof, and look for ways to eliminate it through improvements in systems, equipment or people behaviour. *This exercise needs support from the top management, but needs involvement of the lowest possible levels.*

Boeing builds aircraft which do not fail, so claim its manufacturers. The Boeing 777 is an assembly of 1,50,000 uniquely engineered parts and three million total parts (including rivets and bolts), all of which have to combine perfectly with each other, to form electronic and mechanical systems. The effort of planning, designing, building and assembling, brought together individual engineers, designers, fabricators, machinists, suppliers, engine makers, mechanics, sales personnel and even customers, to contribute with ideas, from the stage of concept development, right through to flight testing of the assembled aircraft. Some of the fabrications are made in countries thousands of miles away. It is similar to space flights. This kind of complex activity needs collaborative effort among all related persons, and strict adherence to the minutest specifications. They assure error-free services.

❑ *Checklist and Steps* ❑

International consultant and author, John Humble, had, in association with the Management Centre, Europe, developed checklists to enable organisations and individual managers to carry out fast audits of the true extent of their commitment to service. The checklists are based on the following concepts:

1. Core services and product features, which determine value for money, have two components:

   - performance viz., quality and reliability, design, availability,
   - sense of caring viz., problem solving, courtesy, listening.

2. Key business issues are:

   - external viz., selling and promotion, location, access, delivery methods, timeliness, supplier relationships, customer support systems and images,
   - internal viz., culture, human resources capability, team work, effectiveness of production, organisation, information and technology, quality standards and control, innovation.

3. Delivery of service is a resultant of key business issues and cause customer satisfaction, perceived values, as well as repeat business and profitability.

The checklists raise specific questions on

   - how explicit are quality and service part of the company's mission statement,
   - how sharply defined and measured are the criteria of customer (target), quality and service,
   - methods to track the needs of customers,
   - post-sale concern for customer as compared to pre-sale concern,
   - checking of reliability of services, vis-a-vis promise,
   - communication of policies to staff and their training,
   - convenience of location and delivery arrangements,
   - checking of quality at distribution points,
   - control on incoming materials and components,
   - involving staff in information and decision making,
   - handling of customer grievances,
   - extent of innovation,
   - use of technology,
   - awareness of competition.

On each item, the present state and the desired state can be determined. The action to be taken, will be to bridge the gap between the present and the desired states. The action plan will include the persons who should be responsible for each part of the action.

The steps to be taken by top management to enhance quality of service include:

- defining strategic intent,
- monitoring customer needs and expectations,
- measuring quality and customer satisfaction,
- refocussing organisation structure around the customer,
- finding new roles for middle managers,
- achieving productivity benefits,
- measuring pay-offs, making service cost effective,
- establishing a loyal customer base.

❏ *Strategic Intent* ❏

Strategic intent is to be defined through the objectives of the company and the detailed operating systems. In one company, the organisation chart places the customer at the top, followed by the front line contacts like salesmen, service personnel, branches and ending with the corporate office. The Chairman and the Board are at the bottom of the chart. In another company, all statements of objectives emphasise customer first and turnover, new products, systems improvements, productivity, cost reduction, profits, etc., as following therefrom. Operating instructions will confirm whether these statements are seriously intended or not. One company has posters all over its premises, talking of customer service as its motto but

- has cut down on service personnel,
- cautions employees to beware of 'unscrupulous' customers,
- frowns when an employee exercises discretion and initiative to satisfy a customer.

The manager who makes quick adjustments to handle the unexpected rush of demands from customers, instead of getting irritated at the pressure, is defining strategic intent. The BEST personnel at key bus stops in Mumbai, with authority to redirect or call for additional buses, according to passenger demands, are indicative of strategic intent. Reward systems to personnel as well as infrastructural facilities for service, like location and access, define intent. Public servants who are engaged in cleaning up streets and localities just before the minister is expected to arrive, also define strategic intent.

Every provider of service does not have to be a Disneyland in entertainment, the Taj in hotels, or Thomas Cook in the travel business. The quality standards are to be defined in terms of the target market. If the hotel is catering to pilgrims visiting a temple, spartan food would satisfy more than a luxurious four-course service in the restaurant. The arrangements at Shirdi, providing a locker to keep one's belongings, clean toilets and bathrooms with 24-hour water supply, and a space to sleep, seem to meet the requirements of large numbers of people who travel light, want to wash up before a *darshan* and look for a safe place to rest. A supplier of security guards for housing colonies, does not need the sophistication of computerised personnel inventory that a placement service for top executives may need. A mofussil bus service can do with much less chrome and polish in its exteriors and offices than an international airline, and yet be perceived as of high quality.

Having identified the target market, the provider has to answer questions on how far he proposes to meet the needs of and expectations of that market. Those answers will constitute strategic intent. The intent has then to be translated into measurable quality standards. Benchmarking is done by comparing with other similar organisations. While benchmarking may show what is possible, it need not be chosen to be the level of service offer. At the chosen level, the offering must be flawless and satisfying, the best if possible. In the Shirdi premises, the security of the lockers has to be perfect, the cleanliness and hygiene properly taken care of, the water supply uninterrupted at least during the specified hours, which should match the pilgrims' convenience and requirements keeping in view the programmes in the temple. In addition, care should be taken to see that the pilgrims' enquiries are easily answered, the booking procedures are not cumbersome, too much crowding is avoided and so on.

The strategy will answer the questions, 'Why should customers choose us?' and 'How are we different?' The strategy should aim at communicating a message of uniqueness, of a brand. Subhash Ghai or Rajashri are brands in cinema. These names are associated with certain kinds of cinema, spectacular ones in one case and simple delight in the other. So also are Jaslok or Apollo brands in hospitals, Mudra in advertising, BEST in city bus services, IIMs in management education, IMRB in market research and Infosys in software consultancy.

❏ *Monitoring Customer Needs and Expectations* ❏

Customers' needs and expectations can be monitored through

- market research and surveys,
- observation of customer behaviours and responses,
- data on offers from competition,
- complaints,

- personal contact with customers,
- focus groups,
- comment/feedback forms from users.

Monitoring will try to identify critical areas of expectations, and see what elements could be built into either product features or processes to satisfy those expectations. These elements would then be the parameters of quality. The earlier chapters have dealt with the limitations of various methods normally employed, as well as the practical options.

Monitoring has to be done by people sensitive to both explicit and implicit messages. Most customers do not usually articulate clearly what they want, but they do react adversely when they do not get it. The needs and expectations have to be inferred from casual remarks, behaviour and involuntary signals. It is said that the late Mr M.S. Oberoi, founder of the Oberoi chain of hotels, used to watch the expressions of people in the restaurant. When he noticed a frown somewhere, he would go to the person concerned and find out what was wrong. When a visiting lecturer is found hanging around the accountant's table, the director should understand that there is some problem with regard to payment of honoraria. When a consultant sees that his client is reading the proposal again and again, and asking apparently innocuous questions, it should be obvious that there are matters which the client is uncomfortable about. They could be the level of fees or access to sensitive areas of operation. This activity will take care of *Gap 1* as well as *Gap 2*, referred to earlier.

❑ *Measuring* ❑

Measuring quality and customer satisfaction is complimentary to monitoring of needs and expectations. While monitoring may suggest what elements need to be added, the measurement will indicate the extent to which the elements are effective. Specifically, therefore, the measurements may focus on the pre-determined parameters of quality, particularly changes or additions decided upon recently.

Services, being intangible, measurement would seem to be impossible. However, bad service and the consequent dissatisfaction will be reflected in behaviours like fights, complaints and early termination of arrangements. These can be observed and measured.

Measurements have to be made on a scale. No accurate scale is available for satisfaction. Customers can be asked to comment on specific elements on a five-point scale, anchored with words like 'Very Satisfied' or 'Excellent' at one end and 'Poor' or 'Very Unsatisfactory' at the other. Alternatively, the five points may be described as 'Excellent', Very Good', 'Good', 'OK' and 'Poor'. Customers may be allowed to comment freely on the element in question. None of these methods are perfect, but they do give some idea of customer experience. Taken repeatedly and periodically from large numbers of customers, the measurement is good enough as broad indicators of trend as well as of problem areas.

It is worthwhile to work out a Customer Satisfaction Index (CSI), based on factors identified as critical (moments of truth) and indicative of satisfaction. The factors could be experience of transactions or attitudes that build relationships. CSIs can be worked out continuously or periodically. Both provide valuable data.

Measurements may be made of the service overall. Measurements may also be made of the specific changes made in the recent past. It is necessary to draw the attention of the customer to the changes made and confirm that he experiences the changed features, or processes. The customer should take note of the changes, as evidence of the provider's concern for quality of service provided.

Regular measurements would also indicate changes that may have occurred without deliberate intent. The way things happen are not always the way management thinks they should happen. Systems put into place at one time do not remain so throughout. Gradual adjustments can happen, influenced by those who operate the systems as well as the forces and events within and without. Areas for correction will emerge from these measurements.

An effective way to test quality is to use dummy customers and to report. The dummies may be briefed to create abnormal situations to test how the systems and people stand up to stresses and strains.

❑ *Refocussing Organisational Structure* ❑

Structure refers to the arrangement of responsibilities and functions. The structure clarifies

- who will do what,
- who will report to whom,
- what each person is responsible for,
- what authority is vested in whom.

Responsibility is for achieving results. Authority is to commit resources of the organisation. This means that the person with authority can instruct people, can issue orders and will have some discretion to decide how anything should be done and how the resources should be used.

It is said that structure follows strategy. It is equally true that strategy follows structure. If there is a mismatch between structure and strategy, either may change to suit the other. The functional equilibrium that emerges may not be what the management desired. When the service strategy is defined, it is necessary to ensure that structure is appropriate. Only then will the strategy remain in focus and be acted upon.

If strategic intent is to provide credit approval within a couple of hours, the structure and systems should be such that this can happen. This will not happen if the clearance has to come from a distant office to which papers have to be sent physically, because the two offices are not connected by fax or e-mail. A promise to replace defective goods immediately, has no meaning if the replacement is subject to approval from someone else, not available at the point of sale, or if the stocks are not available to provide replacements. A promise to attend to repairs within two hours must be supported by a structure whereby persons receiving the requests from customers, are also aware about the location of the service personnel in the field and are authorised to deploy such personnel, as per the priorities they may decide upon.

If the structure is appropriate for the strategy intended, the staff attitudes would also change accordingly. When the LIC changed its structure bringing about decentralisation of functions to the branch offices, time lags reduced, accuracy of information improved and the attitude of staff changed from, 'We will let you know when we hear from the divisional office', to 'Tell me your problem and I will help you now'.

The structure should be around specific customer needs and segments. Small units with responsibility for a clear customer group, equipped with essential resources to perform the tasks, and given clear performance objectives, will function with a better sense of cohesiveness, perhaps with a healthy sense of competition. The structure should enable, not hinder, quick responses to unfamiliar and unexpected situations. Systems that require considerable paper work shift emphasis from the personal to the impersonal aspects of working, the latter being unsuitable for the service business.

While structuring the organisation, one needs to identify

- key activities that produce results, where excellence is required and bad performance not acceptable,
- support activities which enable the key activities to be performed.

Key activities impact on customers directly. As a matter of principle, *the key activities should not be subordinate to non-key activities. Revenue earning activities should not be subordinate to non-revenue earning activities.* Conscience activities that clarify and establish values of the organisation should not be subordinate to anything else. They are top management responsibilities.

In many organisations, key activities are made subordinate to non-key support or control activities. The commercial department's preference for economy should not override the marketing department's preference for speed. The credit department's penchant for complete data should not delay the negotiations for a major industrial deal. A ship should not remain grounded because the purchase department is processing tenders for spares that are urgently required. In a hospital, the key activities relate to the medical attention and treatment of the sick. These are also revenue-earning activities. However, filling up of forms and payments of advances at the time of admissions are given greater importance. Negligence in these procedures may invite punitive notice, while neglect in the ward may go unnoticed. Expensive equipment purchased for medical purposes remain idle and unused because the sanctions and budgets for repairs or operators are not forthcoming. Expenditure on non-key activities tend to increase faster than on key activities. Almost all public sector organisations have ever increasing activities in Hindi translations, compliance with reservation rules, response to queries from parliamentarians and so on, infructuous expenditures that override the priorities of the primary business. Operating personnel feel inhibited by and accountable to, audit and vigilance officials. A senior official who tells his customer that he is unable to help because the rules do not permit him to, is the victim of an inappropriate structure. That emphasises internal rules (controls) over customer needs (results).

Some of the dimensions of structure are:

- Centralisation—the extent to which decisions are shared with different levels in the organisation.
- Formalisation—the extent to which activities/relationships are governed by rules, procedures, contracts.
- Specialisation/Differentiation—the extent to which tasks are divided into unique elements.

These in turn influence

- Effectiveness—the extent to which results are achieved.
- Efficiency—the relationship between inputs and outputs.
- Adaptiveness—the ability to adapt to changes in the environment.

More centralisation leads to better control and coordination. More formalisation leads to more efficiency. More centralisation and formalisation are helpful, when uncertainty in the environment is low and tasks are repetitive. More specialisation and differentiation help in adaptiveness. In view of the radical changes taking place in the environment, organisations have to remain very adaptive. Otherwise, competition will have an advantage. Effectiveness is paramount. Efficiency is not less important, because that is the way to keep costs down. Both centralisation and formalisation hamper adaptability. Specialisation improves efficiency and often effectiveness also. However, specialisation is fast becoming obsolescent because of the changing situations. An appropriate balance has to be found.

Mr Hiroyuki Itami, Professor of Management, Hitosubashi University, Tokyo, addressing a meeting of the Mumbai Management Association, said that Japanese firms employed the following principles in their internal organisation and market transactions.

- People, including both managers and workers, who contribute to the organisation with their expertise and energy, should have priority in determining the course of the firm, compared to the stockholders who contribute with capital.
- Money, power and information on environment, technology, etc., are shared and distributed inside the firm, in patterns that are very dispersed, not concentrated, affecting personal relationships and social structures within the firm.
- Firms dealing with other firms as suppliers or purchasers tend to build long-term cooperative relationships.

The structure of a good quality service organisation has to be such that enterprise and initiative would not only flourish, but would always remain focussed on the customer, however large the scale of operations. The flow of information within has to be carefully organised. The less time taken for information to reach relevant decision points, and back to action points, the more satisfying the service is likely to be. Computer networks provide a number of possibilities, if properly programmed, linked and maintained. It is useful to locate authorised personnel close to points where moments of truth may occur, who can notice, receive reports, apply correction, give guidance, make amends and enhance quality almost instantaneously. In other words, the large operation may be divided into smaller units of operations and made fairly autonomous for day-to-day functioning.

❏ The Middle Manager ❏

The middle manager's role has traditionally been one of integrating top management policy with operations of the subordinates. The focus therefore, had been to supervise activities of subordinates, control results, solve problems and so on.

In a service industry, *the control has to be on the process that delivers the outcome*, which then produces satisfaction. Problem solving has to be done on the spot by the employee in contact with the customer, during the process of delivery of the outcome. Also, the quality of service has to be continuously improved upon. Every contact point is a source of satisfaction as well as a source of potential problems. It would be the role of a middle manager to

- analyse operations and processes,
- identify the contact points,
- determine how the contact point has to be managed and what level of quality is to be maintained,
- visualise the possible errors, what may go wrong,
- find ways of avoiding the errors,
- find ways of compensating for the errors, if not avoided.

The middle manager can do this best when he involves the operating personnel into his thinking and decision-making processes. The fact is that they know what is happening, perhaps in more intimate detail than he knows. They should know what should happen. They alone can make it happen. They are willing to make it happen. They need to know what caused the happenings, and the risks involved in the proposed actions.

The middle manager will have to be as good as a nurse or a doctor in building empathy, as a salesman in handling rejection, as a marriage counsellor in resolving conflicts, as a psychotherapist in listening, as a coach in providing leadership and as a teacher or journalist in communicating ideas.

Lead more and manage less, is the principle. Leaders improve communication and trust while managers rely on command and control. The information and the decision should be shared. Let subordinates be a part of managing. They should understand and accept the quality standards, as the superordinate goals of the organisation. Only when they accept, will quality be delivered. Without them, quality will not be delivered.

To find out what is good, very good and WOW, and how to move the whole process repeatedly to WOW experiences, is the middle manager's role in a service organisation. Make quality part of the agenda in all meetings. *Do not ever say,* even by oversight, 'Don't bother, the customer will not notice'. Do not run down suggestions just because the improvement is small. *No improvement is too small to be ignored.* Hundreds of half per cent here and a quarter per cent there, add up to substantial figures. If a customer is fumbling with a form to fill, there is an opportunity to improve. Perhaps, the questions are not clear. Perhaps they cannot be answered.

The middle manager must remain sensitive to customer behaviour and be able to interpret the real meanings in their expressions and comments. They should train their subordinates also to be equally perceptive and empower them to suggest, to improvise, to take initiative and to remain customer focussed. They should be encouraged to report their observations of customer behaviour and comments. They would be thus involved in monitoring customer feedback and expectations. Monitoring should be seen as everybody's business, not because someone higher up says so, but because everybody genuinely and voluntarily owns the responsibility for customer satisfaction. Involving operating personnel into thinking about improvements in service, is one sure way to

- make them customer focussed,
- reinforce the message that management is committed to quality service.

Let stories of exceptional quality performance by employees, or WOW experiences of customers, be known to others, preferably in short meetings held periodically, specifically for these purposes. It increases internal communication and shows possibilities for others to emulate. These practices give meaning to corporate slogans on customer service like 'We respond to guests' needs' (Hilton Hotel) or 'We try harder' (Avis car rentals). It should lead to competitiveness in one trying to excel, but not the competitiveness where one tries to pull down another.

Middle managers would have to lead by example. They have to walk around in the areas where customers contact the service, intervene as soon as problems seem likely and convert such situations into opportunities for excellence. There is a principle that says that out of a 100 activities and a 100 results, 20 per cent activities account for 80 per cent of the results, while the remainder 80 per cent of activities account for only 20 per cent of the results. This is called the Pareto's Principle or the 80–20 rule. Eighty per cent of taxes that are paid by 20 per cent of the payers; 80 per cent of problems come from 20 per cent of the staff or customers; 80 per cent of traffic use only 20 per cent of roads; 80 per cent revenue is collected from 20 per cent of the products. This principle should help identify the critical areas to pay maximum attention.

One of the areas needing constant attention is to lay down standards of performance. Refunds within 48 hours, pick up the telephone within four rings, check in within two minutes of arrival at hotel lounge, six minutes at peak hours, queues not more than two persons per outlet, letters replied within six hours, waiters to attend within 60 seconds of seating and service within 20 minutes of taking orders in a restaurant, telephone enquiries to be passed on to not more than one person, baggage delivery within 10 minutes of arrival of aircraft, every pillow to have 1.8 kg of down, all upholstery scotch guarded. These are samples of benchmarks or standards to be determined and adhered to. Banks have found it possible to issue demand drafts and freshly printed cheque books within minutes.

None of these are easy to implement. All of them would require some rearrangement of systems. Every failure to comply with the benchmark target should carry with it *a penalty to the service provider as an organisation—not the employee concerned*—and a reward to the customer. Every failure to comply should be studied as a systems problem. Even if it is an individual error, the correction should come via management practices. Once these standards become part of the routine, the effort must be to improve further.

It is said that the reprinted 72-page catalogue of Bon Marche of Seattle, stated the revised price of Sony 5-disk Carousel CD player, which was till then selling at $199, as $99, instead of $179. The cost of the item to the company itself was $149. When the shop opened the next morning, there was a long queue of customers and 4000 pieces were sold at $99. Orders were booked for later delivery, when the stocks ran out. The mistake cost the company very dearly. However, it was turned to their advantage. The printer's devil became common information soon and *The New York Times* carried a story about this incident. The loss of $2,00,000 paid high dividends in terms of credibility of the store. This reflected the values of the company.

The quality of service depends on a person's behaviour. Behaviour depends on a mix of physiological and psychological factors. Stress and fatigue affect behaviour to the extent that normal skills may not become available. Middle managers have to monitor the physical and mental conditions of the persons assigned to customer contact jobs. Such monitoring has to be done on a continuous basis. If the conditions at a given time, are not appropriate for courteous, helpful behaviour, the employee must either be restored quickly to his normal best or excused from the front line jobs for that time.

Customers are not always deserving of courtesy and respect. Yet the service providers treat them with due consideration. It is possible that stresses may develop. Middle managers must be able to notice such situations and avoid any eruptions of stress becoming severe. That is why, in the service industry, *the supervision has to be more on enabling the person who is the resource, to excel, and not so much on controlling the work.*

The middle manager is responsible for maintenance of records. Study of problems and areas of improvement need comparisons and analysis, which can be done only through proper documentation. Documentation is the memory for an organisation, by which the experience (learning) continues even when the individuals concerned have changed. Documentation for the purpose of memory, is less likely to be tampered with, compared to reporting activities for control and appraisal purposes.

❏ *Tools for Quality Control* ❏

A number of tools are available to help one to analyse, understand and intervene for the maintenance of quality. Middle managers can do better if they are familiar with these techniques. It will help more if the team members are also introduced to them.

Data can be analysed with the help of tables using Pareto's Principle (the 80–20 rule). Trends would become clearer through histograms, scatter diagrams and other statistical representations. Cause-effect analyses are facilitated by affinity diagrams, inter-relationship diagrams, tree diagrams, matrix diagrams, fish bone diagrams, process charts, flow charts, etc. Affinity diagrams sort out data on the basis of associations or relatedness between different data and help determine patterns. Brainstorming is used to find the associations and later the groupings are gradually refined.

Inter-relationships diagrams are drawn to establish priorities. Any one idea or issue may affect more than another idea and the magnitude of effects can vary. The ideas/issues are written and directional arrows are drawn connecting one and the other. The arrows with the maximum advantage (weightage, strength and connection) need priority attention. If issues are too many, the matrix method is used to illustrate the inter-relationships.

In the case of services, the tangibles are few. They are also not the critical ones. Therefore, statistical methods that handle measurable data, have less application. The other diagramatic procedures help in diagnosing the problem areas and suggesting possible solutions.

Indices help in understanding the situation from time to time. For example, the CSI prepared regularly will indicate significant trends. There can also be a Customer Loyalty Index showing how many of the customers are coming for repeat purchases. New customers may also reveal whether they were told about the service from earlier users of the service. Such referrals indicate customer loyalty. The factors to be used in building these indices, have to be carefully chosen and checked for validity periodically. Many studies are misleading because the data is not collected from the customer. The adage, *The desk is a dangerous place to view the world. Hit the road* is an important one.

❑ *Customer Charters* ❑

As a result of persistent demands from consumer groups for accountability, transparency and quality in services, government departments and public organisations, like hospitals, banks and insurance companies, had formulated what are called charters, which they would try to satisfy as rights of customers. These are in effect standards of performance, which these organisations pledge to adhere to. The charters also include redressal mechanisms. The Delhi Development Authority (DDA) commits itself to provide every allottee/ purchaser 'effective, prompt and courteous service with dedication, integrity and fairness, quality product at reasonable cost'. The LIC promises to 'strive to deal with customers in an open and transparent manner'. These are vague expressions, difficult to interpret in specific situations and are therefore, hollow. The charter of the DDA also contains specific commitments like 60 days for completion of all formalities to give letter of possession, 15 days to give possession after receipt of premium and documents, 60 days for issue of certificate of completion, etc. The LIC promises to settle survival claims before the due date and death claims within 30 days. The New Delhi Municipal Corporation (NDMC) had committed to fill all potholes within one day, replace defective water meters within 15 days, attend to leakage in main water pipes within 48 hours, and so on. These charters have to be known by and taken seriously by every employee. The specifications have to be treated as outer limits and sought to be improved upon continuously, if the perceptions of quality are to be sustained.

Commitments made in these charters will be believed if there is also an assurance to compensate the customer in the event of failure to comply. The charter then assumes the nature of a guarantee. Several service organisations, including hospitals are trying to offer such guarantees. One simple compensation is to refund the money collected for the service. The guarantees have to be quantifiable, unconditional and related to customer need. The penalties or compensations should be easy to invoke and easy to collect. Guarantees are possible only if the relevant variables are controllable. In the case of services, the role required to be played by the customer and co-customers may introduce variables, which are beyond the control of the service provider. Charters and guarantees thus, have the effect of bringing about better focus on the parameters of services.

❑ *Handling Complaints* ❑

A customer has a grievance when he does not get what he thinks he is entitled to get. A grievance may also be recorded when he witnesses some other customer's dissatisfaction as for example, when he hears the cashier and a customer arguing loudly about the correctness of the bill. In this case, the facts may also not be known, but the assumptions would be to the detriment of the service provider.

A grievance has to be taken seriously because

- it means that quality is not perceived as satisfactory,
- it gives clues as to what is going wrong,
- it indicates what customers expect,
- otherwise customers may be lost.

A grievance is an opportunity to examine and rectify errors in the system or process. A grievance has to be handled in a manner that: (*a*) the person aggrieved feels good at the end of it (this is called recovery); and (*b*) there is improvement in the system/process. A complainant's satisfaction depends on how he perceives

- distributive justice: referring to the equity in the final resolution or outcome,
- procedural justice: referring to the manner (speed, flexibility) in which the grievance has been handled and the extent to which the complainant is involved in the process, and
- interactional justice: referring to the explanations given, honesty and politeness, the sincerity of the effort, the attitude of the persons concerned, the empathy shown, etc.

When a customer voluntarily expresses his grievance, it is a complaint. A complaint is an accusation and a demand for redress. Those who complain may be about five per cent of those with grievances. The rest just decide that the provider of the service is unlikely to bother and is unworthy of further patronage. They may also tell their acquaintances about it. Those who tell their acquaintances about their grievances far outnumber those who talk about their satisfactory experiences. The memory of adverse experiences lasts much longer than of satisfactory experiences, unless the latter are of the WOW level. Adverse experiences also wipe out memories of the earlier satisfactory ones.

When a grievance is attended to quickly and taken seriously, there is satisfaction which, in turn, wipes out the memory of the adverse experience. The adverse experience is then treated as an aberration and forgotten. The story in the box below is an example of this kind.

> The dinner ordered at 9 p.m. and expected to be delivered at 9.30 did not arrive till 10 p.m. When contacted, the caterer expressed surprise, as he had sent it half an hour earlier. It arrived at 10.30 p.m. The food was cold and wet as it was a rainy night. The host shouted at the caterer and threatened to return the food, but he did not do so as the food was necessary for the guests. Then, three days later, the host received from the caterer a supply of food, which was a repeat of the earlier order and with a lengthy letter of apology, explaining what happened on that night (cycle puncture). The letter was signed by the manager of the caterer and all the twelve employees.

A customer's grievance may not be valid. He could have, by his own actions, created the situation. There is no point in establishing the fault on his part. A grievance should neither be denied nor ignored. An explanation about the circumstances, may mollify others who are witness to the incident, but not the aggrieved. An admission of error and doing something to avoid repetition is likely to be more satisfactory. A compensation, if possible, to offset the adverse consequences, will go a long way to convey that the error is genuinely abnormal and regretted.

Mark McCormack, Chairman of the International Management Group, has an interesting story of an order for flowers every month being repeatedly delivered at the wrong address. Every month, when the error was pointed out there would be an apology, an assurance of the correction having been noted and a second bouquet sent to the right address. For twelve months he got double the number of bouquets and twelve apologies and twelve assurances, without correction. *Repeated expressions of regret and compensation do not satisfy.*

Since grievances matter and because grievances are not voluntarily articulated, many service providers seek to find out and hear grievances. Customers may refrain from sharp comments even when asked for. They do not want to 'blame' or harm somebody, who may be taken to task. The hospital superintendent who goes round all the wards every morning asking how patients feel, generally receives a smile and 'fine' as responses. Response forms with scalar ratings give overall impressions, but are not detailed enough to identify the elements that need correction. Customers would be willing to express themselves, if they perceive that the management is keen to improve the quality of services and genuinely wants to know the deficiencies. They will talk when they are met during periods when they are not engaged otherwise. They can be met during or after they have used the service. Airline passengers can be met when they are waiting for the baggages. Rail passengers can be met even while they are travelling. In educational institutions, neither the parents nor students are good enough. The former may not know and the latter may not tell. Past students are excellent for feedback.

A hospital arranged to meet discharged patients at their homes after two or three weeks and enquire about

- progress since discharge,
- experience while in hospital.

The questions about experience were:

- did they get enough information about their sickness and the course of treatment?
- did they feel cared for or were treated as an intrusion?
- did the conditions/behaviours of the other patients disturb them?
- how good was cleanliness, nursing, other attendants?
- how convenient, or not, were admission and discharge formalities?

A well-known Japanese motor cycle manufacture surveyed those who had bought motor cycles, of any make, one year earlier. The survey included items on how customers were handled by dealers and evaluation of quality of repair work. Legend has it that Mr Brij Mohan Lall Munjal of Hero Cycles used to sit in the cycle repair shops and listen to the conversations there, to find out the experience of owners of bicycles, what they wanted, what they were happy about and what they were not happy about.

Customers are not inclined to complain. They are however, not averse to helping with information for correction and improvement. Contacts made after the service had been experienced, like the hospital did, has the flavour of asking for help to improve.

Several organisations have created separate cells for handling grievances. Some have practices that are helpful; not so in other cases. Some of the unhelpful practices are:

- A public notice giving the names of complaints officers, arranged in a hierarchy, and the specific dates and specific times when they will receive complaints. Complaints cannot wait for the convenience of the provider to be attended to. If it can wait, the complaint is not serious. A notice like this has the message that the customer's problem is less important than the convenience of the organisation. There is a suggestion that the system is bureaucratic. The rigidity of a bureaucratic system/procedure is not conducive to handle complaints.
- Insistence on the complaint being in writing. Writing is necessary to prove or establish fault. Neither is a complaint nor its redressal, ever founded in writing. They are in actions. Proving fault is not the important thing to do. Identifying fault is the important thing, which does not need written documentation.
- The emphasis is on complaints received and complaints disposed of. Disposal may mean anything from mere acknowledgment, reference to someone else for verification and reporting, issuing a warning to someone, sending a letter of apology, explaining the relevant rules or procedures or law, to closing the matter because 'the complainant did not personally appear at the enquiry'. Disposal is real only when there is recovery as well as correction.

Helpful practices are of the following kinds:

- Treating a complaint as a gold mine from which the organisation can benefit a lot.
- Grievances are noticed even before it becomes a formal complaint. The body language of the customer will show the developing adverse experience.
- Complaints are received on dedicated telephone lines, paid for by the organisation.
- Complaints are processed keeping in mind: (*a*) the need to 'recover' the complainant; and (*b*) the need to improve the system, not punish some one.

'Recovery' means getting the complainant's loyalty back. Recovery can be made via apology, empathy, urgent reinstatement, symbolic atonement and/or follow up. The first two can be done in all cases, but not the other three. The faster the recovery action, the more its effectiveness. Motor car manufacturers were reputed to be indifferent to complaints till the 1960s and the 1970s. The growth of competition from Japan and the growth of the consumer movement have changed these attitudes. When serious complaints are received, the whole range of cars in the market may be withdrawn and parts replaced.

Sometimes complainants are unhappy with the response of the service provider and seek intervention from third parties like courts of justice and arbitrators, seeking directions for performance and even punitive damages. This situation represents a break in the relationship with the customer. This should be avoided as far as possible, but is not always avoidable.

The Consumer Protection Act, 1986, provides for speedy and inexpensive redressal of grievances, in cases where the services suffer from deficiencies and customers have suffered loss or damage as a result of any unfair practice. Voluntary agencies also exist to assist consumers in exercising their rights, providing them with moral, legal and financial support. The rights of the consumers are being extended and elaborated regularly through case laws. The test of quality of service will be when no customer feels the need to resort to third party intervention.

7 REALISING PEOPLE POTENTIAL

❑ *Most Critical* ❑

Jan Carlzon, President of the Swedish airline, SAS, had this to say in the *Moments of Truth*

> Last year, each one of our 10 million customers came in contact with approximately 5 employees and this contact lasted, on an average, 15 seconds. Thus, SAS is created in the minds of our customers 50 million times a year, 5 seconds at a time. These 50 million 'moments of truth' are the moments that ultimately determine whether SAS will succeed or fail as a company. They are the moments when we must prove to our customers that SAS is their best alternative.

The concept of 'Moment of Truth', has already been explained in earlier chapters. The importance of these moments of truth could not be put more effectively than in the lines quoted above. These moments are created by people who render services. A service is performed during an interaction between a person belonging to the organisation offering the service and a customer. The nature of this interaction decides how satisfactory the service is to the customer. Satisfaction and quality of service, being the outcomes from the interaction, the persons involved in the interaction become the most critical factors in determining the quality of service. Thus, five of the 10 factors identified by Parasuraman et al. (1985) referred to in Chapter 4, relate to people and their behaviour. Rosenbluth International, dealing in travel services, says, that in its priorities, the customer comes first but the employees are more important. Reason: only *WOW employees can deliver WOW services to customers.*

The person in the organisation, who is in direct interface with the customer, contributes to experiences of quality. In service organisations, a very large number of employees are in this interface. They have 'boundary spanning roles'.

Some studies estimate this at about 90 per cent. These include not only those visibly in contact, like the receptionist or the waiter or the messenger (in a courier service), but also those who are not visible, like housekeeping (in hotels), the accounts clerk (whose wrong billing can create problems), the telephone operator, the laboratory assistant (who reports on blood samples), the baggage loader of the airlines, the operator who feeds in data, the mechanic in the garage, the florist whose illegible handwriting may cause a delivery failure, the clerk whose carelessness with the marksheets upset examination results, the lightman who controls the light effects on the stage, the technician who does not notice interference (of sounds) during a broadcast, the one who projects the picture of a dacoit on the TV screen while the news is about a politician, and so on. These are the people who make or mar quality. The quality of service may be evaluated by a customer—perhaps forever—by the interaction he has with just one employee down the line.

❑ *People are Managers* ❑

Studies show that nearly 70 per cent of customers shift patronage because of dissatisfaction with attitudes and behaviour of employees, while only about 15 per cent shift because of dissatisfaction with the tangible aspects of the product. This would mean that employees play a major role in retaining customer loyalty in the service business. Several times, customers walking into a store, walk out without any transaction, because the apparent attitude of the counter salesmen put them off. An employee has the capability, through his behaviour, to make people want to come back or never to come back again. Satisfied customers also generate a lot of referred business through their friends. Every employee contributes directly to the success and the growth of the business. In effect, every employee of a service business, including the messenger who delivers courier packets, is a manager of a business, capable of generating more business. They provide the primary source of competitive advantage.

Several little things add up to a total experience. Any one of them can go wrong. They go wrong, because of one individual not doing it right. This colours the perception of the total experience and is called the weakest link theory. Technology, equipment, systems etc., cannot strengthen these weak points. They may help to circumvent some of the weak points by replacing the people performing those functions, like ATMs in banking. The invisible people who man and maintain these machines cannot be eliminated. Many weak points will remain. The guests of the premium segment rooms in hotels, who are allowed the free use of the business centre and health club services, cannot relish the premium offering, if the persons manning these services are unaware of their identities and entitlements.

Technology, equipment and systems cannot substitute for the intimate recognition that a personal contact may provide. A fully computerised report from a diagnostic centre on one's health, like a computerised astrological read out, does not satisfy. A doctor or an astrologer must read through it, explain the import of what is written and answer some questions. A well-indexed library without a librarian, or a self-service departmental store without shop assistants to help, lack warmth.

❏ *People are Resources* ❏

Organisations normally invest heavily in buildings, equipment and machinery, but not adequately in people. Almost all organisations formally state that people are their most valuable resource. One chief executive had said, rather succinctly, that his most valuable assets walked out of his premises every evening at the close of working hours. *The belief that is formally articulated in the mission statement, is usually, not reflected in practice.*

Expensive equipment and machinery will function only as well as the people who operate them. The more expensive the equipment, the greater is the care and technical skill required to operate them. The external appearances of a building and its internal decor do not provide enough evidence about the quality of the education being imparted within, or the judicial system that it houses.

People with technical skills may not always use these skills at work. It is also not possible for the supervisor/manager to ensure that the skills are used. *People at work use more of their knowledge than their physical skills these days.* This trend is expected to increase as time goes by. It is difficult, almost *impossible, to supervise knowledge work.* The supervisor cannot know, if the operator has identified the problem with the machine, but is pretending ignorance. There have been cases where operators have got the collaborators to modify the designs of equipment, to avoid problems of clogging or heat loss. Some of these changes were very simple and retrospectively, quite obvious, *but needed an employee to notice the need for change.* There have been cases of employees noticing these losses and not bothering about them. The difference can be attributed to the attitude of the persons concerned. However, these attitudes are caused to some extent, perhaps a large extent, by the styles and policies of management. Such attitudes spell disaster in a service business.

People, are, in terms of productive capability, unpredictable as well as potentially infinite (both high and low). A person's capacity can change. Today's typist can be tomorrow's publicity professional. People learn. They create new knowledge. They innovate. They make other resources functional and productive. They also deteriorate, due to changes in values, or attitudes or physical condition. An employee who is dissatisfied or worried, may not apply himself fully at work. If he is angry, he may even use his skills to damage the process. In other words, capabilities of people are not constant. They are variable over vast ranges. Their application at work cannot be taken for granted. *This is one resource that may not only not depreciate, but may appreciate beyond any expectations.*

❏ *People are Product Elements* ❏

In the service business, because of the criticality of the people factor, the adage that people are the most valuable resource, is particularly relevant. The person interacting with the customer, is in a cross-boundary transaction, also called a boundary-spanning role. At that time, he is alone and is also effectively the organisation. If he does not know what to do, or does differently from what the organisation would like him to do in such a situation, he is creating in the mind of the customer, perceptions that do no justice to the organisation. What he does, is what the customer sees as the organisation's offering. *His behaviour is an integral part of the product.*

Standardised procedures do not address this problem adequately. To a barber, every head is different. To a doctor, every patient's appendix is different. To a teacher every class and every student is different. Every guest, every patient, every tourist is different. None of them conform to a standard or average that the rules visualise. The person dealing with a customer has to adjust to this variability. It requires skill, discretion and preparation. It does not help to follow the rule book. Albrecht considers *the rule book as one of the seven sins of the service business,* the other six being apathy, brush-off, coldness, robotism (meaning mechanical behaviour), runaround and condescension.

The computerised reservation system in Mumbai was closed on the 10 January, 1998. The software was being upgraded 'for better service'. On that day, manual systems were put into operation, but only to attend to needs of passengers leaving by trains up to 12 noon on 11th. A person who had booked the train leaving at 7 a.m. on the 12th could not avail of the manual facilities for cancellation. If he had done so, he would have lost Rs 30 per ticket. He could do so only on the 11th and as per the rules, he would lose 25 per cent or Rs 400. When he went to cancel it on the 11th, the 'systems were down'. If he did not cancel the ticket on that day, the cancellation charges would go up to 50 per cent. He pleaded with the local officers to certify on the ticket that he had come to cancel the same, and that he would make a separate claim for a refund later. However, this could not be done, as per the rules. Only the ticket collector on the train was authorised to endorse on the ticket the fact of non-utilisation. Nobody could help beyond stating the rules, the procedure and their helplessness.

At the time of interaction with the customer, the employee is alone. In the course of that interaction, he cannot refer to the rule book or the manual or the superiors for guidance. If he does so, the perception would be that the person is incompetent, not knowledgeable and inadequate. Being required to deal with such a person amounts to a lack of recognition. Placing inadequate people on the front line suggests a lack of concern for the customer, as well as the inability to cope. There is an immediate loss of credibility and quality. There is then a felt need to check whether whatever the person does is to be accepted as final or needs to be got confirmed from someone else. Several services, are fiduciary in nature. Examples are advisory services in investments, technology or projects; agencies like in insurance, banking or travel. Credibility or trustworthiness, in the perception of the customer, is crucial. The person in the boundary spanning role—and he alone—strengthens or erodes this.

For all these reasons, people at customer contact points must be aware of not only what the company's policies are, but also why they are so. The rationale is important to be able to use discretion. It therefore follows that new entrants to the organisation should not be placed at points of contact with customers, without proper training and should, even then, be watched closely by a senior, to make sure that his actions are acceptable and consistent with policy. This would apply even if the new person joining has had a lot of experience in a similar business. The reason is that organisational strategies and methods differ between organisations. Every hotel handles its guests and reservations differently. Couriers have varying practices. Within nationalised banks, there are differences in customer service. There are differences even between different branches of the same bank. One bank dishonours checks for minor discrepancies, while another clears the cheque and requests the account holder to visit the bank and rectify the defect quickly. Freedom and discretion allowed to the employees to differ between organisations. These differences affect the services experienced by the customer and are visible in the behaviours of people and are elements of the service product.

❏ *Releasing Potential* ❏

People may not exercise freedom and discretion at work, even if given to them. Reasons would vary from individual attitudes, fears, aptitudes etc., to organisational practices. The most common organisational practice that militates against the use of discretion, is that 'mistakes' made thereby are fraught with unpleasant consequences, including the accusation of malafides. The potentials remain suppressed. *Organisations that use 'mistakes' to learn and to teach, are the ones in which the capabilities of people are released.*

Peter Singe of the Masachusetts Institute of Technology suggests that command and control will have to give way to increased learning, which is creating and sharing new knowledge. Instead of compliance, people will have to be committed using imagination, courage, patience and perseverance. The challenge to management is to harness the intelligence and spirit of people at all levels.

As more freedom is given down the line, and those freedoms are exercised, the organisation will become more people-dependent and sensitive to customer needs. There will be less rigidity of structure and control. Time is released at a rapid rate, meaning that productive work would be happening faster. People happen to work more effectively in their own work area, instead of cross-checking other people's work or decisions. The gap between 'What I do?' and 'What I can do?' will reduce.

The potential for productive use of discretion will not be released, if people

- are not aware of company's goals and purposes,
- do not get feedback on results and progress,
- receive feedback about weaknesses and see them as opportunities for growth,
- fear that concerns and personal goals shared with superiors may be used against them.

Dr A.P.J. Abdul Kalam, in his book *Wings of Fire*, describes his experiences in these words.

The diameters were quite different and to attain interchangeability, some hard innovations were required. I wondered where I should start. I decided to look around for solutions among my colleagues. I also started asking and listening to anyone who showed the slightest promise. Some of my friends cautioned me on my naivete. I made it an unfailing routine to make notes on individual suggestions. ... We had achieved in a year's time what our counterparts in Europe could barely manage in three years. Our plus point was that each of us worked with those below and above in the hierarchy. I made it a point to have the team meet at least once every week. Though it took up time and energy, I considered it essential.

❑ *Necessary Skills* ❑

All employees in service organisations, without exception, need customer relationship skills. They must

- have an inclination to be of help to others,
- have the skills of pleasing people,
- find pleasure in satisfying customers,
- ensure that correct information is given to customers,
- not try to cover up ignorance with false information,
- feel committed to organisation's interests.

These are the attitudes and skills that need to be reinforced in all man-management activities like

- selection of people,
- training,
- reward systems,
- internal communication,
- other HR practices.

❑ *Selection* ❑

Employers often prefer candidates who have had prior experience in similar positions. It is assumed that they would have already acquired the technical skills to do the job. What one learns in a job is not only the technical competencies but also the culture of the organisation in which the job is done. Learning creates a paradigm, a pattern, which includes the appropriate behaviours in different situations. The appropriateness of behaviour will vary between organisations, depending on the ways in which they have chosen to run the business. There could be differences in the concern for customers, for quality, for people, for ethics and propriety and so on. Therefore, the learning acquired in one organisation may not be fully appropriate for another organisation with a different culture. *If the earlier learning is not 'unlearnt', there could be a hindrance.*

Between technical skills and social skills like the tendency to help, pleasing manners and empathy, the former are easier to instil in a training class. The latter are acquired during experiences not limited to one's work and become part of one's personality. Some people have a tendency to keep smiling and appear cheerful all the time and some others always look glum and severe. Those who are off-beat in their thinking and behaviour may be better suited for customer care, than those who tend to conform without question or those who desist from expressing themselves, for whatever reason. One who prefers solitude and looks upon others as an intrusion upon his concentration or tranquility, will not be suitable for jobs that require being nice to others and sensitive to their feelings. These habits are difficult to change. It is better to focus on social skills more than on technical skills, while making selections. One must look for those who

- have high energy levels,
- are genuinely interested in others,
- possess a mature entrepreneurial instinct that makes them go that extra mile for customer satisfaction,
- have good work habits, in terms of follow through on commitments,
- have an eye for detail,
- are flexible and adaptable to changing conditions, environment, situations and people,
- have the ability to identify problems and make prompt high-quality, on-the-spot decisions,
- can prioritise tasks, set objectives and work towards their completion on time,
- do not shirk doing what they should, for fear of being found fault with,
- can express clearly and effectively without hurting other's feelings,
- can establish eye-contact,
- maintain a pleasant, friendly expression,
- can make others feel important,
- can form accurate impressions about people and their needs, by observing body language,
- listen.

These are best judged during interviews, group discussions, role plays, in-basket and other simulation exercises.

❑ *Training* ❑

Training in the service business has to focus heavily on interpersonal and social skills, on listening, on pleasing and not hurting, on understanding body language, on providing comfort, on sensitivity to feelings, anxieties and fears of others. These requirements have to be strengthened and focussed on repeatedly.

A person's behaviour is the outcome of a number of factors, which include his beliefs, attitudes, assumptions, values and expectations, forming paradigms or patterns of thoughts. Any change in behaviour will happen only when some of these paradigms change. That will happen when part of the past learning is replaced by something new. *Unlearning is invariably necessary before change in behaviour can occur.*

Behaviour occurs in a context. A person is rude or polite in a particular situation. Some justification for that behaviour may be found in the situation itself. Perhaps the customer himself has provoked the resultant behaviour of the employee. It is possible that the employee's behaviour can be the cause of the other's behaviour, pleasant or unpleasant. It can even reduce the intensity of the unpleasantness of the other's behaviour. Employees in service organisations must understand these dynamics and acquire skills in regulating one's own, and influencing the other's, behaviour. Cognitive understanding is not enough. There should be the opportunity to practice, so that internalisation may take place.

The training should focus on not only generalities of interpersonal dynamics, but also specifically on the organisation's practices. For example, the sentries at the gates to the airfield should know how to check the bona fides of passengers coming out after landing in a chartered flight. He cannot ask them for boarding cards. The liftman in a hospital has to be able to identify the meaning and significance of various passes that are issued by the departments, failing which he might stop someone authorised to go in, and create a problem. The gatekeeper should be able to distinguish between a genuine gate pass and a fake piece of paper. Security personnel in offices, who insist on inspecting the bags of visitors must be able to identify, at least suspect objectionable material. People must be familiar with the signals for specific emergencies, their roles at those times, where and how the necessities could be accessed and so on. Regular drills may be necessary.

It is said that it takes four years of training to become a butler to an English gentleman, which includes what not to do (shake hands with a guest, challenge the master's opinion, get familiar, drink during work, address by name) and what to do (acknowledge with 'Certainly, Sir', or 'No problem, Sir', look a lady only in her eyes, bow just a little), how to do things (fold the newspaper without crushing it, serving the dish, pouring the wine without frothing, opening the champagne bottle) and so on. The details relevant for excellent customer service cannot be much simpler in any organisation. Apart from simple matters like dress codes, remaining smiling, controlling voice levels, saying 'thank you', and greeting heartily, training should also focus on the advantages, the risks and the precautions relating to the facilities on offer. The American Hotels and Motels Association have, in collaboration with Master Card International, developed extensive training programmes, to cover every aspect of hotel operations like, front desk and Guest Room Exceptional Attitude Training (GREAT). People will conform to rules and procedures, adhere to and enforce instructions religiously, and explain their actions to customers more satisfactorily, if they knew the rationale and the spirit behind, instead of only the letter of the law.

The training function has to arrange to collect relevant details from the variety of operations in the particular organisation and use it in the curricula. This requires observation and study of every detail that causes satisfaction as well as dissatisfaction. The collection of details will have to be the job of everyone who is in contact with customers and that means, in a service business, almost everybody. Employees must be sharp enough to observe customer reactions and to report the same to seniors, without fear that it may affect the evaluation of their own work. Complaints provide a valuable source to identify such details. Documentation is important to enable better training and also better operations.

Top managements tend to neglect training when business is good. Training cannot be limited to 'slack time'. A continually healthy bottom line is an opiate that induces complacency. This is risky. Customers are becoming more aware, more sophisticated, more demanding. Their loyalties cannot be taken for granted. A new offering from a new entrant or existing competitor may cause a switch in patronage. Even the world's biggest computer maker, IBM, learnt this at a heavy cost of $5 billion, the loss that it made in 1992.

Spain's Banco Bilbao Vizcaya was spending the equivalent of US$70 million to put through their 23,000 employees over 1,75,000 hours of training to be ready for the Euro currency effective 1 January 1999. The Munich-based Allianz spent the equivalent of US$24 million to provide 342 hours of extra employee time to prepare itself for Euro conversion. Problems involved checking old currency notes for authenticity before collecting them for destruction, identifying the Europe wide stock indices that will become global benchmarks, and avoiding the tiny system bug which could otherwise wreak havoc.

There has always been the problem of measuring the effectiveness of training. There is difficulty in establishing that any change that may have happened is because of training. The problem is as simple as that the student's learning may not be what the teacher has taught. The Japanese have taken the view that training is like taking in food or regular exercise. That is assumed to be necessary for the sustenance of a healthy body and healthy mind. *Training is a long-term investment, not a cost.* Another view is that the benefit must be established to determine both direction and continuance. In some functions, where the training is directly aimed at operational skills, the work outputs before and after training may indicate changes and effectiveness. Where output is clearly measurable and attributable to a person, and not a group of persons, as in the case of salesmen, even attitudinal changes can be observed by comparing the performances of trained people with the performances of those who had not been trained.

❑ *Reward Systems* ❑

Anything that gives pleasure or satisfaction is a reward. The opposite is a punishment. A punishment gives pain or denies pleasure. Punishment is given when: (*a*) a person is given something that he does not want; or (*b*) something that he wants is withheld. Theories on motivation suggest that people act in order to get pleasure or satisfaction and in order to avoid pain or dissatisfaction. They *seek rewards and avoid punishments.*

This is so even in the traditional theories on motivation, which emphasised on doing one's duty and serving others. 'Do your duty and seek not advantage for yourself', is the famous dictum in the *Gita*. This dictum is validated by the promise of the highest reward, namely, the grace of God and ultimate bliss and happiness, even one's elevation in the social strata.

All behaviour is goal directed. The goals are determined by the availability of rewards or punishments. Therefore, reward systems are strong influences on employee behaviour. Systems should be such that the desirable or preferred behaviour attract rewards and undesirable behaviour attract punishment. Inappropriate systems misdirect the energies of people. There is the story of a wealthy businessman who instructed his secretary to tip the mail boy everytime he brought in the letters, discovering later that the letters were being delivered one at a time. Wages paid by the hour may cause delays in output. Incentives related to quantity of output may lead to neglect of quality. When salesmen are honoured and decorated at annual sales meets regularly, and those in the service functions (maintenance, repairs, etc.) are not, the message is that the customer is important only till he buys. When employees perceive that the exercise of discretion is liable to be questioned by the senior (this causes embarrassment and discomfort), the tendency will be to avoid all decisions and 'delegate upwards'. There are several subtle and not-very-subtle ways of doing so.

That which provides satisfaction, is not the same for all individuals. Money generally is, but not always. There are people, even at lower levels, who refuse to sit overtime, because they want to get back to their families or because of some other social or religious activities that interest them. Some people suffer pain willingly in order to achieve something more laudable. *Satyagrahis* are examples. Sadists love cruelty. Some people invite disciplinary actions because that is evidence of one's non-conformist 'independent' identity and eligibility for union leadership. An opportunity to represent the company at an important meeting, or a holiday cruise, may be valuable rewards to some, but not to all.

In one company, employees are asked to identify their personal objectives. They are then guided as to how they can obtain those objectives through the reward system, which is adjusted to deliver these needs. The individual objectives and the targets at work correspond.

The value of a reward increases according to: (*a*) cost; (*b*) exclusiveness; and (*c*) visibility. A prize worth Rs 1,000 has more value than a prize worth Rs 200. A gold medal has more value than a mention in the company bulletin. A paragraph of mention is better than a line. To be honoured in public is better than to be appreciated through a letter. A dinner with the chairman is better than a dinner with the manager. A dinner with the chairman sitting in the same table in a party in a posh hotel, is better than a dinner in the guesthouse.

Some published studies indicate that employee dissatisfactions are generally more marked in the areas of compensation, performance appraisal and development (including training), while satisfaction levels are not low in areas of team work, morale and change orientation. Such studies mislead, if consequently, attention is directed towards correction in the areas of apparently high dissatisfaction, because no system or practice in respect of compensation and performance appraisal can become acceptable to the majority of employees. Under any system of appraisal, half the people will be below average. Team work, morale and change orientation are not identified as unsatisfactory, even if they are really so, because these are seen to reflect employee behaviour and attitudes rather than managerial practices. These areas provide much more scope for effective intervention by management and the improvement will influence the perception about compensation and appraisals.

❑ *Empowering* ❑

An organisation that emphasises customer service, needs people who, while rendering service at the front line, use discretion and take initiative, out of concern for the customer's satisfaction. Employees must look for opportunities to satisfy customers. The person at the front line will do so, only if he feels 'empowered' to do so.

Empowerment will not occur through a formal delegation of authority. A person may not exercise authority delegated to him, if he does not feel empowered. A peon who takes the responsibility to direct the fireman in a burning office, to areas housing the most important documents, is acting without formal authority. He does so, because he has a sense of dedication, feels it is his duty to save the organisation as much as possible and feels that he is doing the right thing by directing the fireman. He feels empowered. The security guard, who, noticing a fire in the conveyor belt carrying coal from the ship to the dump, cut the belt to isolate the fire, was also acting similarly, without formal authority, but out of a feeling of 'That is my job'.

Those who do not feel empowered, do not challenge or attempt to modify the proposals of others, even when aware of the need to modify. They do not pass on information that could be important and relevant for decision making, because they do not see it as their job. They allow opportunities to pass by. A comment made by a customer on a matter concerning the service being performed at that time, may be ignored by one employee, while another may listen to it carefully and pick up further details. This could make all the difference between a satisfied and a dissatisfied customer, between obtaining or losing valuable feedback on customer perceptions. A missed opportunity and its cost will never be reflected in the accounting data or the output from the management information systems. Investigations conducted after the explosion of the NASA space vehicle soon after take-off in 1985, showed that some of the technicians had noticed a faulty component, but never reported it. This would happen if there is no empowerment.

An empowered employee focusses on results. He is not inhibited by formalities of position, authority or function. He does not consider himself bound by rules and procedures. He believes that the organisation expects him to be aware of the ends to be achieved and to act in furtherance thereof. He 'sees' constraints, but does not feel prevented thereby from doing what needs to be done. Instead, he seeks ways to overcome, not subvert, the constraints. He believes that the organisation will not find fault with him, if he does something new or unusual. On the contrary, he believes that the organisation expects him to do what he is about to do, to take the initiative and ensure that the customer's needs are met. He believes that if he hesitated and the customer turned sour, he would have let the organisation down.

An empowered employee will make demands on management. He may dislike conforming to rules and procedures, which, in his view, restrict his capacity to perform. He is likely to challenge company policies at meetings with seniors. If he is at that time, characterised as arrogant, rebellious or cantankerous, he may tend to conform and feel less empowered. If the initiatives taken and the well-intentioned efforts do not work out as planned, there will have to be tolerance and praise for the effort. On the contrary, if a reprimand follows, empowerment stops.

Empowered employees find solutions to problems, while others will find a problem in every solution. Empowered employees say 'It is difficult, but it is possible' and try, while others will say 'It is possible, but it is difficult' and desist.

It is difficult to monitor the behaviour of empowered employees. They need, *and must be given, autonomy at work.* The decision-making authority must rest with them. They do not operate under the reflected glory of the bosses. The only way to control their behaviour at work is from within themselves. They need to be coached on values and philosophy of the company. An officer posted at the state headquarters to maintain contact with senior government officials resigned his job when he got a letter from the President expressing displeasure at his inability to get certain clearances. He did not withdraw till the Chairman intervened. His point was that the President should have checked with him before taking him to task in writing.

Autonomy should have strong linkages with management systems and work culture. Apart from mutual trust, the supportive elements for empowerment are consultative and participative decision making, cross-functional teams and transparent communications.

The two cases in the box below are examples of empowered employees who were not observing the rules, but did create near to WOW experiences.

> *Case 1.* The airline reservation office located within a five-star hotel, was manned by just a single assistant. He was unable to confirm the booking asked for, because the 'system was down'. He told the client that he had checked that particular flight about half an hour back, that there was enough accommodation on it and that he would issue the ticket as soon as the system revived. After nearly 45 minutes, when the system continued to be 'down',

the assistant issued a confirmed ticket without the PNR number, and told the client that he would make the necessary entries in the computer as soon as it revived.

Case 2. A passenger with a confirmed ticket on an early morning flight from Ahmedabad to Mumbai, could reach Ahmedabad only by 3.30 p.m. because the train by which he was travelling to Ahmedabad from upcountry was marooned in the floods at night. He reached Ahmedabad travelling by special buses arranged by the railways. When he went to the airlines reservation office in town, the assistant wanted to know whether there was any certificate from the railways to confirm these events. There was none. He was then told that, as per the rules, he had to be treated as a 'no show' and there would be no refund on the earlier ticket. He could buy a fresh ticket for the evening flights, both of which were late, and fully booked. He could take his chances at the airport. He agreed. The assistant then endorsed the morning ticket for the evening flights (without any extra charge) and told him to go to the airport immediately and enter his name among the waitlisted passengers. When he reached the airport after about 40 minutes, he found that his name was already among the waitlisted passengers. Apparently the assistant in the office had called up and entered his name in the list.

❏ *Appraisals* ❏

Almost all organisations have systems for the appraisal of employees. Rewards, by way of increments and promotions are given on the basis of these appraisals. Experience shows that the rewards generate more dissatisfaction than satisfaction. This is inherent in the system of appraisals. Managers who administer these systems acknowledge these outcomes, but persist in continuing with the existing systems because they do not see any alternatives and also cannot visualise a situation without assessments of performance. Attempts are on to make the system more reliable, through 360 degree and balanced score cards, with varying degrees of effectiveness.

The problems are many. Any text book on HRD will highlight the problems in appraisal systems. Appraisals are unavoidably subjective, being opinions and performance are complex, being comprised of several elements. Therefore, they are not reliable measures of performance of an employee's contribution to work. If output is a criterion for assessment of performance, the relevant factor may be the number of calls attended in a call center. There is a conflict here between satisfying a customer, whatever time it takes, and the need to record that a higher number of calls had been attended to. The time taken on a call depends on the caller as well. Some callers keep repeating questions. Others get to the point very quickly. Another method used to evaluate employee's ways with customers is to use dummy customers. This one-time contact cannot be a good sample of the work over a period of time.

❏ *Values and Philosophy* ❏

Repeated studies have shown that executives consider that the management of people, values and culture are the most important areas for the future. This was related to freedom and autonomy for the employees. Many Indian organisations also practice this.

Employees represent the organisation while they interact with customers. Customers therefore, expect to and are also entitled to receive the same treatment, regardless of which individual employee is interacting with them. The behaviour of employees has to be consistent and uniform. The traditional method to ensure consistency and uniformity of behaviour was to standardise working procedures and operating rules. Employees were required to comply. The appropriateness of behaviour naturally came from one's knowledge of the rules and understanding of their import. Behaviour will automatically conform to expectations if the rationale for the rules is known to the person concerned and internalised by him. *The rationale for the rules flow from the values and philosophy of the organisation.* When values and philosophy are shared, the emerging behaviour will tend to be appropriate to the ends determined by those values and philosophy. The use of discretion and judgement will be as they should be, consistent with the policies of the organisation.

Members of a community quite easily and naturally conform to the accepted norms of the behaviour of that community. The norms are absorbed and internalised during existence in that community. Behaviour with regard to monogamy, polygamy, obedience to the law, not coveting the other's possessions, acceptance of one's station in life, being decently dressed, being respectful to elders, looking after one's parents, the queue systems—in fact, the whole range of personal, public and social proprieties are observed, not because there are relevant laws with prescribed penalties. The proprieties emerge from values and are different from legalities, which emerge from the law. Laws, to be effective, have to prescribe punishments for transgression. Fear of punishment is not as effective as the strength of one's voice from within, which is what 'values' does. *Control of behaviour is much more effective through values than through rules.*

In the case of companies that are operating internationally, the issue of values and culture has a more complicated dimension. There are significant variations between the cultures of different countries. The Japanese, for example, get offended when asked probing questions. It is not polite to ask 'Why'. The Saudi Arabians do not like to be handed over a document with the left hand. Some people expect to be addressed with formality and are very concerned with the recognition of status and hierarchy. They resent attempts at familiarity. In some societies, people are very particular about adhering to agreed time schedules and do not wait even for five minutes after the appointed time. To be late and to keep others waiting is considered a sign of importance in some communities. Such differences in social behaviour and taboos have to be understood and respected. The company's values and practices have to adjust taking note of the values of the people with whom it is working.

Values are basic fundamental standards of right and wrong which a person holds and which guide his thought processes and actions. In business, they would relate to the business environment, the market, the organisation, the ways to establish a place for oneself in the customer's mind, the importance to be given to participative and consensus building management styles, to relationships with suppliers, concern for socially relevant issues, for safety, for quality, and so on.

If the management believes in certain values or philosophy, and wants their employees to absorb them, then all actions and decisions have to be consistent with those values and philosophy. *Senior management must be seen to practise it.* If there is any difference between action and preaching, the messages from the action prevail. Values and philosophy are clarified—both reinforcement and denial—not by formal statements of policy, but by the behaviour within the community. If corruption is rampant, it cannot be said that community has a value that condemns corruption. Between (*a*) preaching for a clean system; (*b*) actions of the departments that seek to detect and punish the corrupt; and (*c*) the practice of corruption, members observe, perceive and understand, what the operating philosophy is.

Action follows thinking which, in turn, is moulded by words and talk. Language of ownership and property often mislead. Shareholders do not own companies or employees. A public company is a community, not owned by anybody. It has responsibility to all citizens who have rights. Value to shareholder does not necessarily provide customer focus. So also, customer focus and economies in expenditure could be in conflict. A company which insists on a quick response to the customer's needs is not consistent, when it pulls up an employee for having taken a taxi to visit a client in a remote location.

One cannot be arrogant and yet be considerate to and respectful for others. Humility helps in building trust and understanding, with the other customers, colleagues or even bosses. Managers who are impolite and disrespectful to their staff cannot expect the staff to be polite and respectful to customers. One is not likely to listen to others, unless one is listened to by others. If toilets meant for customers are kept clean and aromatic, while toilets used by staff are dirty, the message is clear. It is said that people do unto others as others do unto them, not as they *would* others do unto them. *Employees tend to treat customers as they are treated by their managers.*

There are organisations in which

- figures and data on achievements are cooked up,
- pleasing bosses is more important than pleasing customers,
- status symbols like the size of rooms, shape of the chair, quality of visiting cards and similar other peripherals are more important than the substantial characteristics of work,
- adherence to completion of paperwork is more important than what is done in the field,
- conformity to budget limits are more important than results,
- time taken in an action is more important than the cost of that action,
- getting prior approval is more important than the nature of the proposed action.

These are manifestations of prevalent values. Formal statements may not support these. Sometimes certain practices develop, contrary to the stated philosophies of the organisation. If they are allowed to continue unnoticed and uncorrected, employees learn the wrong values. Their behaviour will then become counterproductive.

❏ *Auditing Values* ❏

How can these aberrations be noticed? One is to have a regular audit of all practices and decisions from time to time. Much simpler and more effective is for managers to spend time at contact level operations. The Chairman of Avis drives cars himself. J.R.D. Tata, when he was the chairman of Air-India, used to be in close touch with the passengers and cabin crew during flights. Senior executives in hotels spend time in the lobbies and the restaurants, watching what is going on and talking to customers. These are all variations of the basic principle of Management by Walking Around (MBWA). This is particularly important in service industries, because the production takes place at the interaction and cannot be checked for quality, either before or after or somewhere else. The company's values and philosophy have to be operative at the front line during these interactions.

Some indication of the values being upheld by employees will be available from the conversations in the canteen, for example. What are they saying to each other about supervision? How do they talk to each other, particularly if they are from other departments? With understanding or with contempt? What do they say about winners and losers? Do they think it is safe to make mistakes or to take risks? How much scope do they think they have, to make suggestions for improvements? What do they say about the trustworthiness of the bosses? What do they understand about the ways to get rewards?

The Customer Service Index (CSI) can be an audit mechanism. The CSI can be built on factors that reflect values. If the CSI is widely communicated and also used to reward employees, the values would be strengthened.

❏ *Getting Commitment* ❏

A committed employee is one who feels a sense of bonding to the organisation; a sense of belongingness. Committed employees contribute more usefully and productively towards achieving corporate objectives.

Commitment is not the same as empowerment. Empowered employees are committed employees, but an employee can remain very committed, even if he is not empowered. Loyal servants are committed but not empowered. They may do nothing without checking for the approval of the senior. They observe the rules and commands scrupulously, even if they do not agree. They take initiatives only to the extent of pleasing the senior. Customer (third party) satisfaction is not their concern.

Committed employees value their association with the organisation. They will not harm the organisation. They would be diligent, even if not very enthusiastic, like children at studies, committed, but not necessarily enthusiastic, about having to study.

Commitment may have three components:

- *Affective,* because of emotional attachment to the organisation caused by personal characteristics and work experience, giving feelings of comfort and '*want*' to continue, with pleasure.
- *Compulsive* caused by perceived lack of alternatives and perhaps linkages (of investment or bonds) which could be broken only at unacceptable cost, having the pressure to '*have*' to continue, with some sense of pain.
- *Normative,* caused by a sense of obligation to continue as a result of socialisation prior to and during entry into organisation, giving a sense of '*ought*' to continue.

Of these, the affective component provides the strongest influence on commitment. The others are relatively more fragile.

Commitment increases when employees are assigned responsibilities and not merely duties. This responsibility is for getting results. In some organisations, the 'responsibility' is fixed when something goes wrong, to find out who is to be punished. The word 'responsibility' is also often misunderstood to mean 'accountability', which is nothing more than the obligation to explain one's actions and decisions to seniors, a factor of reporting relationship. There can be no responsibility without some authority, to use discretion and make decisions. *Tight controls, rigid procedures and very close supervision tend to reduce responsibility and therefore, commitment.*

Employees who are not committed

- do not concentrate on their work,
- remain absent from work stations,
- go through the motions of work in a routine manner,
- are not surprised or perturbed when things go wrong,
- take no intitiative to satisfy customer grievances,
- have ready excuses for failures,
- blame others for things going wrong,
- are cynical about company policies, values and philosophy,
- join with customers in complaining about management.

Commitment of employees tends to increase when

- they are informed of the company's successes, future programmes, etc.,
- they are invited to attend important corporate functions, like celebrations or launches,
- they are aware of company's policies so that they do not get embarassed before customers,
- they are listened to.

Commitment becomes less when employees become aware of company's activities only through rumours, press, etc., when they are not informed by the company, when the trade and media are invited for functions but not the employees, the message is that in the top management's view the employees are not an integral part of the organisation. It is necessary to have organisational support for one to do a job well. For example, the telephone operator has to know when departments or individuals shift from one cabin/space to another. The duty officer at the airport has to be informed of the options that can be offered to passengers, when flights are cancelled. When such support does not become available and the employee feels constrained in his attempts to perform, his commitment reduces.

❏ *Suggestions from Employees* ❏

Problems and defects in the operational systems are noticed by almost all employees. Those at the work spot know, probably more than anybody else, how things are working. They notice problems earlier than senior managers. They notice, for example, that (in self-service stores) the normal practice of stacking heavy items in the bottom-most shelf is not the best arrangement for customer convenience, as it is difficult to bend and pick up heavy items from below. They know that rubber stamps on standard letters are hastily done and not legible. They know that jobs given out on contract are badly executed, because of the emphasis on numbers to be completed. None of these can be known to the supervisors or managers, unless pointed out to them by the employees who know. The MD may not know that his decision had effectively reversed the impact of instructions sent earlier by the head of a department and several consequent actions. Uncommitted employees remain indifferent to such problems. Committed employees are prompted to find solutions. Everybody has the ability to think about problems and to make suggestions, but not all may make them. There are a number of organisations with suggestion programmes, offering attractive incentives. Not all of them receive suggestions. The failure is not with the thinking ability of employees, but with the way the company manages suggestions.

Making suggestions is not the business of top management alone. It is of all employees. If all of them do not get involved in making suggestions for improvement, there is a big loss of opportunity. Clearly the commitment is poor and that should be a matter of concern for management. Employees, in order to make suggestions, must feel that

- top management is keen to receive suggestions,

- suggestions are taken seriously and processed quickly,
- they will be asked to explain before someone discards the suggestion as worthless.

If suggestions are processed in routine through various levels in the hierarchy, without any sense of expedition and the employee concerned does not get any information as to how his suggestion has been viewed, the message is that the management is really not serious about improvements. In one company, all suggestions received in a day, about a 100 on the average, are typed next morning and distributed to all employees. Someone might like to build on these ideas. Techniques are available to encourage employees to come up with ideas. In one company, cards are kept at convenient spots with the heading 'How do we do?' Anybody can note down his comments, which may be either his own (new) or an addition to an earlier comment. An organisation announced an elaborate scheme whereby branch officials would scrutinise suggestions received by them and forward 'the best three' suggestions to the divisional office, where after some further scrutiny, 'the best three' would be sent up to the regional office and so on. Despite reasonably heavy cash awards for the 'best' in the year, the response was practically nil.

Suggestions, cannot be made into a competition for the 'best' to be selected. Even the 'last' is worthwhile, if it can improve even a little bit. Suggestions may relate to lay out, work flow, canteen timings, anything. The authority of 'officials' at various levels is not enough to instil confidence in the ability to evaluate suggestions. Some officials are attitudinally unsuitable to consider suggestions, particularly if they seem to challenge arrangements worked out earlier by them. Vested interests constitute a major impediment to improvement. A simple suggestion that by reducing the strength of electricity, there could be a saving of Rs 300 million per annum, was dismissed off-hand by the production as well as the instrumentation personnel, on the ground that there could be damage to equipments, despite the evidence that for a long period the strength had actually dropped and there was neither loss of production nor damage to the equipment.

Innovation is the opposite of conformity to conventional thinking. It requires a deviation from conventional assumptions and paradigms. While everybody is cutting costs, the innovator thinks of reshaping conditions of operations. While airlines created first class services with large reclining seats and lounges to pamper the customer, a few went the other way, eliminated all frills, even checked in baggage, and captured a big market. CNN changed the format of news presentation with real time news from around the world, 24 hours a day. The deviation from conventional logic and paradigms may be minor, doing better what everyone is doing, or major, affecting the very nature of the market. Exchange offers, which were confined to the auto industry, has changed the promotional strategies in electronic systems, home appliances and other consumer durables.

Innovative thoughts are not easy to implement. The progress from an idea to its becoming an operational reality is fraught with attempts to discredit, to ridicule, to place obstacles of various kinds, and sometimes even to sabotage. These attempts come from rivalries as well as from genuine doubts. Even otherwise it takes a lot of effort and time to translate an idea to a functional reality. There has to be testing and finetuning. Even products like the Xerox machine, the CT Body Scanner, the microwave oven, the Post-It note pads, the Compact Disc and Polypropylene, so popular today, had to be pushed through by their protagonists, against several odds, over several years, in some cases 20 years. *Innovation needs persistence, and that is not a common trait. It has to be nurtured.*

Well-known Japanese companies, who have attained exceptional success in harnessing the creativity of employees to advantage in quality improvement, have systems that

- do not discard suggestions just because the impact is not substantial,
- permit decisions being taken at shopfloor levels,
- involve the suggestion maker in the decision process,
- permit experimentation to test out ideas.

Employees have to be allowed to try out suggestions. This requires that the management trust them to be responsible. Trust is 'less risky', if the authority to try out is left with teams of employees, preferably multiskilled. There can be many teams and involve all employees. *Enable and enhance, not restrain or restrict. Adopt experimental techniques. Prototype, iterate, pilot and learn. Do not be obsessed with costs.*

❑ *Internal Communication* ❑

To remain committed and empowered, people have to be informed properly and correctly, on operationally relevant matters. The nature of their dealings with the customers both behaviourally (responsiveness, sensitivity, etc.) and in content (information given), depends on the nature of the internal communication. Inadequate internal communication can be the cause of failure in service. For example, skincare and cosmetics giants, L'Oreal India and Pond's India have set up advisory cells to provide personalised solutions on skin and hair related problems, free of cost. The personnel manning these cells and responding to enquiries need to possess the correct latest information as known by the company in its laboratories. Otherwise, their own personal levels of knowledge (or ignorance) will become the basis for the advice, which will effectively be the company's advice.

Written circulars, bulletins on notice boards and similar media are useful, to inform about products, plans, procedures, etc. Doubts, if any, have to be handled with authority and competence, to set at rest misgivings. Values and philosophies need to be communicated, so that they are shared. These are best communicated

- at meetings through discussions,
- through experiences reflecting values, which if not direct, could be captured on films,
- by top managers,
- through events that celebrate successes of individuals or operating units.

Some organisations produced video magazines to be shown to all employees in all the offices, sometimes numbering over 2,500 containing interviews with senior executives and excellent performers at various operations, information on new plans and achievements, the socially relevant programmes supported by the organisation, and so on. Another company with a huge residential colony provided with cable TV network, inserted the company's promotional video cassettes between other programmes. The families became familiar with and understood the worth of the organisation.

Communication to be relevant, would involve feedback on customers' opinions, performance data, rationale for rules and principles that govern, plans and budgets, and so on. To be effective, seniors must listen to the subordinates, however time consuming and critical they may be. Mr Rana G.S. Talwar, CEO of Standard Chartered Bank, in an interview to *The Economic Times* (18 December, 1998), said that the Bank was 'developing a culture where people were proud to stand up and talk of their mistakes, so that we do not repeat them. People were earlier embarrassed to talk about what had gone wrong'. Almost all senior executives say words to this effect, but not all succeed in achieving these results. In the beginning, what seniors hear may be very critical and unpalatable. It is necessary to listen to these expressions of anguish and concern and persist in the effort, till it begins to take the shape of a cooperative exchange.

Communication should involve also feedback on employee behaviours. Both erratic behaviour needing correction and commendable behaviour needing reinforcement may be communicated, so that others may know what is expected and what is not. *Bragging sessions communicate. Rewards communicate. Appraisal systems communicate.* Top management has to make sure that the communications through these practices and decisions are not distorted, that they do not mislead. If any event had raised some doubts, such doubts have to be discussed, explained and set at rest. Frequent meetings to celebrate, to exchange ideas and to inform, help. *A celebration is of success and success builds cohesiveness.*

Decisions impinge on operational routines. Operational personnel have relevant facts and opinions about their work. For example, when petrol prices go up, vehicle owners buy less petrol during each visit to the petrol station. For the same volume of sale in a period of time, the work of the filling attendants would have increased. If companies were to relate total staff to net revenue or to margins, there may be a case for cutting down on staff strength, while the actual work load may justify an increase.

The staff like to be involved in matters relating to their work, improving productivity, preparing plans and budgets, assessing and absorbing new technology, layout, work assignments, work flow, etc. They are in a position to contribute to decisions. They will happily do so, if consulted. They may even help management to implement harsh decisions. Let them discuss feedback, MIS and performance data. They can understand the implications thereof and suggest appropriate action. Communications would have improved.

❑ *Flexibility* ❑

Service organisations are well suited to individualism. The structure can be federal in nature, linking many small businesses and creating networks of discrete operations. It can also accommodate part-time workers, even people working from homes and independently, in fairly loosely held connections. For this reason, women with household commitments will find more scope in service industries. They can help in scenario writing or lending voice for a variety of dubbed TV programmes. They can do the promotion of goods, become models, canvas customers, interview people for market research, provide coaching and tuition in person or by mail, be guides for tourists, and so on. The same person can also be engaged in multiple activities at the same time. This would be one way to adjust 'supply' to fluctuating 'demand'.

Service personnel have to be enthusiastic. Part-timers, with flexible arrangements are likely to remain enthusiastic throughout. Others may not remain so, particularly when they notice that there is not enough variety or scope for fulfilling aspirations, even though they may have been very enthusiastic in the beginning to perform and prove their worth. It may be better to let such people go. Turnover of personnel in service industries does not matter in positions that do not need high levels of skills, other than interpersonal skills. Replacements may not be a problem at those levels. Turnover may reduce, if people are rotated to new sites, locations or jobs.

8 STRATEGIES FOR GROWTH

❏ *Determining Strategy* ❏

Strategy is a long-term plan of action to secure the objectives of the future. Strategies will focus on

- mission and directions, including culture,
- methods and practices,
- critical performance measures/indicators like defects per 1000, errors in billings,
- new products, technical excellence,
- guarantees, recoveries, ease of access,
- relationships, customisation.

In a new organisation, the objectives of the future would be determined after scanning the environment as well as making estimates of the resources that could be mustered. In an ongoing organisation, an additional input into this decision process would be the analysis of the present—objectives, achievements and resources. An analysis of the present may indicate possibilities for the future. The danger here is that *the present—which is really the past—may tend to perpetuate itself, dominating the thought processes, and blinding one to the discontinuous future.*

There are many factors on which the present can be analysed. One could do the analysis separately for different products or for different segments of customers, treating each product or each segment of customer, or combinations of each of these, as separate businesses. The patterns may be compared over a period of time for the same segment/business, or between different segments.

There are many ways in which analysis may be made. One could study the growth of business, in terms of resources employed, profits or revenues generated from each of the businesses. Different businesses may show different patterns of growth, indicative of distinct characteristics or features of the different segments. The patterns of growth may be different for each business in terms of revenues earned or profits generated. The analysis could go further and look at the costs in managing each of the businesses. Each analysis will throw up ideas as to whether the business should be continued or hived off. The finer the segmentation, the deeper the insights during analysis.

The patterns of revenues and costs should also be analysed. A scatter diagram can be created by plotting each customer segment and each product on a graph paper, showing costs on one axis and revenues on the other, the two ends of each axis representing high and low. A clear picture would then be available of how the segments and products contribute to profits. Products and customers with low revenues and high costs would seem to be candidates for being hived off. In such a case, the decision may very well be to continue with that product-customer segment, because it is part of a package of total services related to an industry. That is also a segment into which competitors may not be attracted and therefore, could be studied for possible cutting of costs and/or expansion of business. A high-revenue low-cost segment may need attention because that is the segment into which there could be threats of new competition. *The graphic representations do not directly lead to decisions. They only help analysis of the existing systems, which would then lead to decisions.*

The strategic decisions may relate to one or more of the following:

- the segments and businesses to continue with,
- the segments and businesses to withdraw from,
- the segments and businesses to develop or build more intensively on,
- the kinds of resources to build and the ways to do so,
- the nature and processes of communications, external as well as internal,
- the ways to cut costs through better synergies (in business) or modification of processes.

❑ *Classification* ❑

The range and variety of services is vast. A useful framework for examining issues relating to strategy is to group them on the basis of some commonalities and discuss differences in management approaches relevant to the different groups. Also, *through the commonalities, one might observe similarities not observed otherwise. The practices of one business might provide clues on what may be tried in another similar business.* The parameters to be used for such classifications can be varied.

One parameter could be convenience shopping vs speciality goods. Examples are: (*a*) a general hospital vs a diabetes hospital or a children's hospital vs cancer hospital, (*b*) a general departmental store vs a sports store. The target segment is very focussed in speciality goods. It helps to organise the distribution systems as also the retailer to arrange the physical facilities, demonstrations, endorsements and appeals. If a speciality sports shop is manned by a sportsman of eminence, endorsement is strong. Sports clubs, associations etc., are a part of the distribution system. The shop can also become a place for discussions and expert advice in addition to retailing. A cancer hospital can associate itself with related activities like prevention checks and campaigns and rehabilitation.

Some services are long-term purchases, some are for a short term. Frequency also varies. Life insurance, for example, is a long-term and low frequency purchase. General insurance on the other hand, is short term. Risks of transit may be covered for just a few hours. The frequency of purchase may be so high that running accounts are maintained and adjustments of premia made once a month for the total risks covered during that month. This distinction is similar to the retailing of durable and non-durable fast-moving consumer goods. Distribution, communication and pricing strategies vary.

Another parameter could be in terms of the decision-making processes of the buyer. At one extreme is the individual and at the other the big corporation, with its rules, procedures and intervention of multiple roles. The search for alternatives, evaluation and decision processes are different. Most services are bought by both categories of buyers, and therefore need to be organised, marketed and managed differently. Banking services for corporate financing are not to be handled the same way as for individual customers. Services, for approving individual tenements, will have to be separately organised compared to colony developments or for industrial and commercial activities.

○ *Complexity* ○

A simple classification is on the dimensions of the complexity of service and divergence. Complexity refers to the number of steps and sequences in process. Divergence refers to the extent of freedom available in doing a step. Looking at medical services alone, the classification will be as given below:

Complexity

		Low	High
Divergence	Low	X-Ray Out-patient	Forensics, Caesarean
	High	Scan, Diagnostic Centre	Surgery, ICU

The top left quadrant permits more standardisation and automation. The bottom right hand quadrant raises the maximum uncertainty and has the maximum scope for *WOW* experiences. Pathology tests could be in either of the two top quadrants.

O *Nature of Service* O

Using two parameters relating to the nature of the service act, we get a four-way classification as shown below:

Directed at

		People	Things
Nature of action	Tangible	Healthcare, Airlines, Beauty, Restaurant, Tourism	Freight, Repair, Janitors Landscaping, Laundry
	Intangible	Education, Theatre, Museums, Advertising, Fashion	Legal service, Banking, Financial services like Credit card, Stock broker, Consultancy

This grid helps to clarify whether: (*a*) physical or mental presence is necessary for service; and (*b*) if necessary, should it be at the beginning, throughout, or at the end. Accordingly, the location and the schedule of the service, can be determined. In low contact services, where presence is not necessary, the locations can be far away. Mail orders and home deliveries are possible. If presence is necessary, it is a case of high contact. Then, physical facilities and process become more important.

When physical presence is necessary, there is the problem of irregular arrival of customers, like in restaurants, out-patient departments of a hospital, petrol stations or an airport. Customers rarely come regularly. There will be periods of inactivity and then a sudden rush. The problem is one of creating and managing a queue. In some services like restaurants, where the service lasts only for short durations, everyone in the queue can be attended to, with some delays. However, where the service is of longer durations and the infrastructure limited, as in hotel rooms or a hospital ward, some in the queue will have to be returned. The latter have to be diverted to associated service providers, as per agreements for mutual support.

The scope for standardisation can also be examined in the light of such classification. Presence provides opportunities for heightened levels of satisfaction, consequent loyalty and word of mouth publicity.

O *Proximity* O

Some services require the physical proximity of the user and the provider while some do not. Physical proximity may be made possible by either the user or the provider or both moving. The following classification can be made:

Provider

		Mobile	Immobile
User	Mobile	Consultant, Courier, Lecturer	Laundry, Hospital, Car repair, Cinema, Restaurant, Shopping
	Immobile	Construction, Painting, Visiting doctor, Ambulance, Internet, Event Management	Telecommunication, TV, Cable networks, Radio, Credit card, Mail orders, E-commerce

Some services like couriers, consultancy and car repairs could be in more than one quadrant. The provider can be mobile or immobile. Advancements in electronics technology is making long distance provision of services (right bottom quadrant) possible. The Internet will bring many services into the right bottom quadrant. Education, consultations, shopping, library references, etc., requiring physical/mental presence, become possible through the Internet with both the provider and the user immobile. Services can cross international boundaries easily.

Multiple outlets or franchises improve the mobility of the provider. The mobility of the provider improves ease of access, but with the Internet, there is effective mobility, despite real immobility.

O *Membership* O

Another classification relates to the nature of relationship the service organisation may have with the customer. Services like library, insurance, banking are available to those formally approved for the service by the specific producer, while radio and TV programmes may be received by any person without the knowledge of the producer. In the former case, there is a formal admission to membership. Combining this distinction with the nature of service delivery, we get a four-way grouping as shown on the following page.

Relationship

	Membership	Informal
Continuous	Credit card, Banking, College, Insurance, Library, Telephone subscriber, Electricity service, Season tickets, Family doctor, Industrial catering	TV, Radio, Public highway, Police protection
Discrete	Courier, Single journey ticket, Hospital, Consultancy, Hotel	Public telephone, Cinema, Restaurant, Sports event, Taxi, Exhibitions

(left margin label: Delivery)

Encrypted TV, called 'pay channels', need membership. Radios and newspapers, try to get membership through subscription to their bulletins, offering special services. A cinema theatre which organises a club is inviting membership and may offer concessional prices, priority reservations, special showings. Airlines try to increase membership through the recognition of frequent flyers, providing them information on the airlines' latest achievements, new offers, future plans, etc., as well as special privileges in check-in, choice of seats, comfortable waiting, baggage clearance. These privileges may be extended also by hotels associated with the airline. Also, pricing arrangements can be varied for members. Members of clubs and associations may get lower priced tickets for shows staged under their auspices or premises. Members in hospitals may get periodical check-ups or bulletins on healthcare or fitness facilities.

Membership builds long-term relationships and loyalty. The membership relationship provides detailed data on size and preferences of the customer segment. Many services are offered free to members, like the hotline on the Internet, or information on the telephones. They value the data that they so gather about members, which can be used as resource for market research, for promotional mailing lists and for direct marketing.

O *Customisation* O

Another way of classification is on the dimensions of

- extent of customisation, and
- extent of judgement/discretion used during service delivery.

		Customisation	
		High	Low
Judgement/Discretion	High	Consultations, Beauty, Secretarial, Advertising, Tuition	Sports commentary, Tour Conductor, Teaching, Theatre, Industrial Catering
	Low	Air tickets, Retailing, Hotel, Nursing, Boutique, Tailoring, Diagnostic services, Taxi, Library	Fast food, Laundry, Preventive health programme, Car repairs, Cinema, Sports, Public transport, Book publishing

Low customisation is when the service remains unchanged, whoever may be the customer. TV, radios, cinemas, car servicing, etc., belong to this category. Very high customisation, is when the service is practically tailored to the requirements of the customer, as in the case of legal advice, or hospital treatment. In either event, the person in contact with the customer may or may not have some element of judgment or discretion to apply. Teachers will have a lot of discretion in teaching a course, which is prescribed. In a hotel where a variety of services are available for the guest to choose from, the person rendering any one service will have very little discretion. The bank's services are varied, as per the requirements of the customer, but bank personnel will have little discretion to change the stipulated procedures. A doctor may determine the treatment specifically to the needs of a patient, but afterwards, the hospital routine to administer this treatment allows no discretion to the staff.

Where discretion is high, the training of staff and control of processes are important. Where both customisation and discretion are low, standardised procedures and mechanical systems may be appropriate. The customer has a passive role, so he has few options. Therefore, physical facilities assume importance. When both customisation and discretion are high as in the case of surgery, the customer is virtually at the mercy or control of the service provider. The service then has high value and may cost more. Uncertainity of outcomes is high and therefore satisfactions with actual outcomes can be very high.

Consistency of delivery, standardisation and use of equipments can be attempted if the product moves to the right bottom quadrant. If a service can be moved to the left top quadrant, there is enhancement in value. A WOW experience is possible. With high levels of computerisation and 'fuzzy logics', high levels of customisation will become the norm. 'A market segment of one', captures this trend. Students are offered a 'cafeteria' of subjects from which they may choose a specified number to complete a course. Mikissimes Design system, called the 'Eye Tailor' in the US, takes a digital picture of the consumer's face and then adjusts the size, shape and colour of the lens and offers options for nose bridge, hinges and arms of the frame designs. Electronic kiosks enable customers to design labels and greeting cards on the spot, composing their own messages.

○ *Fluctuations* ○

Demand and supply factors are important in the service business, because of the characteristic of perishability. The figures below indicate the classification.

Demand fluctuation

		Wide	Narrow
Normal supply	Excess	Telephone, Police emergencies, Fire fighting, Exhibitions	Insurance, Legal advice, Laundry, Couriers
	Short	Passenger transport, Hotels, Theatre, Electricity, Out-patients	Hospital beds, Education, Event management, Fashions

Demand patterns can be understood properly if market segments are disaggregated. Are the fluctuations predictable or random? Demand may increase because of economic conditions (more incomes) or seasonal variations. Where demand fluctuations are high, it would be necessary to study the cyclical pattern, if any, and adjust staff strength through a core of permanent, plus reserves, available at peak periods. The reserves can be released during non-peak periods to outside agencies or to other jobs within the organisation. There are jobs that do not have to be attended to on a day-to-day basis. Preventive maintenance, overhauling and updating are examples of jobs in which some adjustments in scheduling are possible.

This comparison can be used even to organise work within the same organisation. There are some departments which experience the seasonal pressure of work. Accounts and sales functions are examples. Salary and tax payments have to adhere to tight time schedules and routines. Data processing departments have peak and slack periods. Managing these operations can follow the principles of managing demand fluctuations.

It may be necessary to do temporary demarketing, if supplies cannot be adjusted to meet peak demands. Demarketing may be by means of diverting to other suppliers, with whom alliances may be formed, or to other times. Demand management needs knowledge of the causes of fluctuations, habits or preferences of customers, actions of third parties, or non-forseeable events.

Supply can be managed through

- inventories (having spare capacity),
- scheduling according to demand,
- use of part-time employees,
- lease of extra facilities or equipment,
- subcontracting excess demand to other organisations (on reciprocal basis),
- peak-time routines (doing only essential jobs),
- increased customer participation (self-service).

Excess demand can be managed through

- extending the waiting period,
- pricing variations,
- prior appointments (reservation),
- substituting goods (automatic teller),
- diversifying demands (entering counter seasonal markets).

Demand can be enhanced through

- incentives of special packages, including price concessions and/or additional services.

Depending on the skills and requirements and availability of people, one might

- chase demand (adjust supply according to demand) or
- maintain capacity at a uniform level and service only demands within that capacity.

The appropriate strategy would be as below:

	Chase demand	Level capacity
Labour skill	Low	High
Job decription	Low	High
Compensation rate	Low	High

Working conditions	Hard	Pleasing
Training required	Low	High
Hire fire costs	High	Low
Supervision level	High	Low
Example	Cashier	EDP

O Labour Intensity O

Yet another classification is based on the amount of labour intensity in service delivery and the extent of interaction with the customer.

Extent of interaction

		Low	High
Labour intensity	Low	Ticketing, Cinema, Courier	Hospital, Auto repairs, Individual banking
	High	Life insurance, Retailing, Schools	General insurance, Doctors, Lawyers, Corporate banking

If interaction is low, standard operating procedures can be evolved. There can be a rigid hierarchy. Physical surroundings and marketing need to be taken care of. The service has to be 'warm'.

If interaction is high, quality of the responses to customer intervention is important. Hierarchy will have to be flat, superior subordinate relationships being loosely maintained. There is a greater opportunity to build customer loyalty. If labour intensity is high, hiring and training methods as well as scheduling become important.

The above classifications can be used to distinguish different departments within a big service organisation, like a bank, transport service, hotel or hospital.

❑ Reengineering ❑

Business Process Reengineering (BPR) was the buzzword in the early 1990s. Developed by Dr Michael Hammer and James Champy, the concept of BPR caught the imagination of the business world, which was keenly looking for ways to cut costs and improve customer satisfactions, in the face of intense competition, change and customer pressure. BPR was, by definition, an attempt *to rethink on the fundamentals of the business processes in critical areas of performance, and to redesign the processes in ways that dramatically improved quality of service, speed and cost.* BPR promised sustained long-term benefits in terms of customer satisfaction, through services characterised by speed and accuracy.

BPR basically uses the same techniques as traditional work study practices, asking questions like

- Is it necessary to do this?
- What purpose does it serve?
- What is the value addition?
- Can this be done in different ways?
- Can the jobs be eliminated?

The difference however, is that the new concept *takes into account advances in computing and information technology,* which make it possible to avoid paper handling as well as to cut down on duplication in data transfers, movement and delays that occur in manual operations. BPR focusses on critical processes that impact directly on customers, like enquiry handling, order fulfillment, invoicing and billing, maintenance schedules, information systems and product development. Equally important are processes affecting suppliers. The bottom line of these efforts were expected to be reflected in better market shares, greater revenues, shorter cycle times, increased productivity, quicker inventory replenishment, reduced waiting time, clearer communications, reduced costs, and so on.

Some examples of the dramatic results achieved by BPR are given below:

1. A company cut down the time it took to submit tenders for contracts, from six weeks to one day. It stopped making detailed drawings which, in any case, were necessary only after orders had been received. It also made a grid from which 95 per cent estimates could be worked out on the basis of standard parameters like length of the valve, diameter of head, raw material to use and nature of finish.

2. By putting data on all appointments at various facilities in a hospital into a computer and making the same available at all terminals, both patients and doctors/paramedical staff had to spend less time waiting. Time spent on attention to patients increased by 80 per cent.

3. A newspaper having multiple editions at multiple locations, collected orders for ads at various centres. Billing, which had to be made according to insertions, source of order, size, subject, etc., used to be delayed by as much as 30 days. This was reduced to one day.

4. The time taken to receive materials and tools required for maintenance work was brought down from 45 minutes to five minutes.

5. By separating simple and complicated pathology tests, and having the simple ones carried out by the nurse in the ward itself, a hospital was able to cut down the time taken to decide on treatment, from one day to five minutes.

6. When the data relating to purchase orders placed, delivery received, checking of specifications, etc., were fed directly into the networked computer system, payments could be speeded up from 25 days to two days.

7. Pillsbury, a $5.6 billion food manufacturer, brought down its stock from 64 kinds of starch, to 12.

8. A life insurance company, reduced its resources for processing applications from 30 steps, five departments, 19 people, 24 hours and a turnaround time of five to 25 days (only 17 minutes in process) to one man, one step (expert system in computer), four hours and two to five days.

9. A provident fund with nearly half a million subscribers, brought down the number of complaints from 50 per day to just two or three.

10. A mortgage company was able to bring down the time taken for processing applications and giving loans from 26 days to just seven.

In the US car assembly plants, there were 2.5 times more inspection workers, six times more scheduling workers, 11 times more janitors, four times more management staff and four times more material handlers as compared to Japanese firms. Ford's accounts department was five times larger than Mazda's and still had heavy accounts payables pending. They were matching advices from purchase orders, material controllers who received the goods and vendors' invoices. They changed to invoiceless processing, with orders received on the computer, and the receiver confirming entry on the computer.

In matters relating to repairs of TVs and refrigerators, experienced operators who receive and attend to calls, may record the problems and the repairs carried out in the data base. Service personnel who are unable to tackle trouble can consult the expert system embodying accumulated expertise and knowledge. Hundreds of salesmen, visiting dozens of retailers each in different towns, pass on information on sales and orders relating to scores of items to regional offices which coordinate with the head office for instructions on pricing, promotion sales strategy, etc. The feedback on the effectiveness of head office decisions are not known for a long time. The solution was that the salesmen can use hand-held computers to record orders and sales. The information got transmitted to the central system overnight.

In all these cases, the normal ways of doing things were scrapped, manual operations were computerised, information keyed into the system at one place was made available at every other relevant place through networks. Standard data stored in the system made it an expert system to assist the operator.

❑ Need for Reengineering ❑

The context for BPR is nothing more than the realities of change. The realities are:

- Nothing is simple any more due to rapid and perplexing change.
- Whatever we do has to be quick and radical, because of the speed of change.
- Marginal or incremental adaptation is not enough.
- Organising should be around outcomes, not tasks.

The imagery for organisations has to shift from that of a well-oiled machine in a predictable environment, to a ship caught in a storm in an uncharted sea on a dark night, with all its navigational aids non-functional. This is the context for future managers. Existing routines, of periodically tightening nuts and bolts, may be inappropriate in the new situation that has a lot of new factors, largely unknown. The jobs in such a crisis will not follow the hierarchy of normal times, but authority will pass to those with competence for functions appropriate to the new situation. These competencies will include new knowledge, innovativeness and even guts. Instead of trying to extract obedience through authority, which will not work in any case, the captain would try to obtain solutions to the new problems, through consultation, rather than reinvent himself. Reengineering recognises that the *market is turbulent, the customers are not predictable, competition is ruthless, margins are shrinking, obsolescence is high and life cycles of products are shortening.*

❑ Steps in Reengineering ❑

The purposes of BPR have to be clear. They are meant to improve effectiveness and to cut costs of operations and processes. Effectiveness is, for all practical purposes, better customer satisfaction. This is true in all cases, when the concept of an internal customer is kept in mind.

The focus is on processes, the ways in which things are being done. To be able to do this, the process has to be understood fully. The way to do it is *Mapping.* Mapping involves asking, with regard to every step, what is being done (task), why it is being done (outcome) and what resources are being consumed (equipment, money, time).

Every detail of the process has to be identified and noted down, *documented*, showing the forward linkages (to activities and to results), and backward linkages (source from which information comes for this activity), the time taken, the number of persons and equipment involved, etc. Mapping will also identify the customer or the stakeholder for that process, and in turn try to identify what the interests or the concerns of the customer might be. The gap if any, between the concerns and the outcomes being delivered, will then be clear.

While studying processes, look for areas and activities which add value. What is the value added by the process, viz. the benefit that it adds to the product/ customer. The data here should be exact, not hunches or assumptions. They need to be tested for exactitude. Non-productive activities and time in process must be isolated and eliminated. *When tasks are fragmented, about 40 per cent of processing time add no value.* Sometimes, only one per cent of the elapsed time is working time.

The next step would be to look at the possibilities of using IT levers, to speed up, to add value, to avoid repetition, to avoid errors, to integrate, to cut costs. In order to explore the possibilities in a particular situation, it is worth assuming that technology is not a constraint in delivering what is necessary. In other words, *the limitations, if any, in organising for the best, would not come from technology.*

Link parallel activities, do not integrate them. Put decision points where work is performed and build control in the process. Capture information once, at source.

The mindset required while working on BPR consists of:

- Nothing is sacrosanct. Everything is changeable.
- All current assumptions are challengeable.
- Life cycles will shorten.
- People are responsible and trustworthy.
- People alone can deliver satisfaction on behalf of the company.
- People are willing to learn and enthusiastic to contribute.
- Errors can, and must, come down to zero.
- Every customer action is reasonable. They can come any time and ask anything.
- Customers do not follow working hours.
- Customer loyalty cannot be taken for granted.
- Customer responds only to quality.
- Customer service is part of product quality.
- Customer service is part of back office responsibility.

❏ *Value Chain* ❏

In the analysis of the value chain, five activities are primary viz., inbound logistics, outbound logistics, operations, marketing and sales service. There are four others which are support services, viz., infrastructure, human resources management, technology development and procurement. This gives a matrix of 20 (five primary multiplied by four support) boxes. Each box is a potential area for improvement.

Customer complaints are indicative of problem areas. If the problem areas are identified by frequency (of errors and/or delays), one can select the 'most frequent' as the one having the highest priority for attention. The costs of these failures, both for correction (after failure) and for prevention (avoiding failure), can be measured. The ones having the highest costs for correction, need priority attention. This is the area which will have the maximum impact, measured in terms of the bottom line results.

When all the data is properly mapped and documented, showing work flows, times taken, activities and value additions, serious questions can be asked about relevance, substitution, alternatives, etc. Brainstorming and benchmarking are methods that help to answer these questions. Brainstorming is a method that triggers original ideas from the participants in a group, by activating their potential for creativity and imagination. Benchmarking looks at the possibilities for learning from some of the practices of other organisations.

While benchmarking, it is useful to remember that no practice can be just copied. The idea will have to be adapted to the circumstances of one's own business. Airfreight compared itself to the self-service systems of retail shops and cafeterias and found it worthwhile to give PCs to big customers, who could print their own airway bills and leave the packet in a bin to be collected at the convenience of the freight company. It eliminated unnecessary repetitive visits.

The adaptation has also to take note of one's own culture. For example, it is said that in the advertisement business in Europe, there is one person for every $1 million business, while it is seven in India and three in the Far East. The comparison is valid only if costs of advertisements in media are similar. It is like the head of a family of hens pointing out the egg laid by an ostrich in the nearby farm and suggesting better productivity.

Thinking about the possibilities for change, is not the exclusive privilege of senior managers. Anyone familiar with the process, either while making it work, or while receiving its outcomes, can think and suggest, invent and reinvent. *All such persons should be involved into the process of change, not by compulsion, but creating a climate of wanting to contribute.* Make it easy for employees and customers to complain. Make it easy for them to do and derive benefit, without the involvement of anyone else.

❑ *Reengineering in Services* ❑

BPR was popularised mainly in the context of manufacturing, to cut costs, to enhance quality of customer service and to improve bottom lines. However, the focus was on processes that deliver quality to customers. Processes are services. The concepts of Reengineering apply to services. Service businesses like hospitals, hotels, couriers, airlines, railways, tourism, public services, credit cards, retailers and contractors, have considerable scope to improve their effectiveness, through concepts from BPR.

The core processes that BPR focusses on are, in the context of services—the moments of truth. The kitchen is not core, in a hotel. The kitchen is important for consistency in quality of food. The core is the processes of taking and executing orders, the way the order is processed in the pantry and kitchen and brought to the table, particularly if the execution of the order involves non-standard specifications and/or more than one operational area.

❑ *Risks in Reengineering* ❑

BPR programmes have not always been successful. Some of the reasons for failure are as follows:

- The change programme did not take note of all related impacts.
- The competitor had come up with a more effective response, in product or service.
- Market conditions had changed, due to technology, customer preferences etc.
- Economic cycles.
- Government regulatory systems.

Some of the factors involved in these circumstances will be outside the control of the organisation. However, the reasons stated hereunder are always within the control of the organisation, but are neglected:

- The momentum for change is not sustained. Change will not automatically follow the decisions to change, even if the changes proposed are clearly beneficial to the organisation. Resistance is likely for a number of reasons, from different quarters. Even if there is no active resistance, the inertia will tend to impede the processes of change. Therefore, the change processes have to be monitored and managed carefully till they become institutionalised.

- The technical considerations in change are important. However, equally important are the human factors and managerial practices. No change will take place truly, unless the mindset, attitudes and behaviour of the people within the organisation change. The mindset will not change, just because the seniors ask for it.

- Managerial practices and structures have to be supportive of reengineering. The appropriate practices and structures would be such as would emphasise the primacy of customer satisfaction as well as of employee commitment and initiative. The way people think about, organise, inspire, measure and reward value-adding operational work may require change. The appropriate culture has to be built up.

❑ *Branding* ❑

In Chapter 5 reference was made to the need for service providers building up brands. A brand exists when the brand name triggers off, in the minds of the consumers, thoughts relating to the attributes, quality and nature of the product. This happens because, over a period of time, a consistent message has settled in the minds of the consumers, partly through the communication and much more through the experience. Such sustained efforts are required to build a brand. Once the brand is built, there is a relatively easier acceptance of the product/service. Building customer relationships and loyalty becomes simpler. Marketing costs also become less.

A brand is a brand only if it is different from other brands. There has to be a uniqueness, which is not available elsewhere. Therefore, there is no competition when a brand is strong. *To maintain that uniqueness and distinctiveness, is the major effort.* When friends decide to go to the Prithvi theatre (in Mumbai) for the evening, there is an implied assumption that the evening's experience, would include clean theatre, decent crowds, excellent drama, etc.

The same provider can brand its different offers. The same hotel may have different floors providing different standards of room service and attention. The 'Maharaja' service of the Air India is a brand. The Taj Gateway hotels are different from the Taj Residency hotels. They are two brands. The platinum credit cards are different from the gold credit cards.

Business class is different from the Economy class. Some may call it First class, providing images of special attention, additional conveniences and priority service.

The distinctiveness may be in the tangibles associated with the service. Banks and airline offices maintain distinctive signboards and office decors. Colours in petrol stations identify the service provider. Cover page designs are unique for Penguin paper backs, Prentice-Hall student editions and Addison Wesley publications. Law books and McDonalds' kiosks can be identified from long distances.

A brand does not have to be at the upmarket or premium end. There is place in the market for medium and budget customers who may do without the frills, and concentrate only on the core service. All placement services provide personnel for various assignments. But they may cater differentially to extras for film sets, college students for field work in market research, stenographers, sales persons or high level executives. A boarding house may provide super deluxe hotel facilities, or just a room with sparse furniture and a bath. The latter can have an image of cleanliness, safety, moderate prices, and courteous attention, which are valued by some. That is its brand. The Quality Inn hotels have a lower image than the Holiday Inn, but are equally highly valued and sought after.

It takes time to build a brand. A brand has to be relevant (to the needs of the customer), original (not an imitation of another) and consistent in all aspects. The messages have to be in tune with the perceptions and expectations of the target segment, need strong distinctive visual attractiveness. The imagery, the symbols, the sounds and the colours must be differentiated and recognisable. Together they provide the identification, which in turn, is related to the promises that the brand signifies. The 'Give me Red' shout of Eveready batteries, the dot patterns of Sony and the strains of the music in Titan watch advertisements, are unmistakably unique.

Retail outlets are brands. They have reputations for quality and price. Any product made available from that outlet shares the brand image of that outlet, if it does not have one of its own. When the brand of a retailer is strong, he may consider selling the product with his own brand name, after getting it manufactured by those who supply others.

In the view of James Hemerling of the Boston Consulting Group, it is important to think of the 'overall architecture of the brand'. Citibank has a broad umbrella brand under which each product tends to start with 'Citi', thus being associated with the equity of Citibank. Hotels belonging to the same group can be branded differently. The US-based Mariott hotel and resort chain have developed sub-brands, each targeted at different segments, signalling different price or value propositions. The Midland banking group launched the First

Direct, a deposit scheme, without visibly endorsing it with the Midland name, wanting to position it as separate from any of the High Street brands.

❑ *Focus on Cash Flow* ❑

Several companies with excellent turnover and order books have sometimes found themselves short of cash. This occurs due to inadequate attention to the cash flow, which can be affected by credits and receivables. While every business has its own rules and practices, the retail business may provide some lessons. The finding is that large volumes with small margins contribute to outstanding successes. Volumes are high when customers keep coming back for more. When volumes are high, the retailers clout with suppliers increases. Suppliers are willing to accept stringent terms partly for the reputation of being associated with the retailers, as well as assured high volumes. Established retailers like the 100-year old Niligris with a chain of 18 stores in the southern cities and the RPG Group's Foodworld with a large chain of stores, are showing how retailing is assuming big business proportions like the supermarkets in the developed countries. The 30-year old Vivek is able to have direct negotiations with 50 companies and 128 suppliers. Even a multinational like Hindustan Levers, servicing 100,000 retailers across India, including large numbers in remote villages, is targeting 22 million households for volumes. While small owner-managed one-location retailers operate with margins of 15–20 per cent, supermarkets are able to operate with wafer thin margins, providing better value to the customers. To be able to do so, they also have to keep their costs very low. Large volumes, low costs, small margins and tight cash management are consistent with high quality customer value.

Some hotels have some ingenious ways to cut costs. A guest can leave a card if he thinks that the linen need not be changed. Smaller serving dishes are used for butter and jam. Stained tablecloths are made into napkins, chef's aprons and ties. Guests are lent bicycles, if they do not want to use taxis. Coins and chips are used instead of paper for car parking and coat checking. Garden clippings are made into mulch. Blue floor tiles are made from automobile windshields. Solar energy is used for heating water. Sydney's new Novotel hotel, claiming to be environmentally and socially responsible, reuses 80 per cent of all waste, has systems that automatically cut off airconditioning when the window is opened, has brought down carbon dioxide emission to zero and uses fewer baths to reduce water waste. Ideas such as these are circulated through hotel associations.

Cash flow projections should be part of all decision making. This goes beyond traditional accounting practices. Cash flow will drive stock markets and shareholder returns, yield, dividend and capital gains.

❏ Associations and Alliances ❏

Several organisations were seeking tieups with well known foreign companies, in order to get the advantage of branding. Such linkages have been worked out in Telecom, TV broadcasting, Internet serving, education, software development, hotels and so on. After some time, when one is known on its own performance, the link with the other brand can be severed. Professionals like lawyers and doctors, who practice with eminent seniors for some time before branching out themselves, follow the same principle.

The association can be in the nature of a strategic alliance or joint venture. Sometimes licensing arrangements also provide the benefit of an association with the brand. There are varying advantages in each of these arrangements, in terms of costs as well as flexibilities. Associations and alliances make it possible to expand offers without capital involvement. Companies which offer time share holiday arrangements in cities throughout the world like Sterling Resorts or Mahindra Resorts, operate on this basis. Airlines and couriers resort to such arrangements extensively.

Associations also help in strengthening outsourcing arrangements meant to overcome the problems of fluctuating demands. It helps both the one who has capacity and offers and the one who takes the outsourced service. Air India offers ground handling as well as engine overhauling facilities in India to other airlines and receives it from other airlines in other countries. A lot of outsourcing is done in the IT industry, both for infrastructure and for software. When Compaq bought Digital, it was largely to acquire Digital's service setup, more than anything else. Electronic giants like Samsung, Kenwood, LG and Sony share common manufacturing, servicing and retailing facilities. Hotels, called boutiques, may have minimal facilities for room and food, but have linkages with nearby providers, in case the customer wants to avail of health club or business centre services. Even transport may be provided free for the movement to 'on the mall' services.

Apart from the advantage of branding and outsourcing, there is a trend towards creating giant organisations that will dominate the market. When Vodafone bought over the Air Touch Communication Inc., it was one of the biggest mergers in the history of the mobile phones industry, creating a combined sales exceeding $10 billion per year. GE Capital Services, with an asset base of $250 billion and having 28 different businesses in the areas of consumer finance, leases, mortgages and satellite communication, took over SRF Finance in India and established joint ventures with the State Bank of India, availing of the Bank's technical and back office facilities in India for its growth. Insurance companies associate with banks taking advantage of the facilities and 'image' of the other. It is the same strategy to exploit advantages of size that makes companies reduce the number of stockists, so that each stockist may have a much bigger volume of turnover and a better return on investment.

One of the problems encountered by companies transacting business globally, is the difficulty of understanding and adapting to the differing cultures of different communities. Associations help to overcome these problems, because the practices of the local companies are consistent with local cultures. However, strains develop within these associations because the cultures, and therefore the managerial styles and operating practices of the companies in the association, do not match. If serious efforts are not made to integrate cross-cultural differences, the associations are likely to break. There have been several instances of such breakages in India in the 1990s and later.

❑ *Listening* ❑

People in the service business have to learn to listen. They have to listen to the customer and also to the employees. Listening is an act that by itself provides considerable satisfaction to the person listened to, because listening is an expression of recognition, of respect, of taking the other person seriously. There is an immediate response of being inclined favourably to the listener, and also of wanting to speak more. This is what leads to the advantage of authentic feedback, both from customers and from employees, both necessary for enhancing the level of service. Worthwhile correction of deficiencies as well as upgradations, are aided by listening

A good listener picks up cues about customer needs and displeasures before they are formally expressed. *This is sensitivity. It helps build relationships and consequent retention of customers.* Listening is also important for noticing changes in the market place in terms of customer preferences, customer expectations, competitive offerings, technology and so on. Good listeners pick up the signals much faster than others. *There is competitive advantage in listening.*

❑ *Manage through Culture* ❑

In the context of BPR and even otherwise, it is necessary to emphasise that the management of people has to be, not through control of people and activities, that hamper, hinder and restrain, but through value and culture that enables and encourages.

The new culture will be one that encourages, not obedience to chains of command, but relentless pursuit to match customers' elusiveness, through bottomless resources of imagination, smooth teamwork, as well as individual autonomy. The new culture will be strongly *supportive of openness, trust, respect and teamwork.*

The new values also regard employees, including managers, not as instruments for maximising benefits to the shareholders, but as instruments of society working towards creation of wealth and benefits for the community. This value alone generates an orientation that seeks to provide satisfaction to customers.

Values, if they are truly characteristic of an organisation, would be enduring, widely understood and managed as an asset. It will be embodied in all decisions and activities regardless of the economic consequences. There could be temptations to ignore the stated values for quick short-term advantage. This will not happen if the values are not only understood (cognitively at the intellectual level), but are internalised, at the emotional or behavioural level. When fully internalised, the aggregate of values represent the culture of the organisation. The values and culture have to be managed as assets, to ensure that they never erode or depreciate. This can be done by submitting every decision and policy to scrutiny against the strict standards of the values, in the presence of all the decision makers.

Merril Lynch's core principles underline its corporate culture. They include:

- client focus,
- respect for individual,
- team work,
- responsible citizenship,
- integrity.

This principle was in evidence operationally when it undertook to meet, on its own, all the commitments that it had made on behalf of an insurance company that it was representing and which went into liquidation.

❏ *Ethics* ❏

Ethics deals with issues of rightness, propriety, fairness and justice. Propriety and justice are not the same as legality. A company polluting its surrounding with toxic effluents may be within the limits prescribed by law. However, it would be wrong, if it knows how to, and has the capability to, but does not, reduce the toxic levels further. It would be wrong because it is knowingly causing avoidable harm to the environment.

Ethics is determined in relation to the effects of one's actions on another. *Concern for others is the core of ethics.* It is wrong to harm anyone or anything. One is expected to do good even at some cost to oneself. Selfish actions are rarely the subject of praise. People remembered in history and admired by current society are those who have shown selfless concern for others. Those who have bothered about self-interest at the cost of the society, are generally the butt of public criticism. A Mother Teresa is raised to the levels of sainthood, ultimate goodness, because of the concern she had shown to others, not for the strong and mighty from whom she could have derived benefit for herself, but for the poor and the weak.

Every action of an organisation has an impact on society. Apart from questions of safety and pollution, the way the people are managed have social impact. Employees who spend large parts of their lives within organisations pick up, from what they see within, attitudes relating to concern for others (collaboration and team work), taking responsibility for what one does, instead of blaming others, communal and caste distinctions, material attainments versus the more abiding assets of contentment, happiness and health, loyalties and gratitude, and so on. These attitudes are carried back into the society and reflect the kind of integrating or divisive forces that may develop there.

Apart from the direct social impact from its activities, organisations need to have concern for the well being of society. This is called social responsiveness or social responsibility. It is expected to do good to the society by relating itself to the development of the society. Society expects organisations to support programmes relating to healthcare, literacy and education, local arts and crafts, self employments etc., because organisations are endowed with enormous human, finance and technology resources.

Management styles practised within an organisation can create psychologically healthy (or sick) people, impacting on the family and community outside the organisation. The values supported by the organisation are the values that employees may practice outside. Corruption, personal aggrandisement, greed for material possessions, competitiveness that destroys the other, are also values that people learn from corporate experience.

Organisations that are not ethical, ignoring the requirements of being just and fair in their behaviour, not unwilling to harm others for their own self interests, are not likely to command respect in the market place. They may not survive for too long. They would have created among its employees, people who have not acquired the characteristics of good citizenship. By neglecting their duty to society, they would have harmed its future. Ethics flows out of the values of the organisation.

Ethics has to be built into strategy. The concepts of marketing, which focus on benefits to the customer, automatically lead one to ethical actions. The primary purpose of service to the customer, implies doing good to him. As long as this purpose is not lost sight of, the actions are likely to remain ethical. Problems begin when the focus shifts from this to corporate advantage in the short term. There is increasing emphasis on corporate governance in recent times. The codes and the laws are liable to be violated. Penalties do not guarantee appropriate behaviour. Good governance is essentially ethical, as it shows concern for the public at large.

Ethics and good governance are important for business organisations, because of the large resources (money, technology and human) that are under their control. The effect of their actions on society are immense. The public has very little control on business houses, but has very heavy stakes in their actions and decisions. The management has to be fair. Ethics is more important in the case of the service businesses because

- there are no warranties in most cases,
- the nature of the service offered are not specified in detail,
- information about the offers are limited,
- there is a time gap between purchase and availability,
- there could be conflict of interests,
- there are concerns of confidentiality (safety).

❑ *World Class Service* ❑

World class service connotes

- high levels of customer satisfaction,
- high levels of customer retention,
- high levels of innovation in products and delivery systems,
- clear and often unconditional guarantees,
- very good service image (people talk),
- costs under control,
- people want to work for them,
- quick adaptation to change.

Customer service and support must be integrated into every activity, particularly in the areas of logistics and distribution. The value chain can be analysed and linked to the development of a Customer Satisfaction Index. Establishing the attributes to be measured and the points at which the measurements will be made, requires thinking through the importance of the various points in the delivery chain, and the relative importance of what is being delivered at each of these points. *Be ruthless on 'non-value added' items.*

Simple systems can provide excellent data. If one keeps a complete record of all calls of enquiries or of complaints, who called, when, what time, from where etc., enough data can be generated for some market research. In a busy departmental store, the doorman at the gate presses a counter which gives information about the flow of customers, time-wise and daywise. A little more sophisticated system can also identify customers by family size. A similar counter about exits, with bags and without bags, will provide rough data about the ratio of those who return without purchases.

❏ *To be the Best* ❏

The appropriate strategy to be the best is what has been identified as the characteristics of Nobel Prize winners. They are:

- the courage and willingness to stand alone,
- the confidence to challenge the conventional,
- intense passion to do continuously better,
- perseverance to do as you dream,
- unflinching focus on purpose and direction,
- seeing all constraints as opportunities to prove oneself.

9 MANAGING INFORMATION

❑ *Introduction* ❑

In all business, as in all spheres of activity, information is the basis of decisions and actions. The quality of decisions and strategies depends on the quality of the information made available at the appropriate points at the appropriate times. Information management is a large proportion of costs in business, particularly in services like hospitals, hotels, couriers, airlines and consultancy. The value chain uses information flowing between suppliers, distribution, customers, etc., in both directions. A transporter has to know at a central point how each piece of cargo is moving, or not moving, over several points of handling and transhipment. Lengthening queues caused by clogged processing lines and productive resources remaining unutilised because inputs have not arrived on time, are both matters of serious concern, and can be tackled effectively only if that information reaches the appropriate control points on time. So also, an office administrator or factory manager has to know how the files or work or cash is moving along the various stages of processing. A manager also needs to know about changes and new developments in the fields of materials, market, competition and matters affecting their effectiveness

Information is available from within the organisation as well as from outside the organisation. Information has to be captured, stored and retrieved as and when necessary. Traditionally, the office is where these activities are carried out. The job requires recording of information on paper and in files, copying or transference of information from one paper or file to another, as well as the physical movement of the recorded information from one place to another, for storage or for usage. These, usually manual processes, were subject to the risks of errors and delays. Electronic processing of information has been in vogue for the last 50 years or more, with systems provided by both the IBM and ICL. Since the development of computers, there have been tremendous advances in the capabilities of processing information. Improvements in fibre optics and advances in digital technology have resulted in increased speeds and lower costs of voice, data and video services. Computers can be linked and made interactive through networks of various kinds. Some of them are local connections, exclusively for the internal use of an organisation. Some connect different organisations, but are mainly meant for processing of certain specified kind of information. While earlier, information had to be taken to where the people were, networks make it now possible for people to access the information without any physical movement. The most well-known and widely used is the Internet, which spans the world and has infinite current applications as well as possibilities for the future.

❏ *The Internet* ❏

The Internet today has grown from the ARPA (Advanced Research Project Agency), which the US armed forces developed in the late 1960s, to protect its information network from a possible strike by the Russians. The concept was that data to be transmitted would be split into small parts or packets, which could be sent to various parts of the network through different routes, so that in the event of a particular route being damaged by a nuclear attack, an alternate route would be available. Several computers were used to store and communicate the data. Several people could access and share the information stored, using their own terminals. The procedure adopted to link and operate these interconnecting systems was called TCP/IP (Transmission Control Protocol/ Internet Protocol). The system also enabled the connected persons to exchange messages, which was the beginning of e-mail. ARPA was later merged with the UseNet News, a non-governmental, academic network.

In the late 1980s, the American government set up five supercomputer centres, which became the main nodes of the Internet. All the research and lab networks were connected to these nodes. In 1983 there were less than 500 'host' computers, mostly government laboratories and academic computer science centres. By 1987, there were 30,000 and by 1995 there were five million. A fresh Internet user joins every minute. By the year 2007, there is likely to be at least half-a-billion interconnected computers. Universities and research laboratories found that with this fast, convenient and flexible connectivity, it would be possible to participate in discussions across the network, which meant across the world. They created software and document libraries on the network, accesible to all users.

The development of personal computers in the 1980s opened up the Internet to a wide range of users. Individuals could now get connected into the network.

PCs could be connected between themselves, facilitating communication between different segments of organisations located at distances. In the early 1980s, internal networks began with single LANs, (Limited Area Networks), which developed into extended LANs, and then WANs (Wide Area Networks). In the 1990s, the movement is geared towards Virtual LANs (VLAN) and switched VLAN networks, when users may move between different VLANs, depending on their projects. E-mail has became an easy mode of communication, instantaneous and inexpensive.

MANs (Metropolitan Area Networks) and VSATs (Very Small Aperture Terminals) are further extensions of limited networks. Alongwith on-line services, came the concept of Bulletin Board Service (BBS) for exchanging information, making enquiries, offering services and so on. In 1990, Mr Tim Berner Lee of the CERN, the high energy physics lab near Geneva, developed a software for sharing documents with their colleagues at large. This came to be known as the World Wide Web or www or W3. Developments in W3 include the use of XML (Extensible Markup Language) and the Resource Description Format, which would make it possible for machines to interact without the intervention of humans, leading to filtering mechanisms to meet the concerns of parents and educators; intelligent, comparison-based shopping; smart invoicing across international boundaries; improved purchasing methods; and so on. The web will be able to put people, buyers and sellers, together and solve problems.

The www is a means by which information (words, sound, images, video, animation) can be flashed across the globe, by just placing one soft copy (electronic version) of the document on an Internet web server. Millions of users can use it, download it to their personal computers and even have them printed out. There were an estimated 2.1 billion web pages floating in cyberspace in 2002, compared to only 50 in 1992. The total traffic is estimated to be doubling every year. The www functions on the foundation of 'html' (hypertext markup language), which is a standardised language of computer code imbedded in source material and documents.

The Internet has now become a diversified global entity. Its nodes are supported by diverse authorities, not by the five American supercomputers alone. The Internet is self-sustaining and in a sense, uncontrolled. The millions of computers and wires that connect as smaller networks between themselves, and into the major international networks, follow a simple rule. The TCP/IP lays down that all data shall be broken down into smaller packets, that the first packet will have an address as to where it is meant to go. There is no central control computer to which the data goes. The data travels from one point to another over the web of computers. The principle is the same as the one in which modern large computers are built, a complex array of elements working rapidly in precise and elaborate ways. Modularity enables the system to be broken up into smaller subsystems, that function separately and independently, but integrally as a whole.

All the data is held by 'servers', which are owned by organisations and companies like Microsoft or VSNL in India. When a request is made to these servers for information, the requested information is bundled in small packets with the destination address and sent to the nearest connection to the Internet. When the packet reaches the Internet junction, the address is read by the router and directed to the address. The same routine is repeated at the subsequent junctions till the packet is delivered to the right address, where it is put together again to make up the original information. There is no predetermined path and the individual packets of the same message may follow different paths, depending on the traffic at that node at that time.

❑ *The Domain Name System (DNS)* ❑

The Domain Name System is intended to facilitate identification of one host computer by another. DNS is a distributed database, allowing local control of the overall database, yet enabling availability across the entire network. Every country in the world is identified by two alphabets like 'au' for Australia, 'uk' for the United Kingdom and 'in' for India. There are six top level domains as follows:

- com.   for commercial/business organisations,
- edu.   for educational organisations,
- gov.   for governmental organisations,
- mil.   for the military,
- net.   for the network resources like the service providers,
- org.   for other organisations.

These domains are maintained by the InterNIC. The top level domain 'in' for India is maintained by the NCST as they were the first Internet node in India.

An address may read as bala@bom1.vsnl.net.in. or as palhan@srisim.ernet.in. In the latter case, VSNL is not the server and there is only one node. In the former case, the node is identified as the one in Mumbai, maintained by the server VSNL.

Usages of the Internet

A connection to the Internet enables one to

- send and receive e-mail,

- search retrieve and read data, files, pictures,
- join discussion groups including video conferencing,
- communicate in real time,
- browse through information on a variety of subjects,
- display what one has to offer for the benefit of whoever may be interested,
- buy and sell (e-commerce),
- download onto one's own terminal any relevant information or data,
- 24-hour access for on-line banking, funds transfer,
- Electronic Data Interchange (EDI) for international trade.

Several softwares are available on the Internet to enable performance of these functions. Some of these are:

- Search engines, like Yahoo or Google, providing information about and access to services available in cyberspace,
- Gopher, space on the Internet which is different from and largely replaced by www,
- Java, Internet Scripting Language,
- DRAM, Dynamic Random Access Memory—the basis for Internet,
- Lynx, the versatile browser for www,
- Archie (to find a file you want),
- FTP (File Transfer Protocol),
- Kermit Protocol,
- Veronica (Very Easy Rodent Oriented Netwide Index of Computer Archives),
- WAIS (Wide Area Information Server),
- URL (Universal Resource Locator) which is the unique address of any web document,
- IRC (Inter Relay Chat),
- Pine for e-mail,
- EDI (Electronic Data Interchange),
- PDF (portable document format), used to capture almost any kind of document and can be read through an ACROBAT reader,
- XML (extensible mark up language) useful when parts of the document are standardised and must reappear many times.

Software like SMART (System for Manipulation and Retrieval of Text) can search hundreds of sources for articles on specific topics of interest and deliver them by Fax, e-mail, Internet or any other chosen method.

Other technologies related to the web are:

- Net2Phone—enabling phone (voice) messages being sent over the Internet. The recipient does not need an Internet connection. He only needs a phone.
- Net2Fax—which is a similar facility sending messages to Fax machines.
- Iphone—which enables Internet users across the world to exchange voice messages. The International STD charge comes down to zero in this case.
- Internet relay chat—which is a facility whereby several persons can simultaneously exchange brief notes on specific topics.
- WebTV technology—wherein the TV is attached to a keyboard type of device and the cable TV operator becomes the Internet service provider, allowing users to select a specific programme from a set of programmes.
- Real audio facility—enabling an individual to set up a radio broadcasting station on his own.

New usages and technologies related to the Internet are developing very fast. Netscape which was founded in 1994 developed the Navigator, a web browser, providing easy access to www. Because of the Navigator, the Internet was transformed from a communications channel for scientists and technicians into a network connecting millions of ordinary users across time and space, into an industry in its own right. In the face of possible competition from Microsoft and others, Navigator 2.0, was introduced in January 1996 and Navigator 3.0 in August 1996. They had to introduce the next Beta 0 version of the programme on 14 February 1997. Beta 1 was introduced on February 22 and Beta 2 in March 1997. Netscape's market share had come down from 70 per cent to 60 per cent in 12 months and it was planning to offer to its buyers the source codes free, so that independent providers could improve the software.

It is difficult to keep track of the developments in the Internet system. It has become an integral part of everyday life. Every company of some standing has a web site, from which information about the company can be downloaded. Forms for applications (college admissions or investments) can also be downloaded and even submitted through the Internet. All banking transactions can be made through the Internet. Every individual is expected to have an e-mail address. Some have more than one. Many people who do not have personal computers, access their e-mail through cybercafes.

❏ *Electronic Commerce* ❏

It was estimated that millions of households write and print checks from their PCs, pay bills electronically, collect and organise information about their purchases, expenditures and investments. They use electronic cards called affinity cards, smart cards etc., for electronic commerce. Smart cards are practically electronic cash, and are debited as per usage. They can be enhanced to capture store names, transactions amounts and also retain or download information directly into the PC. This is made possible by Infomediaries like (*a*) 'Quicken', personal finance software, which is cheque-free and Visa-interactive; or (*b*) Microsoft money to manage chequebooks. These softwares make it possible to compare different product offerings, to swap funds automatically between accounts at different institutions. In the event of ongoing relationships, banks are aware of customer's financial transactions, clothing store will be familiar with customer's tastes and frequency of purchase, health maintenance organisations will know about the private medical history and risk profile of people. It will not work if customers question company's professionalism, integrity, or commitment to high quality service.

On-Line Transaction Processing (OLTP) enables the direct placement of orders, immediate response thereto, refilling inventories by suppliers, very large data bases (not merely age and address, but also likely timing and size of orders). Travellers are able to check out facilities and costs of available hotels and make direct reservations on line. Business Interactivity requires secure arrangements, laws and protocols to govern digital signatures and electronic cash. Mastercard and Visa have developed Secure Electronic Transmission Method. Electronic cash is made possible by purchase from one bank being retrievable from another member bank in local currency. E-cash is still not legal currency and is not a negotiable instrument. Internet banking has no offices, no tellers, no queues, free ATM debit card. There is no need to close the account and open another, when you shift residence or work.

The Internet has become a medium for commerce, a market place. One can rent out or buy out a place in the websites where information about one's products are displayed. One is 'invited' to visit the website which would usually have the address as http://www.(your name).com. Orders can be placed and payments made. The Census Bureau of the Department of Commerce, US, reported that the volume of retail sales on the Internet during the three months April to June 2003, was $12.48 billions, being approximately 1.5 per cent of the total retail sales ($858.8 billions) in the country. It is also estimated that by 2007, nearly 5 per cent of all retail sales may happen through the Internet.

Information as to the availability of products or the need for products, can also be posted in the Internet bulletin boards, reading which, offers may be received. It is estimated that, with increasing processing power, multimedia features such as 2D and 3D graphics, digital images, basic video and audio processing and communications will become possible on domestic PCs. The computer will become a virtual gateway in every home, enabling the user to discover new places, explore monuments, shop for anything, from anywhere in the world.

There are web sites that are visited by large audiences. Some of the places frequently visited are *communities* like Tripode.com or Geocites.com and *content sites* like Sony and Disney for entertainment, Weather for forecasts, ESPN for sports and CNN for news. There are other web sites that provide contents or services that appeal to specific segments, that have interests in news, sports, weather, finance and so on. Marriage bureaus and employment exchanges flourish on the Internet, as much as offers and enquiries for trade. Distribution is no longer physical.

Corporates are able to access the same financial markets that banks use. They can do without the services of the banks as an intermediary. Newspapers also lose similarly. Any newspaper or magazine can be read by anyone, anywhere in the world, even before local circulation takes place. About 150,000 persons are said to be reading *The Wall Street Journal* on the Internet every day.

Websites are places most suitable for communicating. The effectiveness of messages placed here is much greater than in traditional media like the press or the TV. More people will see it and also read it fully. Perishability is low. The sheer breadth of choice available to potential customers will create the need for third parties to play the role of facilitators. Facilitators will be required to provide both access to and interpretation for the mass of data that has become available. Hotmail, with its data base of 35 million subscribers, makes it possible for target audiences and advertisers to come together only if there is a commonality of interests. There were 20 million addresses added in Hotmail in 1998, double the total in 1997. The enormous volume of market data available at the click of a button is unprecedented. The amount of junk mail is equally unprecedented.

Value chains are being undermined. They are getting fragmented and refigured. For example, Amazon is an electronic retailer of books on the web. There is no physical store and no inventory. It has a catalogue, offering 2.5 million books, ten times larger than the largest chain store. It sold $15 million in 1997. Customers search through the catalogue by just about any criterion. Amazon orders from industry or wholesalers, repacks them and mails them from a central facility. Customers cannot browse through a book, but they can access book reviews. Barnes and Noble have also started selling books through the Internet. Saab, the car manufacturer, was planning to make the Internet the primary tool to sell and service vehicles, enabling customers to get everything from buying to repairs, without going to the dealer. Hotel reservations can be made by anybody, anywhere in the world, in 500 hotels which share the Access www site, and display photographs of their property, facilities, tariffs, restaurants, etc. Access also enables reservations in Cruise liners, Eurorail, etc. It is becoming a one-stop supermarket for travel-related services.

GE's dealers used to buy truckloads of appliances for the benefit of best price and in order to be committed to that product line. The 'loaded dealer' assumption turned invalid because of competition from independent low-price multibranded chains. With GE's Direct Connect system, retailers no longer kept own inventories of major appliances. They operated on the company's logistics system as though they had a wide range of variety of appliances. They had instantaneous access to GE's on-line order processing system 24- hours a day. They checked on model availability and ordered for 24-hours delivery. They also got the best price regardless of model, and three months credit if they sold nine major products and paid through electronic fund transfer.

The key to the success of companies in the future, particularly those in 'sunrise' industries, is the shortening of the supply chain, which are the entities involved in the flow of materials from procurement to manufacture, to transportation and ultimate sale in the market. The reason for Digital's troubles, which ended with Compaq buying it out at $9.6 billion and the Dell computers, which suffered a loss of $86 million in 1993 and was turned round to a profit of $8 billion in 1997, are said to be the length of their respective supply chains, delaying the response to the market. The turnover of the working capital is affected by the supply chain. The Internet shows a way to cut the chain.

Some of the early entrants occupying websites have had to close down. Some have had to cut down on their sizes and staff. While distribution costs are less on the Internet, marketing and maintenance (of a site) costs are high. The annual cost of maintaining a high profile site could be about $3 million. The barriers to entry in the Internet market, are very low. However, it is not easy for a surfer to find a site. The site will do well if the owner uses other media for promotion.

Experts advise caution in creating websites. There is no guarantee that a website will generate business. A website must be created as carefully as starting a new office. Its location should not be in a place where no one travels. It is a full marketing exercise. The response to a website will not be immediate. Even if income does not flow, there is saving in costs—costs of communication, printing promotional brochures, in generating sales leads, etc. Eastman Kodak estimates that there were 1,76,000 downloads of software drivers for Kodak's digital equipment, saving the company the costs of more than $4 million by avoiding the need for maintenance of telephone No. 800, taking shipment orders, sending software overnight, etc. Also, if the contents in the website are not changed from time to time, it could be as tedious and even painful as the advertisement that is seen repeatedly in the course of a cricket match telecast. The matter on the site should have a clean layout, be functional, have a simple structure and be user friendly.

Every development in technology brings risks as well as benefits. Some see the opportunities for self-aggrandisement existing simultaneously with the possibilities of honest trading. The safety of electronic cash transfer lies in the password. *Passwords and codes can be and are 'hacked'.* The cash can then be stolen without fingerprints and other clues being left behind. Total annual losses in electronic cash thefts is estimated at billions. Internet crime grows almost parallel to the business. Even very strict security barriers as of the Pentagon in Washington and the BARC in Mumbai are reported to have been crossed by hackers. The extent of theft, if any, will not become public information, however, the dangers are obvious. Sometimes crimes are committed by innocent hackers having fun. The Florida telephone system was shut down for seven hours by a 19-year old, surfing cyberspace.

❑ *The Intranet* ❑

The concept of networking, when applied exclusively for processing information within an organisation is called the Intranet. Any office of a courier service, with an Intranet connection, can track the movement of packages, by just keying in the way bill number. It would save in telephone bills (calling other offices) as well as in time. The Taj West End, Bangalore, used to make three copies of every order in the restaurant (for the kitchen, for F&B and for the steward) involving a lot of movement. Now, with all the restaurants including room service, being connected, an order fed into the system is automatically communicated to the respective sites (orders for drinks go only to the bar), and the billing is also done automatically as the prices are in the system's memory. Merrill Lynch could swap different accounts to post credit cards, checks, securities, deposits and update credit limit for each account holder on daily basis. The Intranet is used by Texas Instruments Ltd, for training as well as for sharing inventories in multiple locations. Price Water House has been able to reduce the time taken to respond to customer queries, from four weeks to two hours, because it can now directly access the database at headquarters. The Government of Andhra Pradesh, in its drive to replace the bureaucratic system with SMART (Simple, Moral, Accountable, Responsive and Transparent) systems, has, through the extensive use of technology, achieved tremendous expedition in jobs. For example, the job of searching for and certifying encumbrances on property, which used to take weeks, can now be completed within hours.

Corporates are permitted to have their own networks. They can also subscribe to a provider of VANS (Value Added Network Service), licensed by the government (Department of Telecommunications). In the former case, they control the network and it is highly secure. In the latter case, there are no problems of inadequate utilisation of bandwidth, maintenance, or finding skilled personnel. State-of-the-art technology is now available.

There are companies which maintain all contacts through desktops and e-mail. There is no paper and very few meetings. It is not even necessary to come to the office. Terminals at home are equally effective. The Intranet makes it possible for the same information to be available at every point in the same manner. Organisations like banks and insurance companies, having offices spread throughout the country and hundreds of correspondents and agents, use the Intranet to send communications to all of them. Specific communications to individuals can be sent through the equivalent of the e-mail through the Intranet instantly. Instruction and control requirements therefore, change drastically. The logic for a limited span of control also vanishes. Thus, Intranet makes it possible to have relatively flat structures, as well as improve communication in all directions. One of the disadvantages of these developments is that people do not meet and therefore, do not know each other. The social system does not develop and communication becomes impersonal.

Springfield City near Brisbane in Australia, is perhaps the first city, where everybody was linked by the net. Connections are like standard fittings of electricity and water connections. All transactions, enquiries, applications, requests, sanctions, payments, displays, promotions, etc., can be made through the net, many of them automatically. The possibility, as visualised, is that a modem on the lamp-post will inform the control room when the bulb has fused.

❑ *Resource Planning* ❑

Developments in clients/server systems have given rise to the growth of software for managing resources. Innovative process-integrated business solutions have given companies greater flexibility to be more responsive to customers and market changes, as well as to eliminate wasteful unnecessary activities. SAP's R/3 system was the software industry's first client/server software designed to integrate all business functions of an enterprise, taking advantage of relational databases and graphical interfaces. Between 1992 and 1997, it went through seven releases, each time reducing the technical problems associated with upgrading. Earlier approaches looked at Inventories (Materials Requirement Planning) which was MRP-I. The next, called MRP-II, was Manufacturing

Resources Planning, which extended to the shopfloor and distribution activities. ERP extended the gamut to include Engineering, Finance, Human Resources and Projects Management. It is an integrated approach providing a helicopter view, combining financial control with multiplant manufacturing coordination. It handles all organisationally relevant factors, like costs, efficiencies, inventory controls, increased customer service and cycletimes, from a total enterprise perspective, instead of from the perspective of departments, operations, etc. It takes care of causal factors like price cuts and campaigns, non-availability of raw materials, etc.

ERP is versatile. It is also expensive. The software used has to be evaluated for functional fit with the company's business processes, technology, client server capabilities, etc. Some companies have developed their own software, like ITC, for example, to manage the supply chain with manufacturing and logistics activities, linking nine manufacturing plants, 18 branch offices, 800 wholesale dealers, 15 lakh retail outlets, handling 35 brands. Bata, with 1200 models, each of 10 sizes, and with more than 1,000 outlets nationwide, and Maruti, dealing with 1,000 trucks and 1,600 consignments going daily to its vendors and dealers all over the country, use networks to manage their distribution, inventories, costs and billings.

❏ *Internet in India* ❏

The Internet came into India in the late 1980s in the form of the ERNET, which was a joint undertaking of the Government of India and the United Nations Development Programe (UNDP). All major nodes of ERNET were connected to each other. International access was provided from the National Centre for Software Technology (NCST), in Mumbai. Over 75,000 scientists in 800 academic and research groups had access to ERNET. These numbers were expected to increase to 275,000 and 3,000 respectively, by the year 2000.

On 15 August, 1995, VSNL launched the GIAS (Gateway Internet Access Service). Nodes were established at Mumbai, Delhi, Chennai, Kolkata, Bangalore, and Pune. Each GIAS node is connected to the Internet, via high speed MCI circuits. Users in remote areas in India could access GIAS service via I.NET which connected 99 cities and was maintained by the Department of Telecommunication (DOT). In the process of liberalisation, the Government of India allowed other organisations to become servers. Mahanagar Telephone Nigam Ltd, Bharat Sanchar Nigam Ltd., Satyam Infoways and many others, are now Internet providers. Those who provide cable television connections offer Internet connections as part of the cable service. Cellular telephone companies offer Internet services along with the telephone. The whole country can now access the Internet with or without a separate telephone.

As of June 1997, there were 35,000 dial-up subscribers and 90 leased-lines, each having many users. In July 2003, it was estimated that there were five million subscribers and more than 16 million users of the Internet. Trade and commerce is carried out among people using their personal computers and communicating through the Internet. Known as e-commerce, this business is very different from traditional trading practices. Either party will have little knowledge of the other transacting party. The extent of e-commerce in India is not considered to be significant, but is expected to grow very fast, because of its convenience and speed. Estimates by some consulting groups are that globally, e-commerce will be approximately US\$6.8 trillion by 2005 and that India's share would be around \$40 billion.

The stock market is an example of how the Internet makes transactions faster and more transparent. The number of transactions in the two main stock exchanges of the country, the Bombay Stock Exchange and the National Stock Exchange, exceeded 300 million in 2002. This was the third highest in the world, next only to the NASDAQ and the New York Exchange. The on-line electronic system with terminals in all cities, has made it possible for people located anywhere in India, to trade on real time basis and to have the settlements made by the next day. The electronic forms in which the shares are held by depositories, makes transfers also much easier. There is saving in time, in the movement of physical objects and also in clerical work. The efficiencies of these exchanges have made the regional stock exchanges redundant.

Companies having business interests in the rural areas have developed technologies appropriate for the Indian countryside. ITC, for example, has developed what they call *choupals*, to cover a sixth of rural India, by 2007. Community information centres organised by the Government of Andhra Pradesh, provide access to information related to land ownership, employment, health care, farming, financial supports, etc. When any organisation sets up a communication network, it is used by others as well. For example, the ITC's *choupal* is used by the LIC.

The Internet is used by banks (24-hour banking), insurance companies (forms and details of various plans), educational institutions (prospectus), financial intermediaries, government (for public comments on proposed legislations) and so on. Books and rail tickets are purchased and auctions are conducted on the Internet. All these require payments. There are issues relating to the validity of the instructions and authorisations. Some of these transactions are in the nature of agreements or contracts. Contracts have to be signed. The parties in these web-based transactions do not even meet and exchanges of messages by e-mail can be altered deliberately or accidentally. The Indian Information Technology Act, 2000, provides the legal framework for such transactions being valid and safe. The Act

- Provides for the legal recognition of the transactions carried out by alternatives to paper-based methods of communication and storage of information.
- Deals with contractual frameworks, evidentiary aspects, digital signatures, time of dispatch and time of receipt of electronic records.
- Lays down authorities for certification, regulation, licensing and their duties.
- Clarifies cyber contravention, civil and criminal, lays down penalties and adjudications.
- Appropriately amends the Indian Penal Code, 1860; Evidence Act, 1972; Banker's Book Evidence Act, 1891; and the Reserve Bank of India Act, 1934.

Publication of obscene information, hacking, destroying or altering data are all offences punishable with fines and/or imprisonment. If an employee is found guilty of such offences, the employer may also be liable.

Under the Prevention of Terrorism Act (POTA) passed in 2002, authorities are allowed to monitor all kinds of electronic communications, without legal constraints. There are concerns of human rights violations in these provisions.

Under the Indian Contract Act 1956, when an offer is accepted, the contract is complete. This Act clarifies what constitutes an offer and what constitutes the acceptance of an offer, when carried out through electronic media. Acceptance is binding on the offeree, when it enters the information system, that is, when he sends it out. It is binding on the offerer when it enters the computer resource designated by the addressee, or when it is retrieved by the addressee, if it had gone to some other computer resource.

The condition that the information has to be in writing, whenever applicable, is deemed to be satisfied in an electronic record, if it is accessible so as to be usable for subsequent reference. The use of zeros and ones is considered to satisfy the requirements of the General Clauses Act, which states, in Section 31(8), that a document includes any matter written, expressed or described upon any substance by means of letters, figures, or marks, or by more than one of those means, for the purposes of receiving that matter.

An electronic record will be deemed to be secure and the integrity of the information accepted, if any security procedure is applied. Security procedures are normally applied through cryptography techniques, which include encryption and decryption. Every user uses two keys, one public and the other private. These two keys are mathematically linked. The public key is known to all, like the e-mail ID. The private key is secret and known only to the user. When a message is to be sent by A to B, A uses B's public key and A's private key. B will be able to access the message using his two keys. Nobody else can. In India, the Department of Technology regulates the authorisation for encryption.

Digital signatures are permitted and recognised by the law. Certifying authorities are appointed in India to validate digital signatures. Certifying authorities in other countries have to be recognised in India. The Cyber Regulatory Authority as well as a Cyber Regulatory Appellate Authority have been provided for under the Act. Appeals against the decisions of the Appellate Authority can be made to the Supreme Court.

❏ *The Software Industry* ❏

The Indian software industry is one of the fastest growing in India as well as globally. This is also considered to be the main driver for the country's economic growth. Several foreign companies find it worthwhile to set up software business and development centres in India or to engage Indian personnel for the jobs abroad. There is a shortage of people in the software industry worldwide. The expertise is in areas of data base handling, client server architecture and in special applications like Y2K, Java programming and networking.

Export earnings from this sector crossed US$2 billion in 1997–1998, showing a growth rate of 50–75 per cent in five years. It touched Rs 4.8 billion in 2001–2002 and Rs 3.4 billion in the nine months from April to December 2002. Yet, the comparison globally is not that impressive. India's share in the global software market was only 0.5 per cent. A study carried out in early 1998 pointed out that US firms like Microsoft and EDS employ three and 17 times the number of people, earn 57 and 79 times the revenue and have 40 to 60 times the market value respectively, compared to TCS, which is known to be India's largest company, showing that the linear growth pattern of the Indian industry has to change to an exponential one, as in the US.

❏ *IT Enabled Services (ITES)* ❏

ITES constitutes a major growth area, leveraging India's strength in educated personnel with the knowledge of English. Using computers, satellites and the Internet, ITES cover many activities as follows:

- Call centres growing at a rate of over a 100 per cent from 8,500 employees and Rs 4 billion of revenue in 1999–2000 to 270,000 employees and 200 billion of revenue in 2008.
- Business Process Outsourcing (BPO) growing at over a 100 per cent from 15,000 employees and Rs 9.50 million of revenue to 35,000 employees and Rs 28.50 million of revenue in three years.
- Transcription (medical) employing 5,200 persons in 2001–2002 with revenues of Rs 52 million.
- Content development, animation and design, employing 30,000 people in 2001–2002 and having revenues of Rs 21 million.
- Remote maintenance and education growing at about 50 per cent per annum.

ITES grew at over 70 per cent in 2001–2002 and at 24 per cent in 2002–2003 compared to the software business which grew at 81 per cent in 2001–2002 and 76 per cent in 2002–2003. Globally, ITES was a $13.5 billion business and was expected to grow to $142 billion by 2008 and $200 billion by 2010. The Indian ITES is expected to generate revenues of $17 billion or 12 per cent of the global trade by 2008 and provide employment for one million more people. By 2015, more than three million jobs would have shifted to India, according to some studies Most of the *Fortune 500* companies, like British Airways, American Express, HSBC, America–On–Line, Prudential insurance, Phillips and GE, are setting up their own offices in India for ITES. Major Indian IT companies have set up separate units to handle the ITES. Wipro, for example, has Spectramind, Infosys has Progeon, Satyam has Nipuna and Polaris has Optimus.

Technology Parks or cybercities are places earmarked for ITES. They provide guaranteed uninterrupted electric supply and satellite linkages. The park in Chennai is spread over 200 acres and has an investment of Rs 70 crores. The Technopark in Trivandrum covers 70000 sq. ft of covered space. The Cybertowers near Hyderabad, has office space of 525,000 sq. ft, and was expected to generate an income of Rs 20 million in the year 2000 and Rs 160 million in 2005. Every state wants to set up parks of this kind, both because of the contribution to the economy, as well as the generation of employment. The six North Eastern states are being 'wired' by DOT for technology parks, ERNET and electronic clearing. The Software Technology Park India (STPI) set up three more earth stations and expanded locations in 20 secondary cities in 2000. ITESs are being established in smaller towns like Hubli, Patiala, Vishakhapatanam and many others. The benefits of new technology are reaching relatively distant communities, which makes for significant changes, socially and economically.

States are vying with each other to attract ITES companies to set up operations in their states. Kerala, for example, claims that Kochi has two submarine cables landing points, offering the best in connectivity. States are also very proactive in providing facilities for their people to acquire proficiency in IT operations, with as much passion as providing basic literacy.

BPO services include data management (entry, search, analysis), finance and accounts, cash flow analysis, website and network management, secretarial services, help desk, HR services, processing of pay rolls, insurance claims and credit cards transactions. Call centres provide essentially customer care services, answering queries, providing technical support, receiving and processing orders.

❑ e-Learning ❑

Both the Internet and the Intranet are being used extensively for the purposes of spreading knowledge. Companies which are keen to upgrade the knowledge and skills of their employees so that they can adapt themselves to the new technologies or to the new polices of the organisation, find these media a great help, particularly when the target audiences are huge with 1,000 or more people, spread out over 500 to 1,000 centres. Books, specially prepared notes and learning materials, and programmed self-learning modules can be placed on the net to be accessed and used at the convenience of the employee concerned, without disturbing his domestic or official schedules.

Institutes like the Institute of Materials Management, the Institute of Chartered Accountants, the Insurance Institute of India, that are engaged in the business of distance learning, will find the net useful to disseminate their courses, to answer the queries of the students, and even to conduct the examinations. Access to students overseas, is as quick as access to students in the same town. Experts predict that e-learning will grow at a very fast rate, supporting Indian educational bodies, as well as foreign educational bodies that are trying to market their courses in India.

❑ The Future ❑

Business Today on 6 December, 1998 reported that, in a survey, 92 per cent of chief executive officers, chief finance officers and strategic planners, believed that India's telecom industry was way behind global standards. This meant that the current developments were meagre compared to what is likely in the future. Since 1998, however, the growth has been exponential. The WTO expected that the business on the Internet would be around $300 billion by the year 2000. Forrester Research expected that 5 per cent of the world's commerce will be done on the Internet. That would exceed $500 billion. MIT's media lab, Nicholas Negroponte, estimated the figure to be around $1 trillion. All these estimates have been proved to be underestimates.

It is dangerous to try to predict the future. New developments are happening at a very fast pace. The bandwidth required is expected to grow by a factor of 50 to 100 in three years, overtaking the telephone network, guaranteeing delays of less than 150 milliseconds. The next generation protocol IPV-6 has been developed. SilkRoad Inc has demonstrated 93 gigabits per second over a single 62 mile fibre, without the use of amplifiers to regenerate the signal and without using the WDM (Wavelength Division Multiplexing) technique, whereby a single fibre carries many data streams, each a different colour of light, generated by its own laser. The demonstration carried 830 channels of satellite programming over one glass fiber. Using 'much less equipment', they expect to reach 10 tetrabits per second.

A non-resident Indian, Neil Tagare, in the US created a 28,000 km. Fibre Optic Link around the Globe (FLAG), which will be the single largest optical fibre network, with a minimum bandwidth of 640 gigabits per second and extend services that range from telephony, to Internet connectivity and videoconferencing. When complete, the complex network of under sea and overland cables with 262 landing points in 175 countries, linking every continent except Antarctica, is expected to be 100 times cheaper than the present fibre connectivity systems and will transport the equivalent of 25 million simultaneous phone calls.

The DVD (Digital Video Disc) is called the 'ultimate solution for byte-hungry info-gluttons', representing a qualitative shift from earlier storage media in terms of storage capacity and access speeds. It is the latest generation of optical disc technology that can hold any type of data, audio or video, and will eventually render audio CD, videotape, laserdisc, CD-ROM and perhaps, even video game cartridges, redundant.

Too many people around the world are working on applications of various kinds. There is a growing demand for mobile connectivity and interoperability, getting wireless devices to work with one another. The movement is towards convergent technologies, consisting of compilation and development of digital content for intra-organisational dissemination, cross institutional usage, collaboration projects, public domain information. This will occur because of wireless mobile handsets, the explosive growth of Internet and emergence of wireless application standards. The following expressions will be common vocabulary:

- E-goverance,
- E-commerce,
- E-medicine, referral, primary health centres,
- E-infrastructure dealing with bandwidths,
- E-learning,
- E-security for payments on-line.

There will be more IT applications in genomics, meter reading and billing, broadcasting, rural development, forestry and R&D. GIS (Geographic Information Systems) and GMPCS (Global Mobile Personal Communication Services) are two other popular expressions.

The following observations made by persons in the know are worth pondering upon:

The video games market is rapidly heading towards multiplayer games and the Internet .... The online games market also differs in one important aspect .... Users do not have to purchase the game, but will be willing to pay as they go, similar to coin operated arcade games.

As the Net gets used more and more, there will be times when customers need a certain level of bandwidth guaranteed. The technology to do this exists. Internet researchers have developed a new standard, the Reservation Protocol, to allow certain applications. To 'book' bandwidth across the 'Net', a business class Internet would have to be separated from those travelling economy class, the night time surfers, who access the Net via a low cost ISP and stay on line for hours.

The exponential growth in users is putting severe strains on the routers— devices that direct Internet traffic at each intersection. The routers do not scale well. CISCO, who has supplied 85 per cent of the routers, is pressing for a better IP numbering scheme. ATM (Asynchronous Transfer Mode) reduces dependency on routers.

Academics who were the original users of the Internet, today complain that they can no longer use it for research, because of the congestion .... They need a separate network.

SOME SELECT SERVICE INDUSTRIES

General Insurance

❏ Characteristics ❏

When an insurance policy is sold, only a promise is sold; a promise from the insurance company to compensate for losses as specified, if and when the event insured against occurs. The service of insurance effectively is when the promise has to be redeemed. That is, the service is provided when the claim arises, not when the policy is sold.

The event insured against is usually a tragic one; one that causes damage and loss to the policyholder. The event threatens the future of the person who has taken out the insurance policy. The service takes place in tragic circumstances. The service helps to relieve the impact of the tragedy, partly, not wholly. The service is intrinsically satisfying. Its infinite potential to give cheer and happiness, is often marred by the rigidities of procedure.

The market for general insurance is unlimited. Every person who has an asset of economic value and is engaged in economic activity, needs insurance. The market for general insurance ranges from individuals with personal household assets to corporate bodies with assets worth hundreds of billions of rupees, to producers (agricultural or industrial), traders, exporters. The market is a very big one, geographically and otherwise. Prospective customers are in the remote rural areas as well, engaged in agro-based economic activities. The risks to be insured against, are very varied, from cattle to pumpsets to high tech satellites and oil wells. Market segments need to be carefully distinguished, so that each segment is appropriately catered to.

General insurance is closely linked to international trade. Large amounts of insurance are reinsured globally. When a major accident occurs like an aircrash or an oil field explosion or a gas leakage and deaths as in Bhopal in 1984, several insurance companies around the world will share the loss.

❑ *Marketing* ❑

Marketing of insurance has to aim at:

- making people aware that these unpleasant possibilities could happen to them—a demand has to be created; and
- reducing the pain that may be caused by those events.

The person taking out insurance hopes that there may not be any reason to redeem the promise. He is not keen that the claim should arise. The amounts of insurance are likely to be the minimum necessary under the circumstances. It is up to the company to make him aware as to how much the minimum should be, after examining the risks involved.

The range of products in general insurance is very wide. Each one of the products has unique conditions, terms, warranties, exclusions, etc. The covers are subject to different laws of the country. Every theft is not burglary. There are differences between burglary, theft, larceny, house-breaking and robbery. To the owner of the property, these differences are semantic. Despite considerable standardisation, there are exceptions and exclusions to almost every policy. For example, if you want a Motor Comprehensive Policy, the premium has to be loaded if you have a chauffeur. You are also entitled to a discount if you are a member of the Automobile Association. Similarly, every policy has such specifications. The intermediary in the distribution system has to possess enough detailed knowledge about all the plans to provide the proper cover at the proper rates. *The buyer is not in a position to be aware or to understand these details.* He relies heavily on the insurer and the intermediary to be truthful and fair to him.

No one can remain indifferent to the risk insured against, just because he is insured. He has to continue to take all steps necessary to avoid the risk, to prevent the loss. A person who has taken insurance to cover damage during the transit of goods, cannot neglect proper packaging. When the event insured against occurs, the individual's loss may be reduced because of the insurance system of 'sharing' the loss by others. However, the total loss is not reduced. It occurs. There is a loss of national wealth.

A person taking out an insurance policy hopes that the insured risk may never occur. However, when it occurs, that is the time when insurance starts performing. The insured expects the promise to be redeemed quickly, and as he had understood it. The product called insurance can be experienced only in the process of claim payment. The lesser the formalities for settlement of claim, the better the product. The simpler the forms, the better the product. The speedier the response, the better the product. Factors relating to ease of access are relevant.

The claimant is a person in distress. He will also be anxious about getting the claim. Several formalities in the nature of evidence, forms, documents and statements are required to establish the bona fides of the claim. Some of them may be found to be defective. There may be delays while these are being examined. These may be asked for in ways that appear to be attempts at harassment or 'to avoid the claim'. All these cause anxiety. On the other hand, these can be asked for with courtesy, explaining the need and even helping to obtain them. The behaviour of the person processing the claim can considerably bring down the anxiety of the claimant and thereby enhance his satisfaction. This is as important as the technical proprieties of the claim.

❏ *Sales and Service* ❏

A person buying insurance depends on the salesman to choose the right policy for his purposes. He does not know what is covered and what is excluded by warranties or otherwise. He may not understand, even if he reads the policy. If the coverage under the policy does not match the requirements, it means that: (*a*) the required insurance is not properly arranged; and (*b*) what is arranged is unnecessary. The sale is not worth anything to the buyer. The error (in matching) will be found out by the buyer only when the claim is made and is processed. Until then, he assumes that the promises made by the policy he bought, are the same as the promises he wanted to buy. If at the time of a claim, it is found that the assumption was wrong, nothing can be done to make amends. The policy would turn out to be a dead loss. The insured person, in this case, will feel that he had been cheated. It is like the fire extinguisher that does not work when there is a fire and it cannot be put out. This happens if the extinguisher is not regularly 'serviced'. It is not enough to buy and instal the equipment. There are servicing and maintenance procedures for every equipment, to ensure its continued effective functioning. The contents have to be replaced and the valves checked regularly.

Similarly, also in insurance, a sale is not enough—servicing is important. There are conditions regarding warranties that are obligatory on the insured. He has to do (or sometimes not do) certain things, according to policy conditions. If he is not aware of these, and the warranty is breached, the policy will be void. Under certain 'open' policies, the changes in the amount at risk are required to be submitted to the insurer regularly. This is in cases where the policy covers stocks in a godown, and the stocks (quantities and qualities) vary considerably over short periods of time, or goods of different descriptions are being shipped almost daily in different quantities to different destinations. If the insured fails to do so within the stipulated period, the claim processing will run into difficulties.

There are certain procedures to be followed, when the event insured against occurs. Failure to do the same can create problems in processing claims. The insured must be made aware of these requirements, not when the claim is to be lodged, but even before the claim arises. For example, when the event insured against occurs, there may be requirements of having to file a police complaint, finding witnesses to the event, documenting certain data for details and for verification, obtaining certificates from the port or the carrier about the condition of the goods, etc. If these are not obtained on time, they may not be available when asked for later, and that could prejudice the admissibility of the claim.

'Servicing' after sale of an insurance policy, takes care that these problems do not occur and that the policy is maintained, ready to perform when the occasion arises. In several cases, the insurance cover is not standard. It is tailored according to the specific situations of the prospective insured. This is so in large industries, where the risks to be covered are many and may not fall within standard specifications because of new technology, new processes, automated systems, different layouts and so on. If the risk is real, it has to be covered by insurance, even if it is new and unique. There is a tendency among insurers to say 'Sorry we cannot cover this risk', because they have no experience with that risk. For example, at one time, exporters of tyres could not export tyres to the US without product liability insurance and that could not be arranged in India. Computer crimes—a major risk in countries using computer networks heavily—were not insurable in India. Product and professional liability covers are limited.

In insurance, service is very important. Therefore, the agent is important. In fact, many insured people buy what the agent recommends as good for them, without verifying the correctness of their advice. In other words, *the agent is the main product which the insured buys*. Once the agent is bought, that is, he is accepted as knowledgeable and trustworthy, the purchase of the insurance policy on the advice of the agent becomes a natural consequence.

❏ *Pricing Policy* ❏

The premium is the price of insurance. The premium is based on the rating. If the rate of cover is 40 paise per Rs 1000 and the amount at risk is Rs 10 million, the premium is Rs 4000.

Rate is related to the extent of risk. If the risk is less, the rate is less. The risk of fire in a godown stocking eggs is less than in a godown stocking oil. Determining the amount of risk, is called underwriting. The underwriter decides the rate and the premium is worked out. Underwriting needs experience and knowledge. In a vastly distributed network as in India, it is not possible to have enough people who can examine each risk and make an underwriting decision. Therefore, risks are classified by experts according to certain parameters. The premium can then be determined by any person, after verifying the applicability of the parameters to a particular case. This verification needs much less experience and technical knowledge. The job of classifying risks and deciding the premium chargeable in each case is entrusted to the Tariff Advisory Committee (TAC).

Several risks are not tariffed, meaning that they have not been classified by the TAC. In all such non-tariff cases, the rate is decided by the underwriters of the insurance companies. The rate is not exact. The underwriters build in some margin of safety. If the amount at risk is very large, like a shipping company or a petrochemical complex, a small variation of rate can make a substantial variation in premium. Therefore, the insured would like to negotiate for a reduction of rate.

In tariff risks, there is very little scope to make adjustments for the difference between one insured and another. Everybody is treated as average. However, in non-tariff risks, consideration is usually given to the specific situation of the insured, the standards of its management and so on. Simultaneously, there is also the scope of surrendering to the pressures of competition. The negotiations are facilitated, if records are maintained about

- the past experiences in terms of the risks proposed to be insured,
- the maintenance standards of the insured.

Price cutting in insurance, can be suicidal. If the amount at risk is high, needing reinsurance arrangements, the rating will need the concurrence of the reinsurers.

Insurance is not price sensitive. That is to say, the amount of insurance will not vary according to the premium charged. Insurance, if necessary, will be taken at any cost. If there is a perception that the premium is high, what it really means is that the perception of risk is low, and then insurance will not be taken. The thinking would be 'If the danger comes, we can afford to bear the loss'. For example, if you have a minor cold, you may not go to the doctor for treatment. You might do steam inhalation, or drink milk with turmeric, or *tulsi* water. If someone suggests medicine worth Rs 40 you might say 'Why spend so much for such a minor thing?' However, if the suffering is severe, you will go to a specialist doctor and spend any amount on the doctor and on medicines. Thus, price is not what you pay in monetary terms, but is relative to value. In insurance, the value is not measurable in money terms, but is a sense of assurance that you can face a risk if it hits you. It is like having a watchman. The watchman's salary is high or low, not in absolute terms, but according to what there is to protect.

❑ *Customer Contacts* ❑

The business of insurance is not understood by many. It is not understood, for example, that it is an arrangement of indemnity, not an opportunity to benefit from accidents. If a car is damaged, the owner may expect that the insurer should pay for the replacement of parts with new ones. He will become annoyed when he is told that there will be a deduction for replacements. He would also object to deductions because of under-insurance. He may ask 'Suppose I had over insured, would you have paid more ? Then why deduct for under-insurance?' If the cashier had been swindling him, the employer expects the fidelity guarantee to pay up the loss and he may resent questions being asked about how and when the loss was discovered, the nature of checks and controls, police complaints made, and so on. One expects that he should be entitled to special treatment, because for the last 10 years he had not made a single claim.

Misunderstandings such as these, influence perceptions and opinions about value of insurance. A regular programme of contacts between the insurance company and its customers helps to

- explain each other's stands,
- clarify expectations from each other,
- strengthen favourable relationships.

Such contacts work for mutual advantage. This is more important because of the Consumer Protection Act. It will counter the accusation that there was misrepresentation. The most important purpose, however, as stated earlier, is building up customer goodwill, having a better customer profile and an appreciation of insurer's attitude to customer needs.

Some simple methods which could be adopted for customer education are:

1. To enclose a simple brochure with details of every policy, listing out essential obligations and procedures and also details on

    (i) what the policy covers,
    (ii) what the insured has to do,

(iii) what the insured should not do,
(iv) formalities for making a claim,
(v) whom to contact for information when necessary.

2. To organise in every office a person or counter to answer all queries patiently and correctly.
3. To keep leaflets and brochures ready for distribution for anyone who asks for it (people like written documentation for support).
4. To present small articles with the telephone number of the office which can be kept in places, quickly seen in times of emergency. For cars, this can be in the form of stickers, on the windscreen or dashboard. For offices, they can be paper weights, penstands, etc. For individuals, they can be key chains.

❏ *Surveyors, Tribunals, Lok Adalats* ❏

When an insured makes a claim, under the policy, it has to be examined to check that

- The event has genuinely taken place,
- There has been no premeditated effort to cause the event,
- The event is covered by the policy, and
- The amount claimed is reasonable and admissible.

Occasionally, certain events are stage-managed to make claims on the insurer. This is a convenient method to overcome a cash crunch. The tendency to exaggerate losses is also quite common. On matters like this, there can be disputes between the insurance company and the insured. A dispute does not do any good to the relationship between the insured and the insurer. So the system of surveyors has been introduced. The surveyor will examine the loss and the circumstances and recommend to the insurer, the amount of the claim that would be reasonable to admit.

A surveyor is an independent professional like an engineer, metallurgist, chartered accountant or actuary, appointed by the insurer to survey and assess losses. A surveyor may be an individual or a firm or a company having experts, making his services available to insurers.

A surveyor is expected to record the facts relating to the loss truthfully, without any bias either towards the insurance company, or to the claimant. His work is also often investigative. He has to be sensitive to details that suggest abnormality in the situation. Several frauds have been unearthed by surveyors. Some years ago, an international racket was unearthed when surveyors noticed a pattern in insurance claims involving the loss of ships on the high seas. Ships with full loads, after having set sail from ports, would be reported missing without any trace after a few days. Surveyors thought this strange, particularly as no distress signals had been received by other ships in the neighbourhood (of the position last reported) and there had been no reports of turbulent weather. It was ultimately found, that the ships had indeed not sunk, but had been directed elsewhere, and sold to be scrapped or repainted, refitted and rechristened, to be back in business again.

Tribunals are appointed to arbitrate on disputed claims. The Motor Accidents Claims Tribunal (MACT) is appointed by governments to decide on third party claims in motor accident cases. Such arbitration is necessary as the reasonableness of the damages claimed, are difficult to determine. One way to look at the reasonableness of the claim is to see the economic value of the life of the person who has died. Even if a person is not employed, there is a value to his life, in terms of support and guidance to the family. A housewife's life is invaluable. A student's life can be measured in terms of what he could have been after completing his education. These are values beyond the monetary earning at a point of time. It is assumed that an independent judicial authority might be able to arrive at equitable conclusions on these matters. In September 2003, the MACT awarded Rs 15 million as compensation for an US citizen, who was killed in a road accident in Jaipur. He was a 22-year old carpenter.

Since the mid-80s, a new system called the Lok Adalat has been introduced. It provides for summary and quick disposal of long pending disputes, where no major questions of law are involved. A senior judge decides these cases, which are pending before the MACTs and consent decisions are made. The judge facilitates an agreement between the claimant and the insurer and that consent is given the force of a court decision binding on both sides. The system has had the effect of expediting settlement of claims.

❏ *Future Trends* ❏

The following are some important factors that may compel closer attention:

1. Motor insurance is a loss-making proposition. Upward revision of premiums is not likely to be an answer to the problem. Considerable scope exists for better risk management. The insurance industry will have to liaison with government authorities, to bring about improvements in the licensing of vehicles and drivers, road surfacing, road alignments, patrolling, signboards, and so on. Simpler mechanisms may have to be

devised to ensure that third party coverage is total, cutting down on the costs of individual processing.

2. There would be a much bigger reinsurance market in India, both inward and outward.

3. The 'Individual' segment is relatively neglected. This segment will have to be exploited for two reasons. First, the consumer will ask for it. Second, it is likely to be a large and profitable portfolio.

4. The field force will have to be entrusted with more functions like renewals, receipts and small claims, for reasons of speed and economy.

5. The requirements of points (3) and (4) above may justify the growth of smaller agency and underwriting units who would have qualified competent personnel, who could be engaged to inspect and 'rate' at the proposal stage, just as surveyors assess at the claim stage.

6. There would be a need for wider geographical spread of offices and faster decision-making processes, including the use of computer programmes, as decision support systems.

Life Insurance

❑ *Characteristics* ❑

- In life insurance, unlike in general insurance, the promise has to be redeemed sooner or later. No claim is to be paid on a fire insurance policy if there was no fire during the term of the policy. However, a holder of a life insurance policy will have to be paid earlier, if he dies, or later, if he survives the term.

- The amount payable on a claim arising in life insurance is not in doubt. It is as mentioned in the policy. The amount payable in a claim arising in general insurance depends on the extent of damage and has to be determined through surveys and assessment.

- Most of the claimants have not suffered a loss. They are survivors (of the duration of the policy) asking for the fulfilment of a promise, in circumstances which are not tragic.

- Claimants of death benefits are persons different from the ones who had taken out the policy and perhaps know little about the circumstances and conditions under which the policy was taken or had been looked after.

- Almost all policies are long term ones. Most of the policies are for terms of 15 years or more. There could even be terms of 40 years or more.

❏ *Plans* ❏

Conceptually, life insurance is very simple. There are only two basic kinds of plans. One is a 'term' policy, whereunder the money, called the Sum Assured (SA), is payable, if the insured person dies within a specified period. The period can be specified as without limit. The second is the 'pure endowment' whereunder the SA is payable, if the insured person survives the specified term. When you combine the two, you get an endowment policy, whereunder the SA becomes payable on death (within the specified period) or on survival (of the specified period).

All policies of life insurance are varying combinations of these two basic plans. The available options are:

- Choice of the term of the policy.
- Mode of payment of premium, once, twice, four times or 12 times a year.
- Term of premium payment, same as or less than the term of policy.
- Payment of policy money in lump sum or in instalments.

❏ *Annuities* ❏

When the amount payable on maturity (the insured person having survived the specified term) is to be paid in regular instalments instead of as a lump sum payment, it is called an annuity. A pension is an annuity payable to an employee which, as per the terms of his appointment, commences on termination of appointment, by retirement or on prior death or other specified circumstance. An annuity commences on a specifed date or a specified contingency, and continues

- for a specified period of years,
- till the death of stipulated person(s),
- for a specified period of years and beyond up to the death of stipulated person(s).

❏ *Group Policies* ❏

Life insurance policies are usually sold to individuals. However, a group life insurance policy, called the master policy, can be issued to a collective like: (*a*) a company covering its employees; or (*b*) an association (club) covering its members. The persons to be covered as well as the benefits are specified in the schedule attached to the master policy. Premiums are paid by the company or the association as the case may be, which may or may not be collected from the members. The insurance cover may be term, payable on death (usually during membership), or pure, payable on survival, usually as an annuity.

❑ *Comparative Advantage* ❑

Life insurance generally provides money in the event of death and/or survival. It is a financial arrangement. Being a financial arrangement, comparisons are made with other financial arrangements, which may be perceived, as alternatives. Such comparisons have limitations.

The basic, core life insurance product is the 'term'. It is augmented with the addition of the savings element, pure. It is the augmented part of the product that invites comparison. This comparison is made because many holders of life insurance policies survive the term. The comparisons are made, without clarifying the assumptions relating to several matters like appreciation, inflation, incidence of tax, individual's financial position, realisability, and so on. Very few are similar on any of these factors. Even two schemes of any mutual fund will not be identical.

Since the mid-70s, some insurance companies in other countries sought to offer the pure endowment part of an insurance plan, as an investment for all practical purposes with that part of the premium, sharing in the fortunes of a chosen portfolio of funds. Options existed to switch from one portfolio to another at a nominal cost. Minimum returns were guaranteed. Managing these funds needed exceptional skills, monitoring the trends in the capital market and evaluating the fund status on a daily basis. With unpredictable movements in the money markets in the early 1990s, companies found it difficult to honour the guaranteed commitments.

The product image of life insurance is by and large, blurred. The concept of risk is rather vague. An usual question is 'Where is the risk when a person does not die?' This question is valid only retrospectively. A valid prospective question is 'What is the guranatee that one will not be dead by the evening?' However, this question is usually neither asked nor answered. Only competent individual salesmen can make people aware that the risk is not only very real, but also immediate, prospectively.

Many prospects do not know or understand the implications of the plans available. They depend on what the agent tells them. Before a life insurance policy is bought, the prospect, in fact, buys the agent. The agent, therefore, is the primary product of the life insurance company. The better the agent is equipped to deal with the customer's needs, the better the satisfaction to the customers.

The agent is the intermediary between the customers and the insurance company. The customer–agent link is stronger than the agent–company link, which in turn, is stronger than the customer–company link. Customer loyalty depends on how strong the agent's link with the customer is. The agent has to keep in touch with the changes in the customer's situation including marriages, deaths of relatives, release of mortgages, etc., which may necessitate changes in title to policy moneys and have them properly recorded in the company's office. Otherwise, the promises made by the agent and believed by the prospect, may not be fulfilled. The agent may be seen to be false.

A study made by the Insurance Institute of India in 1987, by interviewing 2,510 policyholders in 26 cities, had the following observations:

- Agents do not maintain regular contact with policyholders, although they are seen as available, whenever necessary.
- Of these, 50 per cent said that if they had any work to be done, they would go to the office directly rather than get in touch with the agent.
- Agents are perceived as knowledgeable, but also as concerned more with their own benefits than those of policyholders.

❑ *Principle of Uberrima Fides* ❑

The business of insurance, both life and general, is based upon the principle of *Uberrima Fides* or Utmost Good Faith. This principle says that the contract of insurance is entered into by the insurance company by accepting on faith, the averments made by the proposer in the proposal, for insurance. Accordingly, if on a later day, any of these averments made in the proposal for insurance are proved to be false, and material facts are shown to have been suppressed, the contract will become null and void. This is in contrast to the normal commercial principle of *Caveat emptor* or 'buyer beware' whereby, it is incumbent on the buyer to check on facts which are material for his purpose. Insurance is treated on a different footing because of a number of valid reasons. One of the reasons is that the physical condition of a person, which is the main basis for underwriting an insurance contract, cannot be known to a third person, even if examined by a doctor, if the person chooses to hide the reality. This is so in general insurance also. The insuring person can change the contents of the godown or package to be insured, after the inspection is over. The more important reason however, is that a life insurance company is deemed to be a trustee on behalf of the community of policyholders and any attempt by an individual to mislead through the suppression of facts, will be detrimental to the interests of that community.

The same principle of trusteeship should pervade all dealings of the company with its policyholders. An attitude of trying to avoid claims on the pretext of irregularities, which may not be material, is contrary to this principle. *Uberrima*

Fides demands that genuine claims are not denied on grounds of minor improprieties. If a premium cheque is dishonoured, because the clearing bank had made a mistake, the policy can be strictly treated as lapsed. However, that would not be fair. The insurance company is obliged to pay every claim that is legitimate and due, and at the same time, deny every claim that someone is trying to collect improperly.

The same principle of trusteeship requires that the insurance company resist pressures from the courts and other bodies to compromise on principles of propriety. There is no place in an insurance business for social concerns. Social concerns, if important can be funded separately and not made part of insurance funds. Attempts at fraud in insurance claims are, like other frauds, clothed in apparently perfect evidence. They need the astute mind of an experienced claims manager to detect and find, first suspicion, and then evidence to support the suspicion. The standards of evidence that judicial processes demand are difficult to uphold here. Due to this, several insurance claims are fought in courts and ordered to be paid. The strictures made by some of the courts accusing the company of taking 'hyper-technical views', suggests that there is a lack of appreciation about how the insurance business is to be managed.

The obligations of 'good faith' and trusteeship are such that claims arising out of suppressed information should be repudiated. The amount being 'paltry' is of no consequence to the validity of the decision. In insurance, the community of customers gets precedence over individual customers.

❑ *Security* ❑

The principle of trusteeship has to be practised in the way the insurance funds are managed. Safety and security have to be the primary considerations. Therefore, there would be some sacrifice in respect of yields in the short term. Prudent insurance managers may appear to be somewhat non-dynamic and averse to taking risks. They are also laughed at by 'smart' operators, particularly at times of economic boom. Insurance companies which invested substantially in equity in 1980s in the US, taking advantage of bullish stock markets, came to grief in the 1990s. Many of them went into liquidation. The customers lost. Those companies which were criticised for their conservatism and unwillingness to adapt, are the ones who continued to grow and redeem their pledges. It was easy to point out the foolishness of not investing in junk bonds and making quick money. The 'foolish' are the ones that survived when the junk bonds went into the junk yard.

In connection with the Indian scam of 1993, the names of many leading banks appeared in the press. However, the insurance companies did not figure in the suspect list. The reason perhaps, is that the management of insurance funds is traditionally averse to the 'new', until the 'new' has been tested as safe. The laws permit only limited freedom to invest in new companies without a history of profitable operations. These limitations were introduced into the statute by insurance managers.

❑ *Pricing* ❑

The price paid by the policyholder to the insurance company, in consideration of the promise to pay on death or survival, is called the premium. To the insurance company, premium is cost plus. If 1,000 persons are insured for Rs 50,000 each, for a period of 25 years (means SA payable at the end of 25 years or earlier death) then the premium (P) has to be such that the promise can be met from the fund accumulated from the premium paid by 1,000 people in the first year and surviving policyholders in each succeeding year. The factors involved are therefore, the number of persons who may die each year during the next 25 years (called the mortality rate), the rate at which the fund will accumulate (interest rate), and the expenses of managing the fund (salaries, rent, stationery etc.). The P once decided cannot be changed for the next 25 years. Therefore, assumptions are made as to what might be the mortality, interest and expenses levels in the future. These assumptions are made to be on the safer side, providing cushions for adverse experience. A riot as in December 1992/January 1993, or the bomb blasts in Mumbai in March 1993, can suddenly increase the deaths. The cushions help the company to meet such abnormal variations.

Since the premiums are calculated on the basis of assumptions, insurance companies undertake to examine each year the variation between actual experience and the assumptions. Due to the margins built into assumptions, the actual experience will be usually favourable, which means that the actual premium collected would have been more than necessary. The fund accumulated through this extra collection is called a surplus and usually returned to the policyholders by way of bonus.

The mortality, interest and expense factors that go into the calculation of premium, reflect the experience of the company. The particular segment with which the insurance company transacts business, may have a mortality rate different from that of other segments, which would be different from that of the total population. A nationalised insurer like the LIC of India, also does business only with selected, not all, segments. Ladies and children, farmers and poor people, do not figure prominently among LIC's policyholders. The rural segment had in the early days, only marginal representation. This is now increasing. The urban professionals and the salaried class still constitute the major segments.

When other segments enter into the LIC's community of policyholders in large proportions, the mortality experience will change, perhaps in an adverse manner. So also, interest rates prevalent in the market are not as relevant as the rates within the policy of investment it pursues. The policy of a prudent insurance funds manager, as pointed out earlier, could be very different from that of a common investor. He does not normally transact to book immediate profits. He is a long-term investor and does not speculate.

❏ *Publicity* ❏

Life insurance is rarely bought as a response to advertisements. Advertisements are effective

- as reminders to intimate change of address, pay premium, make nominations, etc.,
- as general information on bonus declaration, special revival schemes, etc.,
- to build the corporate image as financially strong, as a responsible social citizen, etc.

Those who have received policy moneys on the death of the life insured, are the best endorsements for a life insurance company. They are the ones who experience what life insurance means and what it can do differently from other financial arrangements, how a previously determined amount comes in at a time when the future looks bleak with debtors swooping on heirs, threatening to foreclose mortgages and attach property. Satisfied claimants are powerful and effective as word-of-mouth media. Their stories persuade others strongly.

Systems to process death claims should be geared to quick action. Claimants may be ignorant of policy conditions. They may not be able to locate or produce necessary papers. If a good agent is in touch with the claimant, he can smoothen up difficulties with suggestions for alternatives. Otherwise, the office should take up this role and reinforce the image of a friend in times of need. The tendency to help should not extend to suspicious claims, which may not be frequent, but do occur.

Public Services

By public services are meant a whole range of activities performed by public bodies like government or muncipalities, for the community. These services include police, road maintenance, water supply, sanitation, town planning, public distribution and licensing and registration (of vehicles, drivers). Public bodies sometimes undertake services like schools, medical clinics, city transportation, or telecommunications, services which private bodies may also undertake. In such cases, the difference would be that private bodies would be catering to selected segments which are likely to provide financial surpluses, while public bodies may be serving the entire community or specific segments, which would otherwise not be able to avail of these essential services, because of financial or other competitive handicaps. Medical clinics and postal services in remote areas are unlikely to interest the private sector. Many bus routes are run by the state, connecting villages, although they are not economically viable. The promotion of social good, even if not economically viable in the short term, is a primary concern of public services.

❏ *Characteristics* ❏

Public services are characterised by the following:

- They are guided by public policy and funded by public funds, collected through taxes or other levies.
- Application of public funds are regulated by rules and procedures seeking to avoid misuse.
- Decisions are usually centralised. Actions need approval of multiple authorities. Supervisory authorities are many. Discretion is never absolute.
- Application of funds are subject to scrutiny and report by regulatory bodies like audit and vigilance.
- Performance of these services are required to subserve public interest and therefore likely to be commented upon and discussed by the press, elected representatives, politicians, community leaders and so on.
- Public servants who render public services are subject to pressures from vested interests, representing different sections of the community and seeking relatively better advantages for their respective constituencies.
- Public servants are likely to be accused, not always with justification, of having favoured particular sections of the community to the detriment of others. This is done very often to build pressures and obtain conformity to one's own preferences.
- Many of these services are restrictive in nature, curtailing individual freedom and privileges, for the larger benefit of the community as a whole.
- Communication is mostly in writing and along 'proper channels' in the hierarchy. It is therefore, slow and often inadequate.

❑ *Image* ❑

Public services have necessarily to be bureaucratic. In the concept of management, bureaucracy is a fine system of organisation, based on rational, logical and legal principles, and ensuring a consistent, impartial, impersonal performance. Even organisations in the private sector are, to a considerable extent, bureaucratic, with clearly defined rules of procedure, responsibility allocation and authority. Yet, the word 'bureaucracy' has over the years, acquired infamous connotations, and represents wooden, insensitive administration, unresponsive to the realities of the situation.

Public servants operating with public funds cannot be given much discretion in the use of those funds. The community has in some form or other, to decide on how the funds have to be utilised and the officials will have to conform to those decisions. Public accountability cannot be diluted.

Those who criticise the bureaucratic nature of public service would be the first to highlight every variation from the laid down procedure, as if the variation is, ipso facto, proof of malafide and impropriety. This invariably happens when the decision of the public servant was different from what one had canvassed for. The public servant's valid defense of bona fide always, is that he acted according to rules. Thus, *public servants try to be correct as per rules and procedure, even if they miss the purpose for which their activities are organised. Efficiency (doing things the right way) gets precedence over effectiveness (doing the right things).*

The image of 'bureaucracy' and the implied connotation of poor effectiveness, has evolved partly out of the commentators and opinion makers focussing on non-performance. Incidents of non-performance are plenty. However, the incidents of performance far outnumber those non-performances. No conscious note is taken of the fact, for example, that in December 1992 and January 1993 during the riots, when most of the normal activities were at a standstill, offices and shops were closed and people hardly stirred out of their homes, the municipal services continued to be almost normal. Water supplies were maintained, there was a smooth supply of electricity, garbage did not accumulate, hospital services were able to cope with the much heavier load of emergencies and even bus and train services were almost normal. Again, the services were very effective in responding to the explosive situation on 12 March 1993, during the bombs blasts in Mumbai. Statements were issued by the government and the police reassuring the people. While the authorities did a commendable job in investigation and identification of the persons involved, some newspapers were looking for discrepancies in details between the various statements, suggesting that the authorities were not competent enough. *The point is that public services run the risk of their weaknesses and failures being noticed and highlighted. The successes are ignored, or taken for granted. The consequence is a poor image.*

Another lasting image of the public services is that public servants are corrupt, that they do not do their duty, unless influenced through money (bribes) and/or otherwise powerful persons. Instances are aplenty to justify these impressions. Media like the press and the cinema, strengthen these impressions. Here again, is an instance of Pareto's Principle, *more than 80 per cent of media attention is on the less than 20 per cent who are deviants, while more than 80 per cent of the duty conscious public servants, get less than 20 per cent of media attention.*

❑ *Pricing* ❑

Pricing of public services is subject to approvals from authorities outside the operational management. They are not based on the costs of providing the services, rather on the affordability of the customer and other social considerations. Subsidies are inbuilt, but not always explicit, because costs are hidden within multiple centralised operations. The costs of recruitment of staff, of reservations for various groups, of banks operating in remote areas, of procuring and holding stocks of grains etc., are not well defined. Prices are also subject to political considerations, like not alienating certain constituencies.

The pricing of public services is not based on economic considerations, but on considerations of public policy. Making a profit is not considered appropriate, while providing subsidies (for services to the poor and the agriculturists) is often considered not only appropriate but also desirable. As a consequence of such policies, differential pricing is quite common, in hospitals, in taxes, in electricity charges, in the public distribution system, in schools, and so on.

❑ *Public Support* ❑

The offerings of the public services (supply) are:

- inadequate to meet the demands of the customers, and
- without alternatives to the customer.

The demand for public hospital services is always more than the supply because

- poorer sections cannot afford the private hospitals,
- certain services like immunisation or attention to police cases, are available only there,
- public funds to invest in hospital services are limited.

In many cases, there are no alternatives, even if one could afford them. Examples are police services, the judicial system, town planning, water supply.

In situations like these, the providers of services experience heavy demands on their time and efforts. They also have to cope with relatively meaningless queries and exasperating behaviour from ignorant, misinformed customers. They may tend to treat the customers with some indifference, perhaps, with some arrogance. Customers having few options to avoid the service, either suffer these indignities or attempt, not very gently, to assert their rights to more courteous and earnest service. This is a vicious cycle that does not help to improve consideration for each other.

If the community of users of the services are not satisfied, the pressure on public servants will increase through their representatives and the media. On the contrary, if the community of users are satisfied, the pressure will work in support of the public servants, enabling them to resist the pressures from vested interests. There have been instances when the public have openly demonstrated support for the public servants, when they were being subject to false accusations and unfair instructions.

While an income tax officer cannot get the laws changed, he can make it easier for assessees to deal with the income tax office, in answering queries, making forms available, helping them to fill them up, speeding up assessments and being more empathetic to assessees. A summons from the tax official need not, but does, cause anxiety. The large volume of litigation on income tax matters, it is said, is due as much to assessees trying to avoid legitimate dues, as to assessors misinterpreting the law and facts, unfairly against the assessees.

The police force needs support of the community for it to be effective. The support cannot come through methods that instil fear. Mothers persuade children to behave properly, even to drink milk, by threatening to call the police. The police has to be perceived as friendly, helpful and good to cooperate with, not to be feared. User-friendly practices have to be introduced. *Customer-oriented behaviour is essential. An attitude of responsiveness has to be inculcated.*

❏ Media Contacts ❏

Public services may not do much advertising. State governments at times, advertise achievements of the current ministries. These carry little conviction but reinforce the conviction that vested interests misuse public administration systems. However, public services can do much by way of public relations and publicity. It is good to build relationships with the local press and the public and feed them with data on what is happening. A press which is favourably inclined is a great asset.

Public servants have to learn to handle the media and provide accurate information. False information can easily be discovered and the ensuing embarrassment can be very disturbing. Public servants have to become adept in handling the media. They should be seen as cooperative and transparent. A responsible media will welcome such contacts and respect the requirements of secrecy when explained. It is not possible to protect public servants from the limelight of public attention; it is better to prepare them for it. In modern times, aggressive reporters with video cameras confront public servants with probing questions. Embarrassed officials are shown fumbling in thier answers, giving impressions of either incompetence or falsity.

The media does not accept reticence. They need information. If public servants do not help, they would publish what they have. The result is that false, distorted information goes unchallenged. Surreptitious contacts continue and documents are leaked, sometimes with the intention of discrediting public servants.

An important outcome of allowing public servants to be in contact with the media is that they are likely to become more professional and duty conscious. A public servant's professionalism is in perfoming his tasks as the policy, rules and his better judgement require him to, not as his political bosses may, unauthorisedly, tell him to. Several public servants, including officials of public sector enterprises have yielded to the suggestions and pressures from politicians, hoping to be in their good books and hoping also to be protected from criticism. These hopes have often been frustrated. Anyone who had acted contrary to own judgement, would find it difficult to justify himself when questioned by third parties. Exposing public servants to the public gaze through the media, would be enough incentive for them to adhere to their professional judgement.

❑ *People* ❑

Rewards by way of additional increments or quicker promotions may not be possible in public services. Yet, employee motivation can be sustained through the grant of responsibility, providing the opportunity to grow and to enhance one's knowledge/skills in areas of one's choice. Public servants have access to information and perspectives that are more complete than in any other organisation. It also gives them an advantage in providing inputs in seminars and conferences. This is an opportunity which could well be lost if one's concerns do not go beyond one's daily routines. Here is a motivational tool largely ignored. The human resource also is wasted. An opportunity for recognition at a conference of professionals is highly valued. Very few people would spurn that kind of growth and development, which is a bigger reward than increments.

Such opportunities should not be made available only to a few. Questions of equality and equity would arise.

❏ *Quality* ❏

The customer's perception of quality of public service is generally poor. All gaps relevant to satisfaction from service are wide in the public services because

- there are customer segments, widely varying in expectations,
- there are too many layers between customer contact points and decision making points,
- there are laws and regulations defining the parameters of service offer, which do not adapt easily,
- objective data necessary to satisfy the multiple layers of supervisory and control authorities at distant points, cannot capture the intangible and heterogenous nature of service transactions,
- communication channels are not free and open,
- personal contacts are infrequent,
- communication outside the organisation, has to be approved by specific authorities not always close to points of service delivery.

Nevertheless, individual service outlets (offices) can, within the laws, regulations and policies, make differences in customer satisfaction levels if

- they present more acceptable physical surroundings,
- between themselves, employees decide to be more responsive to customer needs, not necessarily to grant what is asked for, but to patiently explain why, whatever is done, is being done that way,
- employees decide to accept and distribute responsibility for various service operations, avoiding role ambiguity and role conflict,
- employees support each other as in a team, and share the credits that may accrue,
- there is encouragement for efforts to identify elements of customer satisfaction and to find ways to include those elements in service delivery,
- employees review, from time to time, their own operations to identify waste, duplication etc., and try to improve systems,
- employees decide, as a team, on how to resist pressures from vested interests and political bosses.

Making this happen would need employee cooperation. The senior-most public servants will have to take more responsibility. He should focus on what could be done instead of what cannot be done, attempt to move forward with every suggestion and not block it for perceived constraints. Seniors, who claim to have a 'realistic' view of the constraints and risks of public service, and refuse to shift from the traditional methods, are the real constraints. The system does allow innovation and better quality. In fact better quality is the best guarantee against unwarranted criticism. The cleaning up of the city of Surat is an achievement that shows that public service is capable of outstanding performance, despite all the constraints. There are other examples as well.

❏ The British Experience ❏

The UK has implemented a range of initiatives, designed to focus the attention of the civil service on their core tasks, clarify responsibility for expenditure, improve the efficiency of key operations, delegate management responsibility to the appropriate levels, emphasise the needs of the user of the service, develop staff capabilities to meet the demands of the new ways of working and encourage organisations to cooperate with others working with the same customer groups. The approach selected was the European Foundation for Quality Management's Business Excellence Model (BEM). The steps included fixing specific targets in identified areas of measurable performance, getting a database of assessment scores, identifying best management practices, and helping organisations to make contacts with others from whom they could learn. The areas for performance measurement included policy and strategy, customer satisfaction, people satisfaction, and business results. This practice enabled benchmarking with companies in the private sector.

Hospitals

A hospital is a place where a person who needs medical attention goes to stay, so that he may get medical and nursing attention and be restored to normal health.

The usual requirements in a hospital are:

1. Rooms for patients to stay, equipped with beds, small cupboards, (for medicines, fruits, clothes), chairs (for visitors).
2. Doctors of various specialisations.
3. Nursing and menial staff (for cleaning operations).
4. Administration personnel.
5. Operation theatre equipped with appropriate machines, instruments and furniture.
6. Equipment for investigations, X-ray, SCAN, pathology.

7. Essential drugs for emergency.
8. Kitchen for food service.

Of these 1, 2 and 3 are essential. The others are optional, depending on the level of service offered. In small nursing homes, doctors and nurses perform also administrative functions like billing and collection.

On items 1 and 8, the hospital is like a hotel, offering

- different classes of rooms, single, common like a *dharmsala* (general ward), or luxurious, deluxe with decor, carpets, airconditioning, music, TV, refrigerator, etc. (special wards),
- choice of food, ala carte or standard spartan (like *thali* meals) with a limited range as may be prescribed by the dietician. If food is on offer, unlike a restaurant, the customer for food is captive. There wll be no waste of supplies.

Unlike a hotel though, people do not come to a hospital for room or food service. These do not constitute the core product. These only augment the core product, which is medical attention. Other elements that augment the core services are admission processes, permission for attendants to accompany patient, visitors timings, facilities to answer enquiries (about patient's condition) on the telephone and also parking facilities.

A hospital may be a general hospital offering services for all diseases or a specialised hospital attending specifically to diabetes, eyes, ENT, gynaecology, neuro, cardiac or cancer problems.

A person seeks admission in a hospital only if the medical attention necessary is difficult to arrange at home. These are of the following categories.

- needing surgery or other procedures requiring multiple skills, support and equipment, difficult to assemble for a single patient for reasons of cost and/or availability,
- needing intensive care because of acute physical or mental disorder,
- needing constant observation of parameters (temperature, BP, sugar levels, cardiac behaviour) for check up and/or diagnosis.

❑ *Customers* ❑

A patient is the main user of the hospital. He is a person in distress. He expects comfort, care, and cure from the hospital.

His distress is more if

- he is not attended to, but left alone,

- the attending personnel do not ask him what his trouble is,
- the attending personnel do not listen to him when he is narrating the problem,
- his troubles (complaints) are not taken seriously. (Patients are sometimes told that they are exaggerating),
- he does not experience quick relief,
- he is not told what is being done about him,
- he is not told what he can expect in terms of attention and cure,
- there is an atmosphere of pain and distress around, particularly in general wards,
- there is an atmosphere of filth and neglect (unkempt surroundings, dirty linen, pests on food and walls),
- the discomfort through illness is accentuated by mosquitoes, loud noises like *Diwali* crackers, marriage and *pandal* music.

A patient is the customer of the hospital, in the sense that he is the primary user of the hospital's offerings. He is not however, a regular customer like that of a hotel. When a patient is being discharged, the hospital staff would not say to him 'Hope to see you again soon'.

A regular customer of the hospital is the doctor. He needs facilities to treat his patients, and these facilities are offered by the hospital to the doctor for his use. If he is satisfied with these facilities, he advises his patients to be admitted in that hospital. A doctor is a customer in the sense that he makes the decision for the patient to buy the hospital's services. However, he does not directly provide revenue to the hospital. The customer providing revenue directly is the patient.

A patient is expected to be a one-time buyer. Repeat sales are provided by the doctor, who continues recommending patients, if he is satisfied with the services of the hospital. Thus, promotion should be targeted at doctors.

Other customers of hospitals would be large business houses or insurance companies who are obliged to provide for medical care to their members and can persuade them to use the services of the specific hospital. These organisations may seek :

- concessional tariffs,
- preferential treatment.

They may also avail, for their members, regular check-ups, as part of a continuing package. Some of these institutions may even sponsor rooms and facilities.

❑ *Doctors* ❑

The quality of the core service depends on the quality of the doctors there. Doctors 'visit' hospitals. They make their services available to the patients or other doctors there, whenever required. The doctors benefit, because they are able to obtain admission to their patients and use facilities which they do not possess.

A doctor's reputation has some linkage to the standard of the hospital which he visits. The reputation of the hospital depends on the stature of the visiting doctors. Both are complementary to each other. The doctor is both a supplier to, and a customer of, a hospital.

A hospital can attract a good senior doctor to be associated with it, if the doctor

- finds that the facilities and standards are in keeping with the nature of his practice and the requirements of his patients,
- is able to influence the hospital's management in maintaining appropriate standards and facilities,
- can get his patients admitted, when recommended.

Every hospital will have resident doctors, usually junior, and on a salary. Junior doctors will join a hospital if they find that

- the opportunity exists to work with eminent senior doctors,
- the hospital has enough cases of the kind in which they want to specialise.

In other words, they are looking for experience, learning and growth. Hospitals are interested in junior doctors, as they are the ones who provide basic medical attention on a continuing basis. Since they are in the premises for long periods, they can carry regular checks (monitoring) and attend to emergencies till a senior doctor may arrive.

❑ *Skills* ❑

The skill levels required in a hospital vary. They are:

- unskilled—to clean, wash, sweep, carry errands,
- skilled—for elementary nursing, technicians in laboratory, office staff, etc.,
- highly skilled—medical professionals of various specialisations.

All of them contribute to patient satisfaction and to quality of hospital service.

The needs of these personnel are different. Their motivations are different. Their availability for replacement or expansion, is not the same. They have to be managed differently.

The out-patient department (OPD) in a hospital is different from a doctor's clinic, to the extent that a doctor offers a limited service and refers patients elsewhere for other services, while the OPD is like a polyclinic, offering all services which the hospital will. The OPDs are usually manned by

- junior doctors who will refer the small percentage of complicated cases to senior doctors on call,
- senior doctors by rotation.

In-patients will be either those sent in from OPD or directly referred for admission by doctors attached to the hospital.

Some hospitals try to avoid admission of in-patients. This is because of the high demand for the limited availability of beds. This may also occur in cases where the patient's chances of recovery are very low. Hospitals may try to avoid deaths in their premises, by refusing admission of critical cases, just as the police try to avoid registering cases within their jurisdiction.

❑ *Hospitality* ❑

A hospital is the patient's home as long as he stays there. He needs personal care in addition to medical care. All wards in a hospital provide almost the same medical care, but different wards provide different levels of personal care. People may be tempted to enter a hospital providing for excellent personal care, even if the medical problem is not acute. Some hospitals in Mumbai, and other Indian cities experienced a sudden influx of Arab patients booking into their most expensive rooms, apparently for medical attention, but really for boarding and lodging. They did avail of the medical check up, but it was apparently not the main purpose. They found hotels more expensive.

Even a private hospital, has a social investment. A doctor's education is subsidised by the state. Nurses training is also subsidised. Therefore, hospitals have a responsibility to ensure that their facilities, including rooms, are used genuinely for the purposes for which they are created, even if alternate usages may be profitable. For the same reason, overstaying, beyond the period required on medical considerations, would be improper.

❑ *Customer Profile* ❑

A good hospital should know the profile of its patients so that it can identify the particular segment to which most of its patients belong and then fine tune its service elements to meet the needs of that segment. It should also know which doctors recommend the maximum number of patients and then find out whether

- these doctors prefer particular hospitals,
- the location is important,
- any of the facilities are perceived as better,
- any of the facilities are considered inadequate.

Another outcome of such continuous monitoring would be knowledge of patterns in diseases, and shifts therein. This data helps to

- identify facilities that are used and facilities that are not used,
- strengthen facilities that are used,
- cut down facilities that are not used or do effective promotion for those facilities,
- liaison with local authority to combat reasons for new infections or endemic disorders.

❏ *Flashpoints* ❏

Work is conducted in cells. A nurse and her helpers in a ward comprise a cell. Doctors of a department also comprise a cell. The physiotherapy department is a separate cell. The radiology department is one too. Like in a hotel, the kitchen is a cell and the housekeeping is a separate cell.

Teams are built around cells. These cells have to interact. The interface is a potential flashpoint. Flashpoint can reach customers but should not. They may, because most procedures are multidisciplinary. Managers have to take care of these interfaces.

❏ *Quality* ❏

Some of the small matters which influence perceptions of quality of service in a hospital are:

- While making enquiries or giving instructions, nurses and other staff refer to patients by the bed numbers or by the disease he is suffering. It makes a lot of difference if the patient is identified by his name.
- Letting patients know what they are suffering from, what is being done to them, why particular tests are being conducted, what they can expect in terms of discomfort or because of a particular medical procedure, etc. Open communication is very satisfying.

- Letting patients have an option about treatment or continued hospitalisation, because of the high costs involved. Hospitals tend to treat patients like captives or hostages, who cannot escape and on whom any treatment and any cost can be forced, without their consent.
- Letting accompanying relatives also know about what is being done to the patient and about their options.
- Patients being escorted by someone senior (and not by menial staff) for X-rays, scan etc. and not being left alone in corridors on wheelchairs or stretchers, waiting for their 'turn'.
- Isolate particularly serious cases from the general wards. Patients get depressed when they see other patients in acute distress or in terminal conditions, with a lot of anxious relatives around and medical staff rushing about.
- A primary nurse may be assigned, as an aide, to every patient, to take care of his needs throughout his stay in hospital.
- In the case of a hospital attracting a large number of patients from outside towns, like the Christian Medical at Vellore or the Eye hospital in Sitapur (Uttar Pradesh), or the Tata Memorial (cancer hospital) in Mumbai, the accompanying relatives have a pressing need for temporary accommodation. If the hospital can help, instead of leaving them to touts, that would be a valued service. It can become a business on its own.

Some hospitals chart out what they call 'clinical pathways', as a method to improve patient care. A clinical pathway is a management tool that shows sequence and time of the major interventions of nursing staff, physicians and other departments. This is done for particular case types like heart attacks. They reflect processes which apply in the majority of—not all—cases. Variances from the pathways are observed and studied for revision, if necessary. Experience from medical misadventures, involving injuries to patients can be particularly studied for risk identification and recurrence. Emphasis is also laid on providing appropriate and effective use of pharmaceuticals avoiding side effects. The patient's dignity is as much a concern as his safety.

❑ *Safety* ❑

Another area, for quality in hospital, is safety. Safety is of the patient as well as of belongings of the patient. Patients dying or developing complications because of inferior medicine, neglect in attention and incorrect records are not infrequent. A good hospital does not let this happen. The difference in outcome is due to systems (of purchase and of storage) of recording, of assigning staff, etc.

A hospital is a place where sick people go to become healthy. However, a hospital is also a place with a high potential to spread disease. There is a high concentration of all kinds of germs, injurious to health. Healthy people come to hospitals to work, or to visit relatives and friends. Therefore a hospital is the easiest place to catch an infection.

Hospital management must take particular care about the disposal of contaminated dressings, linen, toilet, utensils, etc. Personnel on related jobs must know what is to be done and also why it is to be done. Many hospitals are lax on this. Liberal use of disinfection a couple of times, is assumed to be adequate precaution. Linen and floors with clotted blood, animals, birds and flies in the wards, gorging on spit, urine, etc., do not reassure patients, their relatives or friends. If materials to be disposed of have to be carried in open bins, through populated places, with the nauseating odour spreading all over, the hospital may seem unsafe.

Hospitals may develop a Patient Service Index (PSI) incorporating the number of elements which it considers is to be included in the offer. A report with the Department of Health, Education and Welfare, Washington in 1974, listed approximately 900 quality related items of nursing care. The PSI can be the benchmark to measure improvements being incorporated.

❑ *Future Trends* ❑

The nature of surgical operations has changed considerably. Alternate procedures, without resorting to conventional surgery, are becoming available, thanks to new technology using lasers, micro instruments etc. Therefore, there is little post surgery care. Patients can return home the same day with little discomfort and hardly any possibility of complications.

Patients are also finding it cheaper to arrange for nurses and equipment at home, because of the heavy costs of hospitalisation. Equipments can be hired. Care provided at home is more comforting.

For these reasons, the occupancy of hospital beds is going down. Similar trends are expected in India. The data on patients, suggested earlier, will point to the need if any, in restructuring the hospitals to meet new usage patterns.

Speciality hospitals are being connected to similar hospitals in other parts of the world, through satellite communication networks. Through data exchanges and teleconferences, doctors in one place can confer and consult with colleagues elsewhere. Doctors from one town visit hospitals in other cities, countries, for short durations, to demonstrate their skills, to teach and to learn.

A good hospital is a place for learning, if the experience in treating a patient is properly recorded and stored in a library. Doctors can enhance their knowledge and skills by accessing such records. The quality of both the doctor and the hospital can be thus enhanced.

Tourism

❏ *Size* ❏

The business of tourism relates to all activities that cater to the comfort and satisfaction of tourists. International tourists, estimated to be 700 million, spent approximately US$675 per head in 2002. This is expected to become the largest sector of international trade. Internationally, tourism employs 112 million people (6.5 per cent of the global workforce) and is a $400 trillion industry. In India, direct employment in the tourism sector is estimated to be 16.45 million in 2002. The number of tourists into India has been, on an average, around 2.5 million for the last five years or so, about 0.37 per cent of global tourism. It is expected to grow to 10 million by 2010. Apart from China, even smaller countries like Malaysia, Sri Lanka and Thailand receive several times more tourists than India. The foreign exchange earnings from tourism is estimated to have been about Rs 14 billion in 2002, compared to Rs 4.5 billion from software exports.

❏ *Profile* ❏

A tourist is a person who travels out of his normal place of residence

- to stay at another place or places, called destinations,
- for purposes other than business, like leisure, holidaying, recreation, sightseeing, pilgrimage.

A destination

- is a place which offers complex of activities that comprise the tourism experience,
- has more attractions on offer than what a tourist requires, so there is plenty of choice,
- is a product by itself as well as a container of products,
- is bought by different people for different reasons, like convention, shopping, culture.

A tourist expects comfort and pleasure when he

- travels,
- stays somewhere,
- eats (in the variety and quality of the food offered),

- visits places of interest and attraction for him (in the arrangements made for him in this regard).

A tourist does not travel on the spur of the moment or too frequently. He makes his plans to travel well in advance. He looks forward to it with anticipation. He is investing his hopes, time and money on the travel. He expects that

- he will be looked after and cared for,
- he will be able to visit places of interest and spend adequate time at such places and engage in activities that interest him,
- there will be no waste of time in waiting for transport, or at places of no interest to him because of bad weather or other reasons,
- he will not be hurried or hustled against his preferred pace,
- the food will be palatable and suitable to his tastes and health,
- others in the group will be good company,
- he will be able to experience, in the new places, the local life styles, culture, food, etc., as per his choice,
- there will be no risk to his person or to his belongings.

The elements that need to be taken care of include

- obtaining passport, visas, health documents,
- customs regulations,
- regulations regarding money that can be carried,
- the amount of money that needs to be carried,
- convenient modes of transportation to and at destinations,
- clothing appropriate to the local climate and customs,
- availability of reliable services (accommodation, food, transport, guides, medical, shopping, currency etc.) at the destinations,
- the cost of those services,
- language barriers,
- propriety of behaviour in the places being visited,
- health precautions,
- safeguards against being cheated through overcharging, misdirection, bad quality, etc.

The tourist needs information about each of these elements. He also needs help in making adequate arrangements to secure them. Making these arrangements himself can be quite a problem, as several different authorities and agencies may have to be contacted. A tourist agency, which undertakes to make all these arrangements in one package, provides great satisfaction.

The travel agency is depended upon for the accuracy of the information and the reservations/arrangements made. It is assumed that the agency would have taken care of all necessary details and that nothing will go wrong. This is the expectation. If the experience matches the expectation, the quality of the service is good. Travel agents and tour operators usually are affiliated with local agents at most destinations to ensure that they do not fail on this account.

○ Product ○

The tourism product includes attractions at the destination, which may be

- nature and geography, for leisure, for sport, for health, for pleasure,
- history, places of importance,
- tradition and heritage,
- events, festivals, excursions,
- sports, entertainment, shopping,
- people—guides and others in the group.

The various providers of service in connection with tourism are

- transporters, airlines, railways, ships, buses, car rentals,
- accommodation, hotels of various grades, private guest houses,
- caterers,
- developers, who manage the infrastructure at destinations,
- guides, personal as well as through brochures and literature,
- shops offering curios, jewellery, local products,
- communication and money exchangers.

All of them provide value and contribute to the experience.

○ Market ○

The tourists' market may be segmented on the basis of

- place of origin of tourists (this is where the demand is),
- destinations (this is where the supply is),
- purposes of tour, holiday, pilgrimage, sightseeing, shopping, adventure,
- economic status, spending tendencies,
- demographic characteristics, age, sex, occupation, attitudes,
- preferences for staying, camping, beaches, luxury hotels, caravans,
- preference of travel, air, sea, road, train.

Demand and supply are separated across space, unlike most other products, and have to be bridged by the rest of the infrastructure, like customs, visa and travel.

A market study would include

- spatial patterns of supply and demand, flows, impacts (who travels, from where to where, why, when, how),
- seasonalities (periods of high and low movement),
- life cycles of products—affected largely by developmental activities as well as by political and regulatory changes,
- attractions, land forms (hiking, beaches, hill stations), flora, fauna (nature, wildlife, sanctuaries), man-made objects (temples, cathedrals, monuments), culture and history, cuisine, music, theatre,
- accommodation—commercial, private (friends), camping, caravans,
- infrastructure—roads, airfields, buses, car rentals, trains, electricity, water supply, communication, medical care.

The market study would reveal

- effective demand (present position),
- deferred demand (could participate now, but does not),
- potential demand (could not participate now, but may later).

The study should show, for example, not only that 87 per cent of the tourists n Aurangabad visit Ellora 10 km away, and 60 per cent visit Ajanta 100 km way, but should also show

- The reasons for this difference.
- The attraction for tourists in both places.
- Whether they are interested in the caves, the sculptures, the paintings, the history, or the setting and the location?
- Whether they go there because they know what is there and are interested in it, or only to experience what is publicised to be an important sight?
- Whether the need be satisfied by a good replica of everything there for detailed observation and study, after a brief visit to the original?
- Whether better accommodation facilities at Ajanta will increase the number of tourists going there?
- Whether the flow will improve if more opportunities are provided for entertainment and trekking?

Studies show that the major attraction at all destinations is sightseeing and shopping. Shops and malls, with casinos, food fairs and fashion shops are becoming tourist attrractions on their own. The Edomonton Mall in Alberta, Canada, has 800 shops, with an enormous parking space for cars.

❏ *Personnel* ❏

Personnel are an extremely important factor. British Airways believed that interpersonal relations were twice as important as the operational aspects of flying and therefore, had programmes to help staff to act empathetically and with spontaneity. With such special concerns, and actions that reduce anxiety, a difficulty could be converted to an advantage.

The personnel deputed to accompany the tour party locally or throughout, is for all purposes the tour operator, as far as the tourist is concerned. The person deputed must

- know the members of the group by name,
- be generally pleasant and helpful,
- be able to manage difficult members in the party,
- speak the local language,
- speak the language of the tourists,
- know the destination well, in terms of its history, geography, culture, tradition, attractions,
- satisfy the needs of tourists for information, shopping or otherwise,
- plan a daily schedule, communicate the same well in advance to the group, and implement it,
- coordinate with other local agencies like caterers, transporters, porters, managers (of museums and sites),
- guide group members about clothing, behaviour, precautions, what to do and what not to do, safety measures (of valuables),
- be able to withstand the stress and pressures of members of the tour party who may demand information or something else simultaneously,
- take care of any emergency occurring due to break down in arrangements, objectionable behaviour, (whether it is a legal offence or not),
- protect the group from local touts, cheats, beggars, temptations of different kinds,
- guide the group about activities that may offend local sentiment.

Non-adherence to schedule is perceived as unnecessary waiting and therefore wasted time and opportunity. This can happen due to

- some members of the party being slack,
- transporter not being on time,
- hotel not providing supplies on time,
- guides not being on time.

The ones who promote the product are not the ones who operate and maintain the product. The former are at the point of origin where the demand exists, while the latter are at the destination, where the supply is. There could be differences and clashes between these two and the effect will be felt by the tourist.

A tourist likes to do things which he normally does not do and not do things which he is normally used to doing. This opportunity for 'inversion' is an important motivation for a tourist, to be bohemian, and not formal as usual; to eat his full and not diet as usual; to loosen the purse strings and not tighten them as usual; to have a daily routine, different from the normal one; to indulge in frivolities, instead of being serious as usual.

❏ Group ❏

While travelling in a group, the others in it can help to enhance or spoil one's enjoyment. While assembling a group for a tour, the operator must try to look for the similarities among the group members. Otherwise, their dissatisfaction will be vented on the operator.

Most activities will be done by the group as a whole but some members may like to have some time for themselves to do things which may not be of common interest for the rest of the group. This could be shopping, visiting or exploring local attractions or just walking around and taking in the atmosphere. Apart from providing time, they also need guidance on how to go about it. Non-availability of time and guidance can be dissatisfying. When a special charter flight arrived in Goa and all the members of the group checked into a luxury hotel for a seven-day scheduled stay, half of them walked out within half an hour and returned only after three days. They had gone to some remote beach and spent time there, while the rest enjoyed themselves with the water sports facilities available at the hotel. They had known where to go and what to do on their own.

❏ Food ❏

Food is a major source of satisfaction/dissatisfaction. Some people may be willing to experiment with any kind of food. They may particularly like something new. Some are very particular about what they will eat, for reasons of health or safety. Therefore, special arrangements may have to be made, if necessary. A tour operator specialising in certain segments of pilgrim tourists, arranges accommodation in high-grade hotels but arranges for special food through cooks carried with the tour group, with utensils and provisions.

Arrangements could have been made with the hotel for the special food, but the tourists would have nothing to do with a kitchen that was not exclusive. If such demands come unexpectedly, from even a single person, after the tour has begun, this could cause severe stress within the entire group.

❏ Schedules ❏

Convenience of schedules is another important factor. These will vary according to the demographic profile of the tourists. Elderly people may like to walk at a leisurely pace with adequate intervals of rest, avoid extremes of temperature and consume food and drinks at regular times. Younger groups may be willing to start early and continue till late in the evenings, and see rest periods as a waste of time and opportunity. A significant portion of time is taken up in travel. All worthwhile experiences at the destinations are forgotten if the bus breaks down. The amount of time spent at a sight/destination will vary. A group, with Mathura in the schedule, will be very unhappy if the conductor simply says, while the bus is speeding away, 'That is the building in which Krishna was born'.

❏ Access ❏

The tourist is a traveller from some distant place. Access to the places he wants to see should not be difficult. Popular destinations can make access difficult because of queues to buy entry tickets or inadequate transport infrastructure. Restrictions and timings, including holidays and recesses, can make access difficult, particularly if they are unannounced. A competent guide makes access easy in museums, heritage and historical sites and safari tours. Beggars, aggressive hawkers, overbearing officials and indisciplined (noisy) co-travellers make access difficult. The following are some instances of how access may be made easy or difficult:

1. A group of Japanese tourists travelling from Mumbai to Nairobi, were given immigration cards by the airline crew. These cards printed in English, were to be presented on their arrival at Nairobi. Everyone in the group, opened a book, in which there was an exact replica of this card, but in Japanese. Through comparison of the two forms, every one, even those who could not read or write English, was able to complete the form. Each reference book had the tourist's name written in English.

2. The Japanese tourist had details about the towns he would pass through while in Kenya, the road conditions, distances, facilties etc., en route. He had brought this book from Japan. Those who travel by road in India, know how inadequate and sometimes faulty the information is about

road conditions and facilities *en route*. Road maps are published by government agencies and automobile associations and are mostly out of date and not wholly reliable. Even road signs are often plastered with posters of various kinds.

3. Germans are able to reach the Kovalam beach, near Thiruvananthapuram, or any of the smaller beaches in Goa, on their own. They have information on every boarding house in that area, however small it may be.

4. French girls are seen travelling through South India on their own, on cheap budgets, because they have books with detailed information on bus routes, places to stay and essential language requirements.

5. A group of Japanese travelling to Delhi after visiting the Taj at Agra, complained that they did not know the best places in Agra or in Delhi for purchases and that they were becoming victims of dishonest people. Government emporia are not the only outlets for items of tourist interest

6. A group of tourists visiting a game sanctuary, were told on reaching there that they could not enter the gates after 6.30 p.m. The hotels were inside the sanctuary. They were forced to make do with some substandard accommodation near the gate at exorbitant rates. This information was not available at the office when the tour was planned.

❑ *Money* ❑

Money is the third area of importance. Tourists do not have inexhaustible supplies of money. They have some understanding of what expenses are included in the cost of the package, already paid for, and what other personal expenses they may have to incur. They carry money accordingly. This money is probably accumulated over some time for this tour. They would not like to be stranded anywhere or find themselves unable to do or buy something worthwhile, because of shortage of money. They do not want to waste it or lose it, but may do so because of

- theft,
- having to spend on what they thought was part of the package,
- being 'taken for a ride' by local people at shops or roads or tourist sites.

A tour party could not depart, as scheduled, from a foreign destination, because of disruption of air services, and the operator called upon the members to pay the additional cost of overstay. The argument about who was responsible for these additional costs did not lead to any satisfactory solution and the tour was 'spoilt'.

Tour operators must make prior arrangements to meet such extra costs. Charging for the package, with built-in margins for contingencies would be one method. The margin, if unutilised can be returned at the end of the tour as a bonus. It is also possible to insure against most contingencies. Someone falling ill, is a serious and expensive contingency, for which insurance is a satisfactory measure.

Tour operators must be able to give advice on how to take care of money and other valuables. Appropriate warnings would be welcome. Hotels make arrangements for the safe custody of valuables as hotel staff or even fellow tourists may steal valuables or cash.

❑ *Marketing* ❑

Marketing of tourism includes

- marketing of a country as a whole,
- marketing of specific towns, locations,
- marketing of specific activities,
- marketing of a tour package,
- marketing of accommodation/food.

Leisure tourists may spend hours in accommodations. Costa Cruises offer the 'world's top rated ships', according to industry magazines and critics, with impromptu entertainment, Italian style pizzas and a grand finale of a Roman bacchanalia.

To a country developing a destination, the real customers are the intermediate providers of tourism services, such as

- travel agents,
- tour operators,
- transporters,
- hoteliers and caterers,
- shops,
- travel guide publishers.

These persons will promote the destination to the tourist.

A provider of tourism services has considerable opportunity for merchandising, and to make the tourist buy additional services, which he may not have originally planned to buy. Maybe he did not know of the availability of the services or did not know enough to evaluate its true worth. If the additional service on offer is unique and exclusive to that location, the additional costs would seem to be negligible compared to the opportunity—the tourist may not visit the place, at least for quite some time in the future. If merchandising is done before the tour commences, the tourist will be ready for it. Otherwise, depending on the availability of money and time resources, he could be disappointed.

❏ *Future Trends* ❏

India expects to welcome 10 million tourists by 2010. Approximately 30,000 hotel rooms would have to be created by then at a cost of about Rs 100 billion. Most of these rooms would be of the 2 and 3-star variety, as 5-star rooms are too expensive and not viable. The target of 10 million however, is small compared to the potential.

India offers, perhaps, the widest choice of tourist attractions in a single country—snow, mountains, forests, wildlife sanctuaries, rivers, beaches, historical sites, palaces, mausoleums, temples, relaxation and adventure destinations, a contrasting juxtaposition of the ancient and the modern. The Thomas Cook Worldwide Cost of Living Index showed that India offers the best value for money. Both the central and the state governments have the responsibility to support the tourism industry. This responsibility is expressed through the creation of tourism development corporations, medium-priced accommodation and taxation policies.

Private entrepreneurs have a major share in creating facilities. Costs involved are enormous in creating hotel rooms, restaurants, vehicles, communication lines, sports equipment and facilities and so on. The tourist will come only when he feels assured that he will be comfortable, and not harassed.

Harassment is experienced when entry formalities (visas, etc.) are difficult, when airport checks and customs clearances are cumbersome, and when schedules are disrupted by strikes, riots, disturbances, etc., when the safety of persons and their belongings appear threatened, and information is difficult to come by.

Domestic tourism (Indians touring within India) will increase at a faster rate than foreign tourists. Domestic tourists travel more because of the increasing grant of leave travel allowances by employers, as well as their religious beliefs. They are less demanding in their requirements of accommodation and food standards. Though the budgets are smaller, domestic tourism contributes significantly to the GDP. The infrastructure required to satisfy domestic tourism is very different from the needs of the foreign tourists.

A heavy influx of tourists disturbs the local way of life. While additional economic activity is generated at these destinations, there can be abuses as well—of the environment, unruly behaviour, loss of traditional living styles and occupations, and so on. The negative aspects of tourism cannot be ignored.

Plans are afoot for space travel. The Lunar Hill resort will have 5,000 rooms in inflatable buildings, with two huge solar panels and its own beaches, tennis courts, golf courses and working farms. Nishamahu Construction Corporation is planning a resort city, Escargot City, consisting of three 10-storey towers. Travel and stay may cost $50,000.

Logistics

Logistics deals with the transport of materials and goods from one place to another, manufacturer to retailer, supplier to purchaser, and so on. Traditionally, this involved arrangements for carriage through trucks (or rail or ships) and warehousing. It is now considered an integral part of the business.

Logistics is a major factor in the determination of costs. It has been realised that it is possible to improve margins through a proper management of logistics. Traditionally, costs were sought to be controlled through economies of scale and sales volumes, apart from negotiations during purchases. The principle was that overheads could be distributed over a larger base. The current thinking is that costs are controllable through a careful scrutiny of effectiveness, value and relevance of each activity and also by looking at the possible alternatives.

Logistics is an important contributor to one's effectiveness. The manufacturer of a motor car, using more than 4,000 parts that are procured from far off areas, even across continents, can implement his production schedule only if the necessary parts are not out of stock at any time. Among the many alternatives tried out, the Just-in-Time system happens to be the most cost-effective, as the inventory carrying costs are reduced to zero. Among the systems that have to be in place for this to happen, logistics is an important one.

Many organisations have found it economical to entrust the entire reposonsibility of logistics to specialised logistics companies. Logistics has developed as an important service business in recent times. Retailers like Wal-Mart, which procure goods from hundreds of suppliers all over the world, in preparation for the sales during Christmas, for example, may not be able to manage the logistics themselves and therefore, use third parties. Even if they do it themselves, they will have a separate division to manage it, as there is need for information and decisions that are totally different from that of procurement and retailing.

The principles relating to logistics were based on the experience during times of conflict and war, when materials for fighting and for supporting men and equipment had to be made available, after being transported across long distances, under hostile conditions, in secrecy, through difficult terrain and with resources which were limited. At the time of the Falklands War against Argentina for example, the British Government had to transport, men and materials, armour, ammunition, food, tents and equipments, over thousands of miles, via sea and air, to almost the doorstep of Argentina. Logistics were the main considerations in the preparation of the US for the operations in Afghanistan in 2001 and Iraq in 2003.

A logistics company takes responsibility for

- collection, transportation and delivery of materials,
- storage *en route*, if waiting is involved, for trans-shipment or clearances,
- documentation for the purposes of customs and other taxes,
- clearances from regulatory authorities like customs, import or export controllers,
- payments and also collections from consignees,
- bulk breaking and repackaging, if necessary.

The effectiveness of a logistics operation depends on the optimum usage of carrier and time, which depends on

- sizes and quality of vehicles used,
- routing, speed,
- a 'handsoff' policy, meaning points of delays, and ways of avoiding or reducing them,
- reducing turn-around-time (also called cycle time) by studying operations of loading, unloading, servicing or equipping carriers in between trips.

A logistics company may

- have its own vehicles or hire vehicles for carriage or avail services of other carriers,
- provide dedicated service for specific clients on a long-term basis or do one-time jobs,
- provide door-to-door service or have their own receipt and delivery points,
- make collections of (own or supplier's) bills along with delivery of goods,
- focus on speedy and error-free operations,
- focus on performance more than on profits,

- look at and control processes,
- seek to build up relationships for mutual advantage.

A logistics company may have internal standards on the following parameters, by which it may evaluate its own performance. This data can also be used while considering getting into long-term arrangements with logistics companies. The internal standards may pertain to

- order cycle time,
- stock availability,
- order size constraints,
- ordering convenience,
- frequency of delivery,
- delivery reliability,
- documentation quality,
- claims procedure,
- order completeness,
- technical support,
- order status information.

Problems may arise because of

- uncertain lead times,
- unreliable transit times,
- multiple consolidation and bulk-break operations,
- multiple mode and freight cost options.

Logistics is an integral part of supply chain management, both in-bound and out-bound. To receive the full benefits of logistics, the receiving company must be able to reduce its inventory to near zero. This really means that the materials which should have been taken out of inventory, are actually on their way from the suppliers and will reach as they are needed. This is inventory in transit, also called 'virtual inventory'. The physical inventory is in fact, replaced by information about requirements and movement of materials. There is no additional cost to the supplier, but there is a saving to the consumer. The communication between the supplier, the consumer and the logistics company has to be on a real-time basis and the schedules strictly adhered to. The commitments are strengthened by clauses that reward compliance and provide penalties for variations. These operations are based on extensive IT networks. Logistics works across functions of an organisation, because user departments have to be satisfied. It becomes an integral part of management.

Studies have shown that logistics can help companies improve their Return on Assets and asset turnover parameters, because it eliminates idle capital which inventories represent. Logistics companies may have to invest in warehouses, carriers and IT in order to fulfil their commitments to the client. Transporting motor cars from Maruti or huge boilers for L&T, require specially fabricated trucks. Tankers carrying petrol or highly inflammable chemicals need to have excellent shock absorbers and specially trained drivers, to avoid the effects of vibrations and friction.

Retailers like Wal-mart and Woolworths have decided that their products should be tagged with Radio Frequency Identifications (RFID) which are small read-write microchips with eight digit store code useful for routing purposes. Developed to ensure the safety of cars against thefts, RFID is seen as the next generation bar code. Wal-mart has decided that all consumer packaged goods in its store be RFID tagged by 2005. Compliance with this requirement is estimated to cost an additional \$2 billion in tags, system integration, changes in existing supply chain applications and the upgradation of storage and analytics software. Logistics companies have to rearrange their systems as much as Wal-mart and the manufacturers.

A logistics company will take note of the following factors while segmenting the market

- nature of materials involved—perishable, hazardous,
- type—importance of logistics to customer, measured by the percentage of logistics cost to value addition,
- extent of value addition after delivery—varies between deliveries to manufacturers and deliveries to retail outlets,
- customer's sensitivity to delivery—varies according to usage at receiver's end.

The IT systems relevant for logistics include

- GIS or Geographic Information System, which gives data about space and is map based.
- EDI or Electronic Data Interchange, which enables the quick interchange between entities, avoiding rekeying of data.
- MRP or Material Resource Planning.
- DRP or Distribution Resource Planning.
- ERP or Enterprise Resource Planning.

The Southern California Logistics Airport (SCLA), located in Victorville, California, is the first case of an airport that is wholly dedicated to the logistics business. Less than a 100 miles from the ports in Northern Ireland Empire region, SCLA is leveraging its access to rail, road and ocean transportation networks to ensure quicker turnover. A former US airforce base, it was redeveloped as a 5,000 acre multi-modal logistic centre and has been designated as a foreign trade zone.

BIBLIOGRAPHY

Ackoff R.L., *Concept of Corporate Planning:* Wiley (New York) (1970).

Albrecht, Karl and Zemke, Ron, *Service America:* Dow Jones Irwin (Boston) (1995).

Albrecht, Karl, *At America's Service:* Warner Books (Boston) (1995).

Ashworth, Gregory and Goodall, Brian, *Marketing Tourism Places:* Routledge (London) (1990).

Balachandran S., *Managing Change:* Business Books Publishing House (Bombay)(1987).

_____, *Managing Ethics:* Sangeetha Associates (Bombay) (1996).

Bhagwati, Jagdish: *International Trade in Services:* Geneva Association Press (Geneva) (1983).

Beryll, L.L., Zeithaml, V.A., Parasuraman A., 'Quality Counts in Services Too', Article in *Business Horizons* (May–June 1985).

Bloom, Paul N., 'Effective Marketing for Professional Services', Article in *Harvard Business Review* (Sept–Oct.1984).

Bradford, David L. and Cohen, *Managing for Excellence:* Wiley Eastern (New Delhi) (1987).

Brown S.W. and Swartz, Teresa A., 'Gap Analysis of Professional Service Quality', *Journal of Marketing* (April 1989).

Carlzon, Jan, *Moments of Truth:* Ballinger (New York) (1987).

Champy, James, *Reenginering Management:* Harper (New York) (1995).

Champy, James and Hammer Michael, *Reengineering the Corporation:* Nicholas Breadley Publishing (London) (1994).

Christopher H. Lovelock, Eric Langeard, John E.G. Bateson and Pierre Eiglier, 'Some Organizational Issues Facing Service Marketer', Article in *Marketing of Services*, J.H. Donnelly and W.R. George (eds.), Chicago: American Marketing Association (1981).

Cowell D., *Marketing of Services:* Hienmann (Oxford) (1991).

Crosby, Philip, *Quality is Free:* McGraw-Hill (New York) (1978).

Denton Dr. Keith, *Quality Service:* Gulf Publishing (Houston) (1989).

Funakawa, Atsushi, *Transcultural Management:* Jossey-Bass Publishing (1997).

Gupta P.K., *Services Marketing:* Everest Publishing House (Mumbai) (2002).

Hall Edward T., *Beyond Culture:* Anchor Books (New York) (1976).

Hamel, Gary, *Alliance Advantage:* Harvard Business School Press (Harvard) (1998).

Harvard Business Review, *Articles:* Harvard Business School (Harvard) (Various dates).

Hiroyuki Tami, 'Managing Business—The Japanese Way', Article in the *BMA Review* (Mumbai) (Jan/Feb 1993).

Hoffman, Douglas and Bateson John, *Essentials of Services Marketing:* Thomson Southe Western Mason (Ohio) (2002).

Hofstede, Geert, *Culture and Consequences:* Sage Publications (California) (1980)..

_____, *Cultures & Organisations:* McGraw-Hill (New York) (1997).

Hope, Tony and Hope, Jeremy, *Transforming the Bottom Line:* Nicholas Breadley Publishing (London) (1995).

Jackson, Harry K. Jr. and Frigon, Normand L., *Achieving Competitive Edge,* John Wiley & Sons (New Jersey) (1996).

Jayaraman M.S., Natarajan Ganesh, Rangaramanaujam A.V., *Business Process Reengineering,* Tata McGraw-Hill (New Delhi) (1994).

Jha S.M., *Services Marketing:* Himalaya Publishing House (Mumbai) (2002).

Joseph Dr. T.M., *Management of Services:* Himalaya Publishing House (Mumbai) (2002).

Kalam, A.P.J. Abdul and Arun Tiwari, *Wings of Fire:* Universities Press (Hyderabad) (1999).

Kanter, Rosabeth Moss, *Change Masters:* Simon & Schuster (New York) (1983).

Kenneth, Albert (Ed.), *Strategic Management Hand Book:* McGraw-Hill (New York) (1983).

Kotler P., *Marketing Management:* Prentice-Hall (New Jersey) (1986).

Leppard, John and Molyneux, Liz, *Auditing Your Customer Service:* Routledge (London) (1995).

Lytle, John, *What do Your Customers Want:* Excel (New Delhi) (1993).

Management Centre, Europe, Report of Global Conference on Services (Brussels) (1991).

Middleton, Victor T.C., *Marketing in Travel & Tourism:* Hienmann (London) (1988).

Nayak Ranganath P. and Ketteringham John M., *Breakthrough:* Mercury (Oxfordshire) (1993).

Parasuraman, A. Zeithaml V.A. and Berry L.L., 'Conceptual Model of Service Quality', *Journal of Marketing* (Fall. 1985).

Peters Glen, 'Customer Service Benchmarking', *Financial Times,* Prentice-Hall (London) (1994).

Peters Tom, *The Pursuit of WOW:* Macmillan (London) (1995).

Pfeffer, Jeremy, *Competitive Advantage through People*: Harvard Business Press (1994).

Porter, Michael E., *Competitive Advantage of Nations:* MacMillan (Hampshire) (1990).

_____, *Competitive Strategy:* Free Press (New York) (1980).

Price Frank, *Right First Time:* Gower Press (London) (1983).

Rastogi P.N., *Reengineering and Reinventing the Enterprise*, Wheeler Publishing (Allahabad) (1996).

Ravi Shanker (Ed.), *Services Marketing:* Manaas Publications (Delhi) (1993).

Roberts, Lon, *Process Reengineering:* Tata McGraw-Hill (New Delhi) (1994).

Rohinton, Aga, *Changing the Mind Set:* Tata McGraw-Hill (New Delhi) (1995).

Roland T. Rust, Anthony Zahorik and Timothy Keiningham, *Services Marketing:* Addison Wesley (Boston) (1996).

Samuels, Dr. Martin, U.K. Public Sector Benchmarking Project, Paper at World Congress on Total Quality (Mumbai) (1999).

Savage, Peter, *Who Cares Wins:* Mercury (London) (1987).

Shank, John K. and Govindarajan, Vijay, *Strategic Cost Management:* Free Press (New York) (1993).

Stanton W.J., *Fundamentals of Marketing:* McGraw-Hill (New York) (1967).

Taylor Bernard, 'Strategic Planning', *Long Range Planning,* Vol. 17, No. 3 (1984).

Vladimir, Andrew, *Complete Travel Marketing Handbook:* Ntc Business Books (Lincoln Wood) (1988).

Waterman, Robert H., *The Renewal Factor:* Bantam Books (Toronto) (1987).

Zemke Ron, *The Service Edge:* Nalpenguin Inc. j (1988).

Virmani B.R. and Seth Premila, *Evaluating Management Training & Development:* Vision Books (New Delhi) (1985).

INDEX

ABOUT THE AUTHOR

S. Balachandran is an independent management consultant based in Mumbai. He was earlier with the Life Insurance Corporation of India as a senior executive. He also served as faculty with the National Insurance Academy and has been a visiting faculty member at various management institutes.

Balachandran regularly conducts training programmes for various organisations in the public and private sectors and has helped to develop course material for several prestigious institutes. He is the author of several books and has also published articles in a number of reputed journals.